Othello

GW00372114

The Moor of Venice

A Tragedy by William Shakespeare

Editor: Patrick Brennan

FOLENS

Editors
Hilda O'Sullivan and Deirdre O'Neill

Design & Layout
Artwerk Limited

Sample Answers
Paul McCormack

© 2012 Patrick Brennan

Folens Publishers,
Hibernian Industrial Estate,
Greenhills Road,
Tallaght,
Dublin 24.

ISBN 978 1 78090 113 8

Produced in Ireland by Folens Publishers

1359

Photos: © Johan Persson, courtesy of ArenaPAL

Contents

Preface

Othello is perhaps the most appealing and intriguing of Shakespeare's "great" tragedies. It concerns the tragedy of love and the corruption of love by the subtle influence of evil. Many related topics of interest to the modern student are explored in *Othello* – human relationships; the role of women and men's attitudes to them; stereotypes and how they are formed; rash judgements of others; the extent of the individual's responsibility for his own actions; how real love can so quickly turn to hate and so on.

The deeper *Othello* is studied, the more interesting it becomes. The characters may seem removed in time and circumstances from people today, but, in motivation, and character traits, they resemble men and women of any age. In a sense, the infinite variety of the human mind and its relationships is portrayed in *Othello*. It is the student's task to explore this intriguing world of drama.

The aim of the notes, which accompany this edition of *Othello*, is to aid the student in exploring the play and forming a personal view of it. Students will find in these notes something to help them in both private study and classroom discussion of the play. This study and discussion will be all the more fruitful if the student can see the play performed in the theatre or on video-tape, DVD or television.

The notes on each scene include:
 (i) A plot summary to help the student to understand what happens in each scene. Students may choose not to read this section and be more independent, even on a first reading of the play.
 (ii) A section on "Dramatic Significance" to help the student to explore and analyse the role of each scene in the play as a whole.
 (iii) A section on "Character Development" to help the student to understand and analyse the character traits of the people in the drama.

The notes for "Further Study" in the final section are designed for the eager student, who wishes to explore the play more deeply. This section requires various skills of research, analysis and understanding. The technique in these sections has been varied to avoid monotony and to present a greater challenge to the more serious student.

This section consists of the following items:
 (i) Tragedy
 (ii) Themes
 (iii) Shakespeare's Craftsmanship
 (iv) A variety of questions – Questions on Scenes, General Questions, Leaving Certificate Questions.

Finally, these notes will have been successful, if the student can confidently say, "I disagree with ..."

Patrick H. Brennan

Part 1
Introduction

Shakespeare's Life and Work

When William Shakespeare wrote *Othello* in 1604, his reputation and popularity as a dramatist were already at a high point. He had already written most of his comedies, history-plays and some of his greatest tragedies. *Othello* is Shakespeare's only "domestic" tragedy and the only one which is set in his own age. Yet the simplicity and directness of its plot distinguishes it among Shakespeare's other tragedies.

While *Othello* cannot match *King Lear* in the universal scope of its vision, it is rich and satisfying as a theatrical experience. It speaks to us of the world we live in, although it concerns a different world. *Othello* attempts to dramatise the inner workings of the human mind by discovering the reality behind appearances and in distinguishing between good and evil in ordinary life. This exploration is of no less universal significance to modern man than the cosmic version of *King Lear* or Shakespeare's other great tragedies, *Macbeth* and *Hamlet*.

Whatever about the scope of Shakespeare's vision in *Othello* in comparison with *King Lear*, for his craftsmanship in language, for his skill in stagecraft and, above all, for his depth of insight into human character and motivation, Shakespeare remains unequalled to this day. Francis Meres in *Palladus Tamia: Wits Treasury* (1598) said of Shakespeare's craftsmanship: "The Muses would speak with Shakespeare's fine-filed phrase, if they would speak English." Since this was written, Shakespeare has continued to be recognised as the master dramatist that he is and *Othello* is just one fascinating example of the infinite variety of his skills, whether literary, dramatic or psychological.

William Shakespeare was born in April 1564 in Stratford-upon-Avon in Warwickshire. His father was a prosperous merchant, who married Mary Arden, daughter of a substantial landowner. Their third child, William, probably attended the grammar school in Stratford, where he learned the Latin language and literature. In 1582 Shakespeare married Anne Hathaway, who was eight years his senior. They had three children: Susanna, Hamnet and Judith. There is little information available about Shakespeare's early married life in Stratford.

Later Shakespeare went to London and, by 1592, he was well established and popular as a dramatist and actor. He was a member of The Lord Chamberlain's Men, a company of actors and dramatists. He became a shareholder in the Globe Theatre and seems to have become quite wealthy. In a period of just over twenty years, Shakespeare wrote thirty-seven plays, some long narrative poems and over 150 sonnets. He retired to Stratford around 1611 and bought New Place, one of the finest houses in the town. He died there on 23 April 1616 and was buried at Stratford Parish Church.

Shakespeare's dramatic writings consist of comedies, histories and tragedies. His reputation, even to the present time, remains as high as ever and he is best known for his "great" tragedies: *Hamlet, Othello, King Lear* and *Macbeth*. Of his poetry, the sonnets, dealing with such themes as love and friendship, art and poetry, as remedies against the ravages of time, are most memorable. His works of literature and drama have stood the test of time and Shakespeare is perhaps unmatched in any language, as a master craftsman of language, stagecraft and characterisation.

The Elizabethan Theatre

Shakespeare's theatre differed radically from modern realistic theatres, with vast resources at their disposal. The outer stage was a rectangular platform which extended out into the area now occupied by the first rows of seats on the main floor of a theatre, now called the "orchestra" or "pit". The platform had no moveable curtain to punctuate changes of scene. Stage properties were basic and simple, lacking elaborate scenery and stage devices.

At the back of this platform was a curtained inner recess (for use as an inner room or tomb). At each side of this were two projecting wings, each with a door opening obliquely on to the stage. Above these was a balcony (which could represent a bedroom or prison). A trapdoor in the stage allowed an entrance for ghosts or devils and a similar trapdoor, in the canopy over the stage, represented the "heavens", from where angels could descend on a rope. Lavish costumes were employed to create the dramatic illusion of being in a different world.

Such primitive stagecraft placed greater importance on the words of the actual play in compensating for the lack of scenery and effective stage properties. The overall effect resembled that of some kinds of modern theatre, with the audience around the stage, no curtains, and entrances and exits being made through the audience's accommodation. The primitive stage properties and scenery of Shakespeare's stage were similar in effect to the modern minimalist use of scenery and props on a bare stage, with only a vague suggestion of the actual scenes.

Before the advent of theatres as such, plays were performed in inns and courtyards by travelling companies of players. When Shakespeare arrived in London, soon after 1585, plays were performed in public or private theatres and the halls of royal palaces and of the Inns of Court. The public theatres around this time were: The Theater, The Curtain, Newington Butts and The Rose and all were used occasionally by Shakespeare's company.

In 1599, the Globe Theatre was erected on the Bankside, across the Thames from the city. The Globe was the handsomest theatre of its time, consisting of a large octagonal building, open to the sky in the centre, and capable of seating a large audience. In 1608 Shakespeare's company leased the Blackfriar's Theatre, which was protected from the weather and was ideal for the winter months.

Shakespeare had a long association with The Lord Chamberlain's Men, later called The King's Men, who enjoyed great popularity in London. Generally players were looked on with suspicion by society and were poor and of low status. However, Shakespeare's company and some others prospered and sometimes performed at Court. Shakespeare's *Othello* was performed at Court on at least two occasions before important visitors – in 1610, and again in 1613 to celebrate the wedding of Princess Elizabeth and Prince Frederick.

The Date and Publication of *Othello*

The first recorded performance of Shakespeare's *Othello* was given by Shakespeare's company, The King's Men, on 1 November 1604, before the Court of King James in the old Banqueting House at

Whitehall. The play was probably written some months before this date, probably early in 1604, or in 1603, just after *Hamlet* and just before *King Lear* and *Macbeth*.

Othello remained unpublished until 1622, when Thomas Walkley published a Quarto edition of the play. In 1623 *Othello* was printed in the First Folio edition of Shakespeare's entire works. A Second Quarto edition was issued in 1630 and in 1655 a Third Quarto edition. Our present editions rely mainly on the First Quarto and the First Folio editions. Scholars agree that both of these were probably printed from substantially authentic copies of the play as written and acted by Shakespeare and his company. Neither text is superior to the other and both contribute significantly to establishing Shakespeare's original text, despite their differences in words or even in whole passages. Scholars continue to search for Shakespeare's original intentions in writing the text of *Othello*.

The Source of the Plot of *Othello*

The original story of *Othello* was contained in a collection of Italian tales by Giovanni Giraldi Cinthio (1504–1573), entitled *Gli Hecatommithi* and published in Venice in 1566. This collection of a hundred stories contained *The Story of Desdemona of Venice and The Moorish Captain*, which forms the basis of Shakespeare's *Othello*. Shakespeare transformed this leisurely tale into an intriguing drama of love, scheming and jealousy through a number of significant alterations:

- The action is more leisurely in Cinthio's tale. Desdemona and the Moor have lived together for some time in Venice before the intrigue of Iago begins. The action of Shakespeare's *Othello* is compressed into just three days.

- Shakespeare created new characters, particularly Roderigo (who, like Othello, is taken in by Iago's plausible schemes) and Brabantio. He transformed others, notably Emilia (who is not aware of Iago's schemes until late in the play), Iago and Othello himself.

- Iago's motivation is much more subtle than the Ensign's in Cinthio's story. In it, the Ensign was simply motivated by a jealous love of Desdemona, the Captain's wife. Iago's Machiavellian schemes in *Othello* are much more elaborate than in Cinthio's tale.

- There is no political background in Cinthio's novella. Shakespeare has made the historic Turkish attack on Cyprus in 1570 the outward occasion of the action of *Othello*. At this period the very Christianity of Cyprus, so sacred to the Venetians, was under threat and so it is a suitable setting for the tragedy of *Othello*, whose Christian principles and behaviour are under stress.

- Shakespeare's Othello is a man of nobility and greatness who arouses tragic sympathy in his misfortune. He is indispensable to the Venetian state and is portrayed as royal, courageous, honest and even exotic.

- Finally, the manner of Desdemona's death and the conclusion of the play are entirely different in *Othello*. In Cinthio's tale, Desdemona is crudely beaten to death. The Moor escapes justice and is eventually killed by Desdemona's family. The Ensign eventually dies of internal injuries due to prolonged torture.

All these alterations and many more highlight Shakespeare's dramatic skill in weaving his plot and characters from a leisurely and sometimes crude moral tale to a romantic and swiftly moving tragic drama of love corrupted by intrigue and jealousy.

The Period and Setting of *Othello*

The action of *Othello* takes place around the year 1570, when the Turks invaded Venice's great care, Cyprus. Cyprus was an outpost of Christendom, rich and vulnerable to pagan attack. It was here that Christian turned Turk and abandoned his tradition. It was here that strange happenings were known to occur. However, it is Iago's scheming and not the actual locality of Cyprus, which brings about Othello's disasters. Cyprus simply isolates Othello and Desdemona from the normality of Venice, helpful in time of crisis.

Act 1 has as its setting Venice, a peaceful, law-abiding and sophisticated city, where justice and fair play for all are paramount. It is this normal world that Othello and Desdemona leave for the mysterious, exotic world of Cyprus. This change of setting is significant in enabling Iago's schemes to work so effectively, not just on Othello, but on Roderigo and Desdemona and even on Emilia.

If Venice stands for peace, justice and reason, then Cyprus stands for war, evil and passion and thus Shakespeare considered the change of scene appropriate to the tragedy. Apart from this, the actual place of the action of the play has no major significance in advancing the tragedy, since there is no real atmosphere of evil or the supernatural associated with either Venice or Cyprus. The change of setting simply enables the values portrayed in Act 1 in Venice to be tested in the precarious atmosphere of Cyprus and this is what happens in *Othello*.

The Plot Structure of *Othello*

The plot of *Othello* falls naturally into the five divisions of classical drama. The division into acts and scenes may be the work of editors and not of Shakespeare himself.

1. The Exposition: Act 1, Scene I – Act 1, Scene III

This section establishes the setting – the time and place of the action – and introduces the characters and their relationships to each other.

Act 1 introduces many motives for action, none of which will dominate the tragedy: Othello's secret marriage; Brabantio's vindictive passion against Othello; the swift dispatch of Othello to counter the Turkish threat in Cyprus. The first wave of Iago's attack succeeds with Roderigo and Brabantio but leaves Othello firm and unaffected, triumphing over his accusers and receiving a mandate from the state to save Cyprus from the Turks. This section establishes Othello as a man of nobility and stature, while Iago appears as a secondary figure in the action. Yet this section carefully creates the conditions from which the tragic action will spring and which will make the outcome seem inevitable. All is not yet revealed, but the setting and atmosphere of Act 1 prepare for the mainsprings of the tragic action.

2. The Complication: Act 2, Scene I – Act 3, Scene II

In this section the action increases and begins to rise to a high point. Complications are introduced in the plot, which will result in drama and conflict.

This section begins with tension as we await the safe arrival of Desdemona and Othello from the storm. Their happy reunion is overshadowed by the second wave in Iago's plan, leading to the brawl involving Cassio. Othello is moved to anger but is still unaffected by Iago's schemes. As Iago weaves his plans for further action to counter Cassio's pleas to Desdemona for reinstatement, Othello and Desdemona talk together lovingly for the last time.

3. The Climax: Act 3, Scene III

The complications set in motion in the previous section reach a turning point on which the future action depends.

In this section Iago cunningly works on Othello's mind and creates doubts and confusion. As these grow, Othello begins to lose everything that he has valued so highly. Othello loses his self-control and begins to disintegrate, believing Desdemona is unfaithful to him. From now on he is in Iago's power.

4. The Resolution: Act 3, Scene IV – Act 5, Scene I

The movement towards disaster gains momentum and the consequences of previous events take place.

Othello's disintegration continues in this section. Manipulated by Iago, Othello vainly searches for peace of mind, through questioning Desdemona coldly and spying on her. Iago uses Desdemona's handkerchief, which she had dropped, to convince Othello of Cassio's and Desdemona's infidelity. Othello contemplates revenge on Desdemona and strikes her violently in public, as confusion and anger rage together in his mind. In desperation, Desdemona appeals to Iago for help, but he does not relent. While Desdemona innocently prepares for the worst, Iago contrives to kill Cassio and Roderigo in the darkness of the streets, to cover up his evil schemes and prevent his exposure.

5. The Conclusion or Catastrophe: Act 5, Scene II

The movement of the action concludes and the consequences of previous events have their inevitable tragic conclusion.

Othello's disintegrating mind fills with grief, jealousy, revenge and a desire for justice and eventually with despair and self-destructive love. Just as Iago's plot is exposed, Othello kills Desdemona and himself *"to die upon a kiss"*. The action concludes with the villain unrepentant, the innocent Desdemona murdered and the misguided but noble Othello dying, caught between despair and an unattainable love.

Part 2

Text and Commentary

Characters

Duke of Venice	
Brabantio	A Senator
Other Senators	
Gratiano	Brother to Brabantio
Lodovico	Kinsman to Brabantio
Othello	A noble Moor in the service of the Venetian State
Cassio	His Lieutenant
Iago	His Ancient
Roderigo	A Venetian Gentleman
Montano	Othello's predecessor in the Government of Cyprus
Clown	Servant to Othello
Desdemona	Daughter to Brabantio, and Wife to Othello
Emilia	Wife to Iago
Bianca	Mistress to Cassio

Sailor, Officers, Gentlemen, Messengers, Musicians, Heralds, Attendants.

Scene: For the first Act, in Venice; during the rest of the Play, at a Sea-Port in Cyprus.

Act 1
Scene I

Venice. A Street.
Enter Roderigo and Iago.

Roderigo Tush! Never tell me; I take it much unkindly
That thou, Iago, who hast had my purse
As if the strings were thine, shouldst know of
    this[1].

Iago 'Sblood[2], but you will not hear me:
If ever I did dream of such a matter,
Abhor me.

Roderigo That told'st me thou didst hold him[3] in thy hate.

Iago Despise me if I do not. Three great ones[4] of the
    city,
In personal suit[5] to make me his lieutenant,
Off-capped[6] to him; and, by the faith of man,   10
I know my price, I am worth no worse a place;
But he, as loving his own pride and purposes,
Evades them, with a bombast circumstance[7]
Horribly stuffed with epithets of war[8]; And, in
    conclusion,
Nonsuits my mediators; for, 'Certes,' says he,
'I have already chose my officer.'
And what was he?
Forsooth[9], a great arithmetician[10],
One Michael Cassio, a Florentine,
A fellow almost damn'd in a fair wife[11];   20
That never set a squadron in the field,
Nor the division of a battle knows
More than a spinster; unless the bookish theoric[12],
Wherein the toged[13] consuls can propose
As masterly as he: mere prattle, without
    practice,
Is all his soldiership. But he, sir, had the election;
And I – of whom his eyes had seen the proof
At Rhodes, at Cyrpus, and on other grounds
Christian and heathen – must be be-lee'd and
    calm'd[14]
By debitor and creditor[15]; this counter-caster,[16]   30
He, in good time, must his lieutenant be,
And I – God bless the mark! – his Moorship's
    ancient[17].

---

[1] Othello's elopement with Desdemona
[2] By God's blood! (an oath)

[3] Othello
[4] important officials or senators

[5] appeal
[6] appealed respectfully

[7] long-winded evasive language
[8] military language

[9] certainly, truly
[10] a theorist with no practical experience
[11] a ladies' man

[12] book-learning
[13] wearing togas; impractical

[14] must be cut off from further promotion (like a ship cut off from the wind)
[15] by an accountant or theorist
[16] a theorist, who counts using counters
[17] ensign, flag bearer

	Roderigo	By heaven, I rather would have been his hangman.
	Iago	Why, there's no remedy: 'tis the curse of the service,

[18] promotion depends on favouritism
[19] seniority

Preferment goes by letter and affection[18],
Not by the old gradation[19], where each second
Stood heir to the first. Now, sir, be judge yourself,

[20] bound in duty

Whe'r I in any just term am affin'd[20]
To love the Moor.

Roderigo   I would not follow him then.

Iago   O! sir, content you;   40

I follow him to serve my turn upon him;
We cannot all be masters, nor all masters

[21] notice
[22] bowing servant
[23] pleased with his own servile behaviour

Cannot be truly follow'd. You shall mark[21]
Many a duteous and knee-crooking knave[22],
That, doting on his own obsequious bondage[23],
Wears out his time, much like his master's ass,

[24] fodder; food and drink
[25] dismissed

For nought but provender[24], and when he's old,
    cashier'd;[25]

[26] let such servile servants be whipped
[27] pretending to be dutiful

Whip me such honest knaves[26]. Others there are
Who, trimm'd in forms and visages of duty[27],
Keep yet their hearts attending on
    themselves,   50
And, throwing but shows of service on their
    lords,

[28] served their own interests

Do well thrive by them, and when they have
    lined their coats[28]
Do themselves homage: these fellows have
    some soul;
And such a one do I profess myself. For, sir,
It is as sure as you are Roderigo,
Were I the Moor, I would not be Iago:
In following him, I follow but myself;
Heaven is my judge, not I for love and duty,

[29] for my personal interests

But seeming so, for my peculiar end[29]:
For when my outward action doth
    demonstrate   60

[30] the true intentions behind my actions
[31] by my outward behaviour

The native act and figure of my heart[30]
In compliment extern[31], 'tis not long after
But I will wear my heart upon my sleeve

[32] I will show my true feelings openly
[33] own; have
[34] succeed in that way

For daws to peck at[32]: I am not what I am.

Roderigo   What a full fortune does the thick-lips owe[33],
If he can carry't thus[34]!

Iago   Call up her father;

Rouse him, make after him, poison his delight,
Proclaim him in the streets, incense her
    kinsmen,

	And, though he in a fertile climate dwell,	
	Plague him with flies; though that his joy be	
	joy,	*70*
	Yet throw such changes of vexation[35] on't	
	As it may lose some colour.	
Roderigo	Here is her father's house; I'll call aloud.	
Iago	Do; with like timorous accent[36] and dire yell	
	As when, by night and negligence, the fire	
	Is spied in populous cities.	
Roderigo	What, ho! Brabantio! Signior Brabantio, ho!	
Iago	Awake! what, ho! Brabantio! thieves! thieves!	
	thieves!	
	Look to your house, your daughter, and your	
	bags!	
	Thieves! thieves!	*80*

[35] changes of fortune; frustrations

[36] terrifying language

Enter Brabantio, above, at a window.

Brabantio	What is the reason of this terrible summons?	
	What is the matter there?	
Roderigo	Signior, is all your family within?	
Iago	Are your doors lock'd?	
Brabantio	Why! wherefore ask you this?	
Iago	'Zounds[37]! sir, you are robb'd; for shame, put on	
	your gown;	
	Your head is burst, you have lost half your soul;	
	Even now, now, very now, an old black ram	
	Is tupping[38] your white ewe. Arise, arise!	
	Awake the snorting citizens with the bell,	
	Or else the devil will make a grandsire of you.	*90*
	Arise, I say.	
Brabantio	What! have you lost your wits?	
Roderigo	Most reverend signior, do you know my voice?	
Brabantio	Not I, what are you?	
Roderigo	My name is Roderigo.	
Brabantio	The worser welcome:	
	I have charg'd thee not to haunt about my	
	doors:	
	In honest plainness thou hast heard me say	
	My daughter is not for thee; and now, in	
	madness,	
	Being full of supper and distempering draughts[39],	
	Upon malicious knavery dost thou come	
	To start my quiet[40].	*100*
Roderigo	Sir, sir, sir!	
Brabantio	But thou must needs be sure	

[37] By God's wounds!

[38] enjoying sexual satisfaction with

[39] alcoholic drinks

[40] to disturb my rest

⁴¹a remote country house

⁴²A north African horse
    (Othello)
⁴³race horses
⁴⁴Spanish horses or mules
    for relations

⁴⁵sexual intercourse

⁴⁶just after midnight

⁴⁷a common servant

⁴⁸permission

⁴⁹contrary to proper
    behaviour

	My spirit and my place have in them power
	To make this bitter to thee.
Roderigo	Patience, good sir.
Brabantio	What tell'st thou me of robbing? this is Venice;
	My house is not a grange⁴¹.
Roderigo	Most grave Brabantio,
	In simple and pure soul I come to you.
Iago	'Zounds! sir, you are one of those that will not
	serve God if the devil bid you. Because we come
	to do you service and you think we are ruffians,
	you'll have your daughter covered with a Barbary
	horse⁴²; you'll have your nephews neigh 110
	to you;
	you'll have coursers⁴³ for cousins and gennets for
	germans⁴⁴.
Brabantio	What profane wretch art thou?
Iago	I am one, sir, that comes to tell you, your
	daughter and the Moor are now making the
	beast with two backs⁴⁵.
Brabantio	Thou art a villain.
Iago	You are – a senator.
Brabantio	This thou shalt answer; I know thee, Roderigo.
Roderigo	Sir, I will answer any thing. But, I beseech you, 120
	If't be your pleasure and most wise consent, –
	As partly, I find, it is, – that your fair daughter,
	At this odd-even⁴⁶ and dull-watch o' the night,
	Transported with no worse nor better guard
	But with a knave of common hire⁴⁷, a gondolier,
	To the gross clasps of a lascivious Moor, –
	If this be known to you, and your allowance⁴⁸,
	We then have done you bold and saucy wrongs;
	But if you know not this, my manners tell me
	We have your wrong rebuke. Do not believe, 130
	That, from the sense of all civility⁴⁹,
	I thus would play and trifle with your reverence:
	Your daughter, if you have not given her leave,
	I say again, hath made a gross revolt;
	Tying her duty, beauty, wit and fortunes
	In an extravagant and wheeling stranger
	Of here and every where. Straight satisfy
	yourself:
	If she be in her chamber or your house,
	Let loose on me the justice of the state
	For thus deluding you. 140
Brabantio	Strike on the tinder, ho!
	Give me a taper! call up all my people!

This accident[50] is not unlike my dream;   [50] event
Belief of it oppresses me already.
Light, I say! light!

[Exit from above.

Iago   Farewell, for I must leave you:
It seems not meet nor wholesome to my place
To be produc'd, as, if I stay, I shall,
Against the Moor; for, I do know the state,
However this may gall him with some check[51],   [51] reprimand
Cannot with safety cast[52] him; for he's embark'd   [52] dismiss
With such loud reason to the Cyprus wars, – *150*
Which even now stand in act[53], – that, for their   [53] are already happening
    souls,
Another of his fathom[54] they have none,   [54] ability and experience
To lead their business; in which regard,
Though I do hate him as I do hell-pains,
Yet, for necessity of present life,
I must show out a flag and sign of love,
Which is indeed but sign. That you shall surely
    find him,
Lead to the Sagittary the raised search;
And there will I be with him. So, farewell.

[Exit.

Enter below, Brabantio, and Servants with torches.

Brabantio   It is too true an evil: gone she is   *160*
And what's to come of my despised time[55]   [55] dishonoured future
Is nought but bitterness. Now, Roderigo,
Where didst thou see her? O, unhappy girl!
With the Moor, sayst thou? Who would be a
    father!
How didst thou know 'twas she? O, she
    deceives me
Past thought. What said she to you? Get more
    tapers!
Raise all my kindred! Are they married, think
    you?
Roderigo   Truly, I think they are.
Brabantio   O heaven! How got she out? O, treason of the
    blood:
Fathers, from hence trust not your
    daughters' minds   *170*
By what you see them act. Are there not charms
By which the property of youth and maidhood
May be abus'd[56]? Have you not read, Roderigo,   [56] deceived
Of some such thing?

	Roderigo	Yes, sir, I have indeed.
	Brabantio	Call up my brother. O! that you had had her.
		Some one way, some another! Do you know
		Where we may apprehend her and the Moor?
[57] reveal his whereabouts	**Roderigo**	I think I can discover him[57], if you please
		To get good guard and go along with me.
	Brabantio	Pray you, lead on. At every house I'll call; *180*
		I may command at most. Get weapons, ho!
		And raise some special officers of night.
[58] reward your efforts		On, good Roderigo; I'll deserve your pains[58].

[Exeunt.

The Plot (Day One – A Street in Venice)

A SPITEFUL CONVERSATION

At night-time in a dimly lit street in Venice, Iago and Roderigo are talking. Roderigo is angry that Iago, whom he bribed to help him court Desdemona, has not succeeded in winning Desdemona's hand in marriage for him. Desdemona, the daughter of a rich Venetian Senator, has just eloped with Othello, a Moor and a general of the Venetian army.

Iago tries to maintain Roderigo's confidence in him, in order to retain access to his money. He explains that he hates Othello, since the inexperienced Cassio was appointed Othello's lieutenant, instead of Iago himself, who had more experience and deserved the promotion. Iago succeeds in gaining Roderigo's sympathy and denounces favouritism in making military appointments. He explains that he follows Othello only to be revenged upon him.

Roderigo envies Othello's success in winning Desdemona. Iago encourages him to awaken Brabantio and tell him of his daughter's elopement with Othello. With relish, both go to Brabantio's house to awaken him with their shouts.

BRABANTIO ORGANISES A SEARCH PARTY

Brabantio, half asleep, appears at a window and accuses Roderigo of being drunk and disorderly. Roderigo had been forbidden to come to Brabantio's house to seek Desdemona. When Brabantio hears about the elopement, he is worried for her safety because of an ominous dream he has had. He enlists Roderigo's help in organising a search party for Desdemona and the Moor. Iago has succeeded in setting up both Roderigo and Brabantio against Othello. Meanwhile he slinks away into the night in order to maintain favour with Othello, who is important in Venice.

And what's to become of my despised time
Is nought but bitterness

(Brabantio, Act 1, Scene 1)

Dramatic Significance

A NIGHT OF INTRIGUE AND SUSPENSE

The scene opens dramatically with Roderigo arguing heatedly with Iago over using his money but letting him down. Later we realise that they have just heard the news that Desdemona, whose hand in marriage Roderigo hoped to win, has just eloped with Othello. They talk of money, promotion and old grudges and create an atmosphere of mystery and intrigue.

Later in the scene, we hear of an ominous dream, racial tension, treason of blood, a midnight elopement, magic charms and a search party by night. The spiteful hypocrisy of Iago in deciding to follow his superior officer just to get revenge for not being promoted, adds to the atmosphere of intrigue and hidden malice.

> *"I follow him to serve my turn upon him;*
> *We cannot all be masters, nor all masters*
> *Cannot be truly follow'd."*

We hear mention too of wars at Rhodes and Cyprus and against Christian and heathen. We learn that the Moor is shortly to embark to the Cyprus wars, which are now being fought. We are curious to meet Othello, who seems to be in everybody's thoughts, and we wonder what will come of the events of this night.

> *"Call up her father*
> *Rouse him, make after him, poison his delight,*
> *Proclaim him in the streets, incense her kinsmen,*
> *And, though he in a fertile climate dwell,*
> *Plague him with flies."*

THE CONTEXT FROM WHICH TRAGEDY WILL SPRING

Several different actions are begun in Scene I, any one of which might provide the dominant motive for a tragedy. Othello's elopement and secret marriage, Brabantio's vindictive fury, Roderigo's rejected love for Desdemona, and Iago's grudges against Cassio and Othello over Cassio's promotion in his place, together create the context in which tragedy is likely. However, the mainspring of the actual tragedy of *Othello* has not yet been wound up by Iago.

It is Roderigo who sets the drama in motion, by accusing Iago of betraying his trust and misusing his money. Roderigo has just lost Desdemona, who has married the Moor. Iago must defend himself, to retain control of Roderigo's money, and so he devises a plot against Othello – the main motive of the tragedy:

> *"O, sir, content you;*
> *I follow him to serve my turn upon him."*

Iago's own personality prepares us for the tragedy to come. His false appearance and his grudge against Othello and Cassio have hidden potential for destruction. He is never what he seems and studies his own interests first.

> *"Though I do hate him as I do hell-pains,*
> *Yet, for necessity of present life,*
> *I must show out a flag and sign of love,*
> *Which is indeed but sign."*

Iago's nature makes mischief very likely and we wonder what he will do next and who will be his victim.

A WEB OF PERSONAL RELATIONSHIPS

In this scene we are introduced to a complex web of relationships: Roderigo desires Othello's wife, Desdemona's hand in marriage; Cassio has been appointed Othello's second-in-command in preference to Iago; Othello has eloped with Brabantio's daughter, Desdemona; Iago is envious of Othello and seems to admire Desdemona. Iago has become involved in each of these relationships in this scene. To put matters mildly, Iago's hypocritical self-interest makes it clear that he is not attempting to do anyone a favour, except himself. Roderigo will be used as a tool to serve Iago's purposes and will then be discarded. Cassio and Desdemona will be used to destroy Othello and Othello himself will be used for Iago's own pleasure in villainy. As yet Iago has not devised any villainous schemes to hurt all around him, but we wait in suspense to learn whom the poisonous spider will trap in his web of deceit and what devices he will use to achieve his hidden purposes:

> *"In following him, I follow but myself."*

Character Development

IAGO
A PLAUSIBLE GRIEVANCE

As the scene begins, Roderigo accuses Iago of obtaining money from him on false promises. Iago plausibly defends himself, claiming that he is just as aggrieved as Roderigo, at the news of Othello's marriage to Desdemona.

> *"'Sblood, but you will not hear me."*

Iago feels insulted that Othello has promoted Cassio as lieutenant, despite his inexperience and the fact that three important persons in Venice had recommended Iago for the promotion.

"I know my price, I am worth no worse a place."

Iago also feels embittered that the promotion was not given by seniority and experience but by *"letter and affection"* for Cassio:

"Why, there's no remedy: 'tis the curse of the service."

Thus Iago wins the sympathy of Roderigo and perhaps we tend to share that sympathy.

A SKILFUL DECEIVER

Despite the sympathy he has gained, we realise that Iago has cheated Roderigo of his money and has not fulfilled his promises to help him to win Desdemona by keeping him informed of her affections:

"Tush! Never tell me; I take it much unkindly."

Iago reveals that his real motives are self-interest and a desire for revenge on Othello:

"Were I the Moor, I would not be Iago:
In following him, I follow but myself."

Roderigo is taken in by Iago's skilful defence of his actions, but Iago's true character remains a mystery.

"I am not what I am."

A ZESTFUL MISCHIEF-MAKER

As the scene progresses, Iago shows his delight in manipulating Roderigo and Brabantio and in creating mischief. He is a skilful mischief-maker, who seems to enjoy causing trouble for others.

"Call up her father;
Rouse him, make after him, poison his delight,
Proclaim him in the streets, incense her kinsmen."

His talent for instigating mischief is matched only by his vulgar humour in describing the runaway lovers:

"Even now, now, very now, an old black ram
Is tupping your white ewe. Arise, arise!
Awake the snorting citizens with the bell,
Or else the devil will make a grandsire of you.
Arise, I say."

Having started the mischief, Iago is shrewd enough not to be found in the middle of it:

"Farewell, for I must leave you:
It seems not meet nor wholesome to my place
To be produc'd, as, if stay I shall,
Against the Moor."

Truly an accomplished villain!

RODERIGO
A DISAPPOINTED SUITOR

Roderigo is a young wealthy Venetian, who has been rejected as a suitor for Desdemona by Desdemona herself and by her father, Brabantio. He shows his decadence in expecting that Iago can use his money to buy Desdemona's hand in marriage.

Naturally he is hurt by his rejection, yet he is polite in telling Brabantio of his daughter's elopement:

> *"Your daughter, if you have not given her leave,*
> *I say again, hath made a gross revolt;*
> *Tying her duty, beauty, wit and fortunes*
> *In an extravagant and wheeling stranger*
> *Of here and every where. Straight satisfy yourself."*

Later Brabantio pays him the courtesy of wishing that he had married Desdemona instead of Othello.

> *"Call up my brother. O! that you had had her!"*

A CONTRAST TO IAGO

Roderigo's politeness and his tolerance of society's ways contrast with Iago's vulgarity and rebelliousness. By these contrasts and through their conversations, Roderigo fulfils an important role in revealing the character of Iago to us. It is Roderigo's complaint at the beginning of the scene which provokes Iago into defending himself and instigating his mischief against Othello. Iago confides in him about his feelings and intentions and thus Roderigo is an important device in the drama, which eliminates the need for too many soliloquies:

> *"Tush! Never tell me; I take it much unkindly*
> *That thou, Iago, who hast had my purse*
> *As if the strings were thine, shouldst know of this."*

A GULLIBLE DUPE

Iago finds it so easy to confide in Roderigo, since Roderigo is so credulous and gullible. Despite his grievance against Iago's misuse of his money, Iago soon has Roderigo firmly convinced that he is worthy of trust:

> *"By heaven, I rather would have been his hangman."*

Roderigo willingly co-operates with Iago's plan to rouse Brabantio in the middle of the night, believing that he can still win Desdemona's hand in marriage:

> *"Here is her father's house. I'll call aloud."*

When Iago shrewdly leaves to avoid being seen to undermine Othello, Roderigo does not protest. Roderigo's stupidity, in believing Iago is on his side and in allowing himself to be used as Iago's willing dupe, is his main fault.

BRABANTIO
SUPERSTITIOUS

When Roderigo succeeds in convincing Brabantio that his daughter has eloped with Othello, Brabantio shows his superstitious nature:

> *"This accident is not unlike my dream."*

He believes that Othello must have used magic charms to entice Desdemona to elope with him:

> *"Are there not charms*
> *By which the property of youth and maidhood*
> *May be abus'd?"*

However, such beliefs were common in Shakespeare's time.

A LOVING FATHER

Despite Desdemona's *"treason of blood"*, Brabantio tries to find an explanation for her behaviour in Othello's use of magic to win her. When he realises he has lost his daughter, he sees nothing to live for:

> *"… what's to come of my despised time*
> *Is nought but bitterness."*

Brabantio's broken speech shows how tortured his mind is by his daughter's betrayal of him. He is torn between love for his daughter and the knowledge that she has deceived him:

> *"Where didst thou see her? O unhappy girl!*
> *With the Moor, sayst thou? Who would be a father!*
> *How didst thou know 'twas she? – O, she deceives me*
> *Past thought! What said she to you? Get more tapers."*

Scene II

Another Street.
Enter Othello, Iago, and Attendants, with torches.

Iago	Though in the trade of war I have slain men,
	Yet do I hold it very stuff o' the conscience[1]
	To do no contriv'd murder[2]: I lack iniquity
	Sometimes to do me service. Nine or ten times
	I had thought to have yerk'd[3] him here under
	the ribs.

[1] a matter of conscience

[2] deliberate murder

[3] stabbed

Othello	'Tis better as it is.	
Iago	Nay, but he prated[4],	[4] talked continuously
	And spoke such scurvy and provoking terms	
	Against your honour	
	That, with the little godliness I have,	
	I did full hard forbear him[5]. But, I pray, sir, *10*	[5] found it difficult to tolerate him
	Are you fast married[6]? Be assured of this,	[6] securely married
	That the magnifico[7] is much beloved,	[7] important official
	And hath in his effect a voice potential[8]	[8] an influence
	As double[9] as the duke's; he will divorce you,	[9] as powerful
	Or put upon you what restraint and grievance	
	The law – with all his might to enforce it on –	
	Will give him cable[10].	[10] scope
Othello	Let him do his spite:	
	My services which I have done the signiory[11]	[11] Venetian government
	Shall out-tongue his complaints. 'Tis yet to know,	
	Which when I know that boasting is an honour *20*	
	I shall promulgate[12], I fetch my life and being	[12] make known in public
	From men of royal siege[13], and my demerits[14]	[13] of royal rank
		[14] qualities
	May speak unbonneted[15] to as proud a fortune	[15] may equal or match
	As this that I have reach'd; for know, Iago,	
	But that I love the gentle Desdemona,	
	I would not my unhoused[16] free condition	[16] unconfined to a house
	Put into circumscription and confine[17]	[17] restriction and restraint
	For the sea's worth. But, look! what lights come	
	yond[18]?	[18] yonder; over there
Iago	Those are the raised father and his friends:	
	You were best go in. *30*	
Othello	Not I; I must be found:	
	My parts, my title, and my perfect soul[19]	[19] my talents, my legal right and my clear conscience
	Shall manifest me rightly. Is it they?	
Iago	By Janus[20], I think no.	[20] A two-faced Roman god

Enter Cassio and certain Officers, with torches.

Othello	The servants of the duke, and my lieutenant.	
	The goodness of the night upon you, friends!	
	What is the news?	
Cassio	The duke does greet you, general,	
	And he requires your haste-post-haste	
	appearance[21],	[21] immediate presence
	Even on the instant.	
Othello	What is the matter[22], think you?	[22] business
Cassio	Something from Cyprus, as I may divine.	
	It is a business of some heat;[23] the galleys *40*	[23] urgency
	Have sent a dozen sequent messengers[24]	[24] successive messengers

[25] urgently

[26] separate

[27] a large treasure ship, i.e. Othello has married the beautiful Desdemona

[28] By Mary
[29] Let us go

[30] we are evenly matched opponents

[31] hidden

[32] speak sensibly; appeal to common-sense

	This very night at one another's heels,	
	And many of the consuls, rais'd and met,	
	Are at the duke's already. You have been hotly[25]	
	call'd for;	
	When, being not at your lodging to be found,	
	The senate hath sent about three several[26]	
	quests	
	To search you out.	
Othello	'Tis well I am found by you.	
	I will but spend a word here in the house,	
	And go with you.	
	[*Exit.*	
Cassio	Ancient, what makes he here?	
Iago	Faith, he to-night hath boarded a land	50
	carrack[27];	
	If it prove lawful prize, he's made for ever.	
Cassio	I do not understand.	
Iago	He's married.	
Cassio	To who?	

Re-enter Othello.

Iago	Marry[28], to – Come, captain, will you go?
Othello	Have with you[29].
Cassio	Here comes another troop to seek for you.
Iago	It is Brabantio. General, be advis'd;
	He comes to bad intent.

Enter Brabantio, Roderigo, and Officers, with torches and weapons.

Othello	Holla! stand there!
Roderigo	Signior, it is the Moor.
Brabantio	Down with him, thief!

[They draw on both sides.

Iago	You, Roderigo! come, sir, I am for you[30].	
Othello	Keep up your bright swords, for the dew will	
	rust them.	
	Good signior, you shall more command with	60
	years	
	Than with your weapons.	
Brabantio	O thou foul thief! where hast thou stow'd[31] my	
	daughter?	
	Damn'd as thou art, thou hast enchanted her;	
	For I'll refer me to all things of sense[32],	

If she in chains of magic were not bound,
Whether a maid so tender, fair, and happy,
So opposite³³ to marriage that she shunn'd
The wealthy curled darlings of our nation,
Would ever have, to incur a general mock,
Run from her guardage³⁴ to the sooty bosom   70
Of such a thing as thou; to fear, not to delight.
Judge me the world, if 'tis not gross in sense
That thou hast practis'd on her with foul charms,
Abus'd her delicate youth with drugs or minerals
That weaken motion³⁵: I'll have't disputed on;
'Tis probable, and palpable to thinking³⁶.
I therefore apprehend and do attach thee
For an abuser of the world, a practiser
Of arts inhibited³⁷ and out of warrant³⁸.
Lay hold upon him: if he do resist,   80
Subdue him at his peril.

Othello   Hold your hands,
Both you of my inclining³⁹, and the rest:
Were it my cue to fight, I should have known it
Without a prompter. Where will you that I go
To answer this your charge?

Brabantio   To prison; till fit time
Of law and course of direct session⁴⁰
Call thee to answer.

Othello   What if I do obey?
How may the duke be therewith satisfied,
Whose messengers are here about my side,
Upon some present business of the state   90
To bring me to him?

Officer   'Tis true, most worthy signior;
The duke's in council, and your noble self,
I am sure, is sent for.

Brabantio   How! the duke in council!
In this time of the night! Bring him away.
Mine's not an idle⁴¹ cause: the duke himself,
Or any of my brothers of the state,
Cannot but feel this wrong as 'twere their own;
For if such actions may have passage free⁴²,
Bond-slaves and pagans shall our statesmen be.
                                        [Exeunt.

---

³³ opposed

³⁴ guardianship

³⁵ the senses
³⁶ it can be proved easily

³⁷ black magic
³⁸ illegal

³⁹ on my side

⁴⁰ immediate trial in court

⁴¹ trivial

⁴² are allowed

The Plot (Day One – Another Street in Venice)

IAGO PRETENDS TO BE LOYAL

Meanwhile, Iago has reached Othello's house and is pretending great loyalty to Othello. He informs Othello of Roderigo's animosity against him. He then warns him that the influential Brabantio will do all in his power to revenge himself on Othello and separate him from Desdemona.

Othello expresses confidence that his services to Venice and his own royal birth will out-tongue Brabantio's complaints against him. A torch-bearing party interrupts the conversation and Iago advises Othello to hide but Othello stands firm.

OTHELLO IS SUMMONED TO THE DUKE

The search party is led by Cassio, who informs Othello that he is summoned to the Senate, since the Turks are about to attack Cyprus. Othello goes inside and Iago and Cassio talk briefly.

Brabantio and his search party enter aggressively and both parties draw swords. Othello orders them to put away their weapons and Brabantio accuses him of stealing away his daughter by witchcraft. Othello will answer these charges but first he must answer the Duke's summons. Brabantio wishes to arrest Othello and put him on trial. However, since the Duke requires them both urgently, he is willing to put his case before the Duke and all depart for the Council Chamber.

Dramatic Significance

OTHELLO STANDS APART

This scene counters the biased views of Othello, which we heard in the previous scene from Iago, Roderigo and Brabantio. Othello is highlighted as an exceptional man of nobility, trust and courage and a fine, accomplished soldier. In this time of emergency, the Duke has sent out three search parties to find Othello, whose services are much needed to counter the Turkish threat to Cyprus:

> *"The duke does greet you, general,*
> *And he requires your haste-post-haste appearance,*
> *Even on the instant."*

Othello rejects Iago's advice to hide from the furious Brabantio and will face any challenge calmly and courageously.

> *"Not I; I must be found:*
> *My parts, my title, and my perfect soul*
> *Shall manifest me rightly."*

When Brabantio and his search party burst on the scene with swords drawn, Othello speaks with authority and even arrogance:

> *"Keep up your bright swords, for the dew will rust them.*
> *Good signior, you shall more command with years*
> *Than with your weapons."*

Thus Othello is portrayed as a potential tragic hero.

IAGO THE CHANGELING

In this scene Iago shows his true colours. He feigns loyalty and concern for Othello in contrast to his spite and animosity in the previous scene. He pretends that he tried to defend Othello against Brabantio's accusations and warns that Othello is in danger:

> *"Nay, but he prated,*
> *And spoke such scurvy and provoking terms*
> *Against your honour*
> *That, with the little godliness I have,*
> *I did full hard forbear him."*

Shrewdly he tries to encourage Othello to take vengeance on Brabantio by suggesting that he threatens Othello's marriage and even his honour:

> *"he will divorce you,*
> *Or put upon you what restraint and grievance*
> *The law – with all his might to enforce it on –*
> *Will give him cable."*

Slyly he challenges Roderigo (to keep him and his money out of danger) when swords are drawn. It is clear that Iago's real interest is self-interest and we now know exactly where he stands.

DRAMA AND EXCITEMENT

This is a scene of drama and tension after the previous scene of intrigue:

— the war in Cyprus seems to have come to a head and three search parties are sent to find Othello quickly. The Council is sitting late at night to deal with the emergency.

— Brabantio and his party rush on the scene and swords are drawn as they attempt to arrest Othello for seducing Desdemona. Othello dramatically quells this mob:

> *"Hold your hands,*
> *Both you of my inclining, and the rest:*
> *Were it my cue to fight, I should have known it*
> *Without a prompter."*

Character Development

IAGO
DOUBLE-DEALING

In the presence of Othello, Iago pretends to be loyal, by professing his anger at Roderigo's *"scurvy and provoking terms"* against Othello's *"honour"*. For this he gains Othello's approval.

> *"Nine or ten times*
> *I had thought to have yerk'd him here under the ribs."*

A little while ago Iago was convincing Roderigo that he was on his side. Not content with this, Iago twice pretends to save Othello from the coming search parties:

> *"Those are the raised father and his friends:*
> *You were best go in."*

Repeatedly, Iago tries to provoke Othello to take action against Brabantio, in order to cause further trouble to Othello:

> *"he will divorce you,*
> *Or put upon you what restraint or grievance*
> *The law – with all his might to enforce it on –*
> *Will give him cable."*

Iago has one purpose in mind – revenge on Othello.

RESOURCEFUL

Iago is quick-witted in turning events to his own advantage. Having failed to provoke Othello either to take action against Brabantio or to hide from him, Iago makes sure that Roderigo is safe during the threatened fight. He pretends to be attacking him but draws him aside to protect him:

> *"You, Roderigo! come, sir, I am for you."*

Even with Cassio, Iago talks casually, giving no hint of his animosities:

> *"Faith, he to-night hath boarded a land carrack;*
> *if it prove lawful prize, he's made for ever."*

Nobody realises that Iago is playing a double game, since his quick thinking covers his part in the mischief-making.

OTHELLO
DIGNIFIED AND STRONG

Othello is not provoked by Iago's assertions of Roderigo's public dishonour to Othello nor his claims that Brabantio's influence will succeed in divorcing Othello. Othello will not take rash action against Brabantio nor will he play the coward and hide. Assured of his own worth, he is prepared to stand firm and meet Brabantio's charges:

> *"I must be found:*
> *My parts, my title, and my perfect soul*
> *Shall manifest me rightly. Is it they?"*

When Othello is accosted by the angry Brabantio, he remains calm and dignified. He prevents a fight and answers Brabantio with courtesy:

> *"Good signior, you shall more command with years*
> *Than with your weapons."*

He realises that this matter is best solved without needless violence, although he is willing to fight, if it were the proper time to fight.

> *"Were it my cue to fight, I should have known it*
> *Without a prompter. Whither will you that I go*
> *To answer this your charge?"*

Othello's dignity and calmness are impressive on this occasion and we are not surprised that the Duke needs such a man to command against the Turks.

HUMAN AND VULNERABLE

In addition to his integrity and strength of character, Othello shows a gentler human side to his personality. He shows no fear of Brabantio's influence and treats him respectfully, despite the insulting accusations levelled against him. He trusts Iago completely and never questions his motives. He is open and honest and expects the same from others and this makes him vulnerable, despite his strength of character:

> *"The goodness of the night upon you, friends!"*

Othello is conscious of his own worth and integrity:

> *"I fetch my life and being*
> *From men of royal siege, and my demerits*
> *May speak unbonneted to as proud a fortune*
> *As this that I have reach'd."*

He openly declares his love for Desdemona, for whom he gave up his freedom as a bachelor:

> *"For know, Iago,*
> *But that I love the gentle Desdemona,*
> *I would not my unhoused free condition*
> *Put into circumscription and confine*
> *For the sea's worth."*

Othello seems to be not only the best kind of soldier but a fine person as well.

BRABANTIO

RIGHTEOUS ANGER

Brabantio's anger is understandable in this scene – he is called out at night to defend his daughter's honour against the spells of the mysterious Moor. He cannot understand how his daughter could have married such a man and his concern excuses his strong language:

> *"O thou foul thief! where hast thou stow'd my daughter?*
> *Damn'd as thou art, thou hast enchanted her."*

REASONABLE

Yet Brabantio is reasonable and is prepared to await the outcome of a trial of Othello:

> *"To prison; till fit time*
> *Of law and course of direct session,*
> *Call thee to answer."*

He feels that the justice of his cause will vindicate his actions before the Duke and the Senate:

> *"Mine's not an idle cause: the duke himself,*
> *Or any of my brothers of the state,*
> *Cannot but feel this wrong as 'twere their own."*

Brabantio earns our sympathy.

CASSIO

OTHELLO'S FRIEND

We learn little of Cassio's personality in this scene except that Othello regards him as a friend. Cassio is just as surprised as Iago was on hearing of Othello's marriage – yet he was involved in the courtship, as we learn later. This emphasises the suddenness of the marriage. Cassio has been diligently searching for Othello, who has been *"hotly call'd for"* by the Duke and Senate and we gather that Cassio is a loyal friend to Othello.

Scene III

A Council Chamber.
The Duke and Senators sitting at a table. Officers attending.

Duke		There is no composition[1] in these news
		That gives them credit[2].
First Senator		Indeed, they are disproportion'd[3]
		My letters say a hundred and seven galleys.
Duke		And mine, a hundred and forty.
Second Senator		And mine, two hundred:
		But though they jump not on a just account[4],–

[1] consistency
[2] credibility
[3] inconsistent

[4] do not agree on the precise number

	As in these cases, where the aim reports[5],	[5] where reports are estimated
	'Tis oft with difference,–yet do they all confirm	
	A Turkish fleet, and bearing up to[6] Cyprus.	[6] coming towards
Duke	Nay, it is possible enough to judgment: 10	
	I do not so secure me in the error[7],	[7] the inconsistency does not make me feel secure
	But the main article I do approve[8]	[8] I accept the main thrust of the reports
	In fearful sense[9].	[9] as disturbing
Sailor	[Within] What, ho! what, ho! what ho!	
Officer	A messenger from the galleys.	

Enter a Sailor.

Duke	Now, what's the business?	
Sailor	The Turkish preparation makes for Rhodes;	
	So was I bid report here to the state	
	By Signior Angelo.	
Duke	How say you by this change?	
First Senator	This cannot be,	
	By no assay of reason[10]; 'tis a pageant	[10] by any test of reason
	To keep us in false gaze[11]. When we consider 20	[11] it is a pretence to deceive us
	The importancy of Cyprus to the Turk,	
	And let ourselves again but understand,	
	That as it more concerns the Turk than Rhodes,	
	So may he with more facile question bear it[12],	[12] more easily capture it
	For that it stands not in such war-like brace[13],	[13] readiness for war
	But altogether lacks the abilities	
	That Rhodes is dress'd in[14]: if we make thought	[14] equipped with
	of this,	
	We must not think the Turk is so unskilful	
	To leave that latest which concerns him first,	
	Neglecting an attempt of ease and gain, 30	
	To wake and wage a danger profitless[15].	[15] to risk a danger, which is unlikely to bring success
Duke	Nay, in all confidence, he's not for Rhodes.	
Officer	Here is more news.	

Enter a Messenger.

Messenger	The Ottomites[16], reverend and gracious,	[16] the Turks
	Steering with due course toward the isle of	
	Rhodes,	
	Have there injointed them with[17] an after fleet.	[17] have been joined by
First Senator	Ay, so I thought. How many, as you guess?	
Messenger	Of thirty sail; and now they do re-stem[18]	[18] redirect
	Their backward course, bearing with frank	
	appearance[19]	[19] directly
	Their purposes toward Cyprus. Signior 40	
	Montano,	

[20] open respect
[21] informs

[22] urgent

[23] so pressing and urgent

[24] swallows up

[25] quacks

[26] without

[27] as you see fit

[28] own

	Your trusty and most valiant servitor,	
	With his free duty[20] recommends[21] you thus,	
	And prays you to believe him.	
Duke	'Tis certain then, for Cyprus.	
	Marcus Luccicos, is not he in town?	
First Senator	He's now in Florence.	
Duke	Write from us to him; post-post-haste[22]	
	dispatch.	
First Senator	Here comes Brabantio and the valiant Moor.	

Enter Brabantio, Othello, Iago, Roderigo, and Officers.

Duke	Valiant Othello, we must straight employ you	
	Against the general enemy Ottoman.	50
	[To Brabantio] I did not see you; welcome,	
	gentle signior;	
	We lack'd your counsel and your help to-night.	
Brabantio	So did I yours. Good your grace, pardon me;	
	Neither my place nor aught I heard of business	
	Hath rais'd me from my bed, nor doth the	
	general care	
	Take hold of me, for my particular grief	
	Is of so flood-gate and o'erbearing nature[23]	
	That it engluts[24] and swallows other sorrows	
	And it is still itself.	
Duke	Why, what's the matter?	
Brabantio	My daughter! O! my daughter.	60
Duke }		
Senator }	Dead?	
Brabantio	Ay, to me;	
	She is abus'd, stol'n from me, and corrupted	
	By spells and medicines bought of	
	mountebanks[25];	
	For nature so preposterously to err,	
	Being not deficient, blind, or lame of sense,	
	Sans[26] witchcraft could not.	
Duke	Whoe'er he be that in this foul proceeding	
	Hath thus beguil'd your daughter of herself	
	And you of her, the bloody book of law	
	You shall yourself read in the bitter letter	
	After your own sense[27]; yea, though our	70
	proper[28] son	
	Stood in your action.	
Brabantio	Humbly I thank your Grace,	
	Here is the man, this Moor; whom now, it	
	seems,	

Your special mandate for the state affairs,
Hath hither brought.

Duke
Senator }
We are very sorry for it.

Duke
[To Othello] What, in your own part, can you
say to this?

Brabantio
Nothing, but this is so.

Othello
Most potent, grave, and reverend signiors,
My very noble and approv'd good masters,
That I have ta'en away this old man's daughter,
It is most true; true, I have married her: *80*
The very head and front of my offending
Hath this extent[29], no more. Rude am I in my
          speech,
And little bless'd with the soft phrase of peace;
For since these arms of mine had seven years'
          pith[30],
Till now some nine moons wasted[31], they have
          us'd
Their dearest action in the tented field[32]
And little of this great world can I speak,
More than pertains to feats of broil and battle;
And therefore little shall I grace my cause
In speaking for myself. Yet, by your gracious   *90*
          patience,
I will a round unvarnish'd [33] tale deliver
Of my whole course of love; what drugs, what
          charms,
What conjuration[34], and what mighty magic,
For such proceeding I am charg'd withal,
I won his daughter.

Brabantio
A maiden never bold;
Of spirit so still and quiet, that her motion
Blush'd at herself;[35] and she, in spite of nature,
Of years, of country, credit, every thing,
To fall in love with what she fear'd to look on!
It is a judgment maim'd and most imperfect   *100*
That will confess perfection so could err
Against all rules of nature, and must be driven
To find out practices of cunning hell,
Why this should be. I therefore vouch again
That with some mixtures powerful o'er the
          blood,
Or with some dram conjur'd to this effect[36],
He wrought[37] upon her.

Duke
To vouch this, is no proof,
Without more certain and more overt test[38]

[29] the full extent of my offence is

[30] have used their strengths for seven years
[31] until nine months ago

[32] battlefield

[33] plain truthful story

[34] magic spells

[35] her natural impulses made her blush

[36] some magic potion
[37] worked

[38] more definite proof

39 weak and unlikely
accusations
40 which seem trivial

41 proper influence

42 continually

43 threatened with death

44 being set free
45 behaviour
46 caves

47 her reaction to my story

48 man-hunters or cannibals

Than these thin habits and poor likelihoods[39]
Of modern seeming[40] do prefer against him.   *110*

First Senator   But, Othello, speak:
Did you by indirect and forced courses
Subdue and poison this young maid's affections;
Or came it by request and such fair question[41]
As soul to soul affordeth?

Othello   I do beseech you,
Send for the lady to the Sagittary,
And let her speak of me before her father:
If you do find me foul in her report,
The trust, the office I do hold of you,
Not only take away, but let your sentence   *120*
Even fall upon my life.

Duke   Fetch Desdemona hither.

Othello   Ancient, conduct them; you best know the
place.

                    [Exeunt Iago and Attendants.
And, till she come, as truly as to heaven
I do confess the vices of my blood,
So justly to your grave ears I'll present
How I did thrive in this fair lady's love,
And she in mine.

Duke   Say it, Othello.

Othello   Her father lov'd me; oft invited me;
Still[42] question'd me the story of my life   *130*
From year to year, the battles, sieges, fortunes
That I have pass'd.
I ran it through, even from my boyish days
To the very moment that he bade me tell it;
Wherein I spake of most disastrous chances,
Of moving accidents by flood and field,
Of hair-breadth 'scapes i' the imminent deadly
breach[43],
Of being taken by the insolent foe
And sold to slavery, of my redemption[44] thence
And portance[45] in my travel's history;   *140*
Wherein of antres[46] vast and deserts idle,
Rough quarries, rocks and hills whose heads
touch heaven,
It was my hint to speak, such was the process[47]
And of the Cannibals that each other eat,
The Anthropophagi[48], and men whose heads
Do grow beneath their shoulders. This to hear
Would Desdemona seriously incline;
But still the house-affairs would draw her
thence;

Which ever as she could with haste dispatch,
She'd come again, and with a greedy ear   *150*
Devour up my discourse. Which I observing,
Took once a pliant hour[49], and found good means   [49] a favourable opportunity
To draw from her a prayer of earnest heat
That I would all my pilgrimage dilate[50],   [50] tell in full
Whereof by parcels she had something heard,
But not intentively[51]: I did consent;   [51] continuously
And often did beguile her of her tears,
When I did speak of some distressful stroke
That my youth suffer'd. My story being done,
She gave me for my pains a world of sighs: *160*
She swore, in faith, 'twas strange, 'twas passing
     strange;
'Twas pitiful, 'twas wondrous pitiful:
She wish'd she had not heard it, yet she wish'd
That heaven had made her such a man; she
     thank'd me,
And bade me, if I had a friend that lov'd her,
I should but teach him how to tell my story,
And that would woo her. Upon this hint I spake:
She lov'd me for the dangers I had pass'd[52],   [52] overcome
And I lov'd her that she did pity them.
This only is the witchcraft I have us'd: *170*
Here comes the lady; let her witness it.

Enter Desdemona, Iago, and Attendants.

Duke   I think this tale would win my daughter too.
                    Good Brabantio,
                    Take up this mangled matter at the best;[53]   [53] Make the best of this
                    Men do their broken weapons rather use   confused affair
                    Than their bare hands.
Brabantio   I pray you, hear her speak:
                    If she confess that she was half the wooer,
                    Destruction on my head, if my bad blame[54]   [54] false accusations
                    Light on the man! Come hither, gentle mistress:
                    Do you perceive in all this noble company   *180*
                    Where most you owe obedience?
Desdemona   My noble father,
                    I do perceive here a divided duty:
                    To you I am bound for life and education;
                    My life and education both do learn[55] me   [55] teach
                    How to respect you; you are the lord of duty;
                    I am hitherto your daughter: but here's my
                         husband;
                    And so much duty as my mother show'd

⁵⁶claim

⁵⁷give birth to

⁵⁸restrict their freedom

⁵⁹wise advice

⁶⁰step

⁶¹gives way to a vain grief

⁶²for joy or grief
⁶³can be interpreted in two ways

⁶⁴strength

⁶⁵recognised capability

	To you, preferring you before her father,
	So much I challenge⁵⁶ that I may profess
	Due to the Moor my lord. 190
Brabantio	God be with you! I have done.
	Please it your Grace, on to the state affairs:
	I had rather to adopt a child than get it⁵⁷.
	Come hither, Moor:
	I here do give thee that with all my heart
	Which, but thou hast already, with all my heart
	I would keep from thee. For your sake, jewel,
	I am glad at soul I have no other child;
	For thy escape would teach me tyranny,
	To hang clogs on them⁵⁸. I have done, my lord.
Duke	Let me speak like yourself and lay a
	sentence⁵⁹, 200
	Which as a grize⁶⁰ or step, may help these lovers
	Into your favour.
	When remedies are past, the griefs are ended
	By seeing the worst, which late on hopes
	depended.
	To mourn a mischief that is past and gone
	Is the next way to draw new mischief on.
	What cannot be preserv'd when Fortune takes
	Patience her injury a mockery makes.
	The robb'd that smiles steals something from
	the thief;
	He robs himself that spends a bootless grief.⁶¹ 210
Brabantio	So let the Turk of Cyprus us beguile;
	We lose it not so long as we can smile.
	He bears the sentence well that nothing bears
	But the free comfort which from thence he
	hears;
	But he bears both the sentence and the sorrow
	That, to pay grief, must of poor patience
	borrow.
	These sentences, to sugar, or to gall,⁶²
	Being strong on both sides, are equivocal:⁶³
	But words are words; I never yet did hear
	That the bruis'd heart was pierced through the
	ear. 220
	I humbly beseech you, proceed to the affairs of
	state.
Duke	The Turk with a most mighty preparation makes
	for Cyprus. Othello, the fortitude⁶⁴ of the place
	is best known to you; and though we have there
	a substitute of most allowed sufficiency⁶⁵, yet

opinion[66], a sovereign mistress of effects[67],
throws a more safer voice on you: you must
therefore be content to slubber[68] the gloss of
your new fortunes with this more stubborn and
boisterous expedition[69].   *230*

Othello   The tyrant custom, most grave senators,
Hath made the flinty and steel couch[70] of war
My thrice-driven bed of down: I do agnize[71]
A natural and prompt alacrity[72]
I find in hardness, and do undertake
These present wars against the Ottomites.
Most humbly therefore bending to your state,
I crave fit disposition[73] for my wife,
Due reference of place and exhibition[74],
With such accommodation and besort[75]   *240*
As levels with her breeding.

Duke   If you please,
Be't[76] at her father's.

Brabantio   I'll not have it so.

Othello   Nor I.

Desdemona Nor I; I would not there reside,
To put my father in impatient thoughts
By being in his eye. Most gracious duke,
To my unfolding[77] lend your gracious ear;
And let me find a charter[78] in your voice
To assist my simpleness.

Duke   What would you, Desdemona?   *250*

Desdemona That I did love the Moor to live with him,
My downright violence[79] and storm of
    fortunes[80]
May trumpet to the world; my heart's subdu'd
Even to the very quality[81] of my lord;
I saw Othello's visage[82] in his mind,
And to his honours and his valiant parts
Did I my soul and fortunes consecrate.
So that, dear lords, if I be left behind,
A moth of peace[83], and he go to the war,
The rites for which I love him are bereft me,   *260*
And I a heavy interim shall support[84]
By his dear absence. Let me go with him.

Othello   Let her have your voices.
Vouch with me, heaven, I therefore beg it not
To please the palate of my appetite,
Nor to comply with heat,[85]– the young affects
In me defunct,[86]– and proper satisfaction,[87]
But to be free and bounteous to her mind;
And heaven defend your good souls that you
    think

[66] public opinion
[67] the guide to what must be done
[68] spoil
[69] tough and violent campaign
[70] hard bed
[71] recognise
[72] attractiveness
[73] suitable arrangements
[74] status and wealth
[75] servants and companions
[76] let it be
[77] my proposal
[78] permission
[79] bold sudden action
[80] disregard for fortune
[81] good qualities
[82] face
[83] idle
[84] I shall be sad in the meantime
[85] lust
[86] youthful desires are no longer important to me
[87] sexual pleasure in marriage

⁸⁸neglect

⁸⁹trivial matters of love
⁹⁰make blind with sexual
   pleasure
⁹¹my eyes and sense (Cupid,
   the god of love, blinded
   lovers' eyes)
⁹²pleasures
⁹³saucepan
⁹⁴head
⁹⁵shameful
⁹⁶attack my reputation

⁹⁷importance and relevance
⁹⁸concern you

⁹⁹care

¹⁰⁰outstanding

¹⁰¹at the best opportunity

	I will your serious and great business scant⁸⁸ *270*
	For she is with me. No, when light-wing'd toys
	Of feather'd Cupid⁸⁹ seal with wanton dullness⁹⁰
	My speculative and offic'd instruments,⁹¹
	That my disports⁹² corrupt and taint my business,
	Let housewives make a skillet⁹³ of my helm,⁹⁴
	And all indign⁹⁵ and base adversities
	Make head against my estimation⁹⁶!
Duke	Be it as you shall privately determine,
	Either for her stay or going. The affair cries haste,
	And speed must answer it. *280*
First Senator	You must away to-night.
Othello	With all my heart.
Duke	At nine i' the morning here we'll meet again.
	Othello, leave some officer behind,
	And he shall our commission bring to you;
	With such things else of quality and respect⁹⁷
	As doth import you⁹⁸.
Othello	So please your Grace, my ancient;
	A man he is of honesty and trust:
	To his conveyance⁹⁹ I assign my wife,
	With what else needful your good grace shall think
	To be sent after me. *290*
Duke	Let it be so.
	Good night to every one. *[To Brabantio]* And, noble signior,
	If virtue no delighted¹⁰⁰ beauty lack,
	Your son-in-law is far more fair than black.
First Senator	Adieu, brave Moor! use Desdemona well.
Brabantio	Look to her, Moor, if thou hast eyes to see:
	She has deceiv'd her father, and may thee.
	[Exeunt Duke, Senators, Officers, etc.
Othello	My life upon her faith! Honest Iago,
	My Desdemona must I leave to thee:
	I prithee, let thy wife attend on her;
	And bring them after in the best advantage¹⁰¹, *300*
	Come, Desdemona; I have but an hour
	Of love, of worldly matters and direction,
	To spend with thee: we must obey the time.
	[Exeunt Othello and Desdemona.
Roderigo	Iago!
Iago	What sayst thou, noble heart?
Roderigo	What will I do, think'st thou?
Iago	Why, go to bed, and sleep.

Roderigo	I will incontinently[102] drown myself.	[102]immediately
Iago	Well, if thou dost, I shall never love thee after. Why, thou silly gentleman! *310*	
Roderigo	It is silliness to live when to live is torment; and then have we a prescription[103] to die when death is our physician.	[103]a right
Iago	O! villanous; I have looked upon the world for four times seven years, and since I could distinguish betwixt a benefit and an injury, I never found man that knew how to love himself. Ere I would say, I would drown myself for the love of a guinea-hen[104], I would change my humanity with a baboon. *320*	[104]a prostitute
Roderigo	What should I do? I confess it is my shame to be so fond; but it is not in my virtue to amend it.	
Iago	Virtue! a fig! 'tis in ourselves that we are thus, or thus. Our bodies are our gardens, the which our wills are gardeners; so that if we will plant nettles or sow lettuce, set hyssop[105] and weed up thyme, supply it with one gender of herbs or distract it with many, either to have it sterile with idleness or manured with industry, why, the power and corrigible[106] authority of this lies *330* in our wills. If the balance of our lives had not one scale of reason to poise another of sensuality, the blood and baseness of our natures would conduct us to most preposterous[107] conclusions; but we have reason to cool our raging motions, our carnal stings, our unbitted[108] lusts, whereof I take this that you call love to be a sect or scion[109].	[105]an aromatic herb [106]correcting [107]irrational [108]uncontrolled [109]a side-shoot
Roderigo	It cannot be.	
Iago	It is merely a lust of the blood and a permission *340* of the will. Come, be a man. Drown thyself! drown cats and blind puppies. I have professed me thy friend, and I confess me knit to thy deserving with cables of perdurable[110] toughness; I could never better stead[111] thee than now. Put money in thy purse; follow these wars; defeat thy favour with a usurped beard[112]; I say, put money in thy purse. It cannot be that Desdemona should long continue her love to the Moor, – put money in thy purse, – nor he his *350* to her. It was a violent commencement in her,	[110]long-lasting [111]help [112]disguise your appearance with a false beard

113separation

114a bitter purgative apple
115satisfied

116a religious marriage vow
117wandering, lustful
118refined

119achieving

120true

121heart-felt

122let us join
123steal his wife

124Get going

125early

126devalue

127fool

and thou shalt see an answerable
sequestration113; put but money in thy purse.
These Moors are changeable in their wills; – fill
thy purse with money: – the food that to him
now is as luscious as locusts, shall be to him
shortly as bitter as coloquintida114. She must
change for youth: when she is sated115 with his
body, she will find the error of her choice. She
must have change, she must: therefore
    put money   360
in thy purse. If thou wilt needs damn thyself, do
it a more delicate way than drowning. Make all
the money thou canst. If sanctimony and a frail
vow116 betwixt an erring117 barbarian and a
supersublte118 Venetian be not too hard for my
wits and all the tribe of hell, thou shalt enjoy
her; therefore make money. A pox of drowning
thyself! it is clean out of the way: seek thou
rather to be hanged in compassing119 thy joy
than to be drowned and go without her.   370

Roderigo   Wilt thou be fast120 to my hopes, if I depend on
    the issue?

Iago   Thou art sure of me: go, make money. I have
told thee often, and I re-tell thee again and
again, I hate the Moor: my cause is hearted121:
thine hath no less reason. Let us be
conjunctive122 in our revenge against him; if
thou canst cuckold123 him, thou dost thyself a
pleasure, me a sport. There are many events in
the womb of time which will be delivered.   380
Traverse124; go; provide thy money. We will
have more of this to-morrow. Adieu.

Roderigo   Where shall we meet i' the morning?
Iago   At my lodging.
Roderigo   I'll be with thee betimes125.
Iago   Go to; farewell. Do you hear, Roderigo?
Roderigo   What say you?
Iago   No more of drowning, do you hear?
Roderigo   I am changed. I'll sell all my land.
Iago   Go to; farewell! put money enough in your   390
    purse.   *[Exit Roderigo.*

Thus do I ever make my fool my purse;
For I mine own gain'd knowledge should
    profane126,
If I would time expend with such a snipe127
But for my sport and profit. I hate the Moor,

And it is thought abroad that 'twixt my sheets
He has done my office[128]: I know not if't be
    true,
But I, for mere suspicion in that kind,
Will do as if for surety. He holds[129] me well;
The better shall my purpose work on him.
Cassio's a proper[130] man; let me see now: 400
To get his place; and to plume up[131] my will
In double knavery; how, how? Let's see:
After some time to abuse Othello's ear
That he is too familiar with his wife:
He hath a person and a smooth dispose[132]
To be suspected; framed to make women false.
The Moor is of a free and open nature,
That thinks men honest that but seem to be so,
And will as tenderly be led by the nose
As asses are.   410
I have't; it is engender'd[133]: hell and night
Must bring this monstrous birth to the world's
    light.

                                                  [Exit.

[128]seduced my wife

[129]regards me highly

[130]fine and handsome
[131]satisfy

[132]refined manner

[133]born

The Plot (Day One - A Council Chamber)

THE TURKISH THREAT

While the Duke and the Senators await Othello and Brabantio, they discuss three different reports which give news that the Turkish fleet is heading for Cyprus. Just then a sailor brings news that the Turks are now heading towards Rhodes. More news arrives that the Turks have reached Rhodes and are joining with another fleet. Excitement mounts as the Senators realise that the united fleet is now making for Cyprus. Othello, Brabantio, Iago and Roderigo arrive and the Duke immediately commissions Othello to defend Cyprus against the Turks.

OTHELLO ANSWERS HIS ACCUSERS

Brabantio immediately raises the issue of his daughter's elopement with Othello and again accuses Othello of unlawful magic. The Duke promises harsh punishment for the offender. When Othello is identified as the offender, all express their regret and the Duke asks Othello to give an account of his conduct.

Othello describes how he courted Desdemona not by lies or magic spells but by love. Brabantio refuses to believe that Desdemona could fall in love with a Moor such as Othello.

I am hitherto your daughter: but here's my husband.
(Desdemona, Act 1, Scene III)

The Duke requires proof of Brabantio's charges and Othello states his case, as Desdemona is sent for.

Othello explains how Brabantio and Desdemona invited him to their house to hear tales of his adventures. Desdemona's interest in him grew and they eventually fell in love but not through any witchcraft. The Duke is sympathetic to Othello and advises Brabantio to leave well enough alone. Brabantio, however, wishes to hear Desdemona's story first.

Desdemona speaks out in defence of her love of Othello. Brabantio bitterly hands her over to Othello's care, warning him not to take her fidelity for granted. The Duke advises Brabantio to forget his grievance and the discussion turns to the Turkish attack on Cyprus.

OTHELLO IS SENT TO CYPRUS

Then the Duke explains the situation in Cyprus. Othello knows the situation there better than Montano, Governor of Cyprus, and must take charge in this emergency. Othello willingly accepts this challenge but wishes that Desdemona should accompany him to Cyprus. Finally the Duke agrees but Othello must leave for Cyprus that night. Desdemona will follow later, when she is ready. Iago and Emilia will care for her in the meantime. The Duke and the senators leave, wishing Othello well, but Brabantio warns him that Desdemona may deceive him as she deceived her father.

IAGO INVENTS A SCHEME

Alone together, Iago and Roderigo discuss these events and form a plan to make Othello jealous. Roderigo is sad at losing Desdemona but Iago persuades him to keep up his hopes. Iago believes that Desdemona will soon tire of Othello and convinces Roderigo to raise money to further his revenge on Othello.

When Roderigo leaves, Iago reveals his true intention of using Roderigo to further his own plan to gain personal revenge on Othello. He decides to hint to Othello that Desdemona is becoming too familiar with Cassio. Since Othello is so trusting, he will easily be made jealous. Iago looks forward with relish to the success of his plan.

Dramatic Significance

A NATIONAL EMERGENCY

This scene opens with an atmosphere of emergency as conflicting reports arrive concerning the impending Turkish invasion of Cyprus. This attack threatens the security of the Venetian

I hate the Moor: my cause is hearted: thine hath no less reason.
(Iago, Act 1, Scene III)

state and Christianity itself. The tension builds up as report follows report and it eventually becomes clear that the Turks have joined their fleets together and are bearing menacingly on Cyprus.

OTHELLO – THE MAN OF THE MOMENT

Amidst the uncertainty and disorder of the Council Chamber, Othello makes his impressive entrance. Straightaway the Duke appoints him as commander in charge of the defence of the state against the Turkish threat:

> *"Valiant Othello, we must straight employ you*
> *Against the general enemy Ottoman."*

Later the Duke highlights Othello's reputation as a skilled soldier and the most suitable to command the expedition against the Turks:

> *"Othello, the fortitude of the place is best known to you, and though*
> *we have there a substitute of most allowed sufficiency, yet opinion,*
> *a sovereign mistress of effects, throws a more safer voice on you."*

Othello instantly and eagerly responds to his duty to the state, even though he has just been married:

> *"I do agnize*
> *A natural and prompt alacrity*
> *I find in hardness, and do undertake*
> *These present wars against the Ottomites."*

Thus Othello is clearly portrayed as a noble and outstanding man of stature, which fits him for his future role as a tragic hero.

LOVE AND ROMANCE WIN THE DAY

Othello effectively counters Brabantio's charges against him:

> *"She is abus'd, stole'n from me, and corrupted*
> *By spells and medicines bought of mountebanks."*

Othello accepts responsibility for taking Brabantio's daughter and explains how he won Desdemona's love by his tales of daring and adventure:

> *"She lov'd me for the dangers I had pass'd,*
> *And I lov'd her that she did pity them.*
> *This only is the witchcraft I have us'd."*

Desdemona confirms Othello's story, making clear that she was half the wooer in the relationship and wishes to go with Othello to Cyprus:

She lov'd me for the dangers I had pass'd,
And I lov'd her that she did pity them.

(Othello, Act 1, Scene III)

> *"I saw Othello's visage in his mind,*
> *And to his honours and his valiant parts*
> *Did I my soul and fortunes consecrate."*

Thus this scene counters Iago and Brabantio's insinuations about Othello and Desdemona's love and makes clear that their love, and nothing shady, brought them together. We hope for their happiness together for the remainder of the play.

A VULNERABLE LOVE

We see in this scene too that Othello and Desdemona's relationship is vulnerable to attack. Desdemona is a young girl captivated by romantic stories, who is bold and daring in her defiance of her father's opposition. She is idealistic and blindly romantic:

> *"That I did love the Moor to live with him,*
> *My downright violence and storm of fortunes*
> *May trumpet to the world: my heart's subdu'd*
> *Even to the very quality of my lord."*

Othello idolises Desdemona and is, perhaps, too possessive and self-centred. He seems to lack self-knowledge. His latent senses are as yet unawakened and potentially dangerous:

> *"She lov'd me for the dangers I had pass'd,*
> *And I lov'd her that she did pity them."*

Othello claims that he wishes not just:

> *"To please the palate of my appetite,*
> *Nor to comply with heat, – the young affects*
> *In me defunct, – and proper satisfaction,*
> *But to be free and bounteous of her mind."*

Desdemona's love centres on Othello but Othello's love centres on himself, through Desdemona. As yet they have not had time to settle down and adjust to each other. Brabantio's warning is ominous:

> *"Look to her, Moor, if thou hast eyes to see:*
> *She has deceiv'd her father, and may thee."*

Othello's reply ironically foreshadows the future:

> *"My life upon her faith."*

We hope that their happiness together will last.

A GLIMPSE AT THE TRAGIC CONFLICT TO COME

Iago advises Roderigo to have courage and patience in his attempt to win Desdemona. He is hoping that circumstances will change to suit their purposes and is conscious of the vulnerability of Othello and Desdemona's love:

> "It cannot be that
> Desdemona should long continue her love to
> the Moor, – put money in thy purse, – nor he his
> to her. it was a violent commencement in her,
> and thou shalt see an answerable sequestration."

He suggests that they work together to achieve their purposes:

> "Let us be
> conjunctive in our revenge against him; if
> thou canst cuckold him, thou dost thyself a
> pleasure, me a sport
> ... We will have more of this to-morrow."

This is our first hint of Iago's aims to revenge himself on Othello.

In his soliloquy, Iago reveals that he is merely using Roderigo as a tool to provide money for his own *"sport and profit"*. He hates Othello, who may have had an affair with Emilia, Iago's wife. He devalues love as lust and he will use his good standing with Othello and Othello's *"free and open nature"* to his own advantage. He begins to form his plan of action to destroy Othello and get Cassio's place, by suggesting that Cassio is *"too familiar"* with Desdemona. Thus we get a glimpse of the nature of the tragic conflict to come:

> "I have't; it is engender'd: hell and night
> Must bring this monstrous birth to the world's light."

Thus the exposition concludes and we are in possession of all the significant facts of character and incident, which are intermingled in such a way that tragic conflict is sure to result.

Character Development

OTHELLO

A HIGH REPUTATION

Othello is welcomed by the Duke before Brabantio and has earned the admiration and sympathy of all. When Brabantio accuses Othello of bewitching his daughter, all cry out in sympathy for Othello:

> "We are very sorry for it."

When the Duke appoints Othello to command the defence against the Turks, Othello's high standing in Venice is emphasised:

> "Othello, the fortitude of the place is best known to you, and though we
> have there a substitute of most allowed sufficiency, yet opinion, a
> sovereign mistress of effects, throws a more safer voice on you."

Othello's reputation is second to none.

A SENSE OF DUTY

Othello does not hesitate to accept the Duke's commission immediately, despite his recent marriage. He wishes Desdemona to be well looked after and is overjoyed that she will accompany him to Cyprus. Yet he stresses his devotion to duty:

> "... Heaven defend your good souls that you think
> I will your serious and great business scant
> For she is with me."

Othello is a soldier first and foremost, when the state needs his services.

AN ELOQUENT DIPLOMACY

Although Othello describes himself as *"rude in speech"*, his defence of his marriage shows a command and eloquence of language. The stories of his adventures and of his wooing of Desdemona captivate his audience and convince them of his integrity and honour in loving Desdemona:

> "She lov'd me for the dangers I had pass'd,
> And I lov'd her that she did pity them."

Othello displays self-control and diplomacy in his replies to the distressed Brabantio. The Duke acknowledges the credibility of Othello's defence:

> "I think this tale would win my daughter too."

Othello's frankness and simplicity win his case most eloquently.

OPENNESS AND TRUST

Throughout the scene, Othello shows his frank and open nature. He trusts others fully and expects the same openness from others.

His account of his wooing of Desdemona is truthful and frank and shows his romance and impulsiveness:

> "... I did consent;
> And often did beguile her of her tears,
> When I did speak of some distressful stroke
> That my youth suffer'd."

Othello has complete faith in Iago's honesty and leaves the care of Desdemona to Iago, as he leaves for Cyprus:

> "My life upon her faith! Honest Iago,
> My Desdemona must I leave to thee."

Iago will later use this trust to shake Othello's faith in Desdemona.

DESDEMONA
NOBLE AND INDEPENDENT

Desdemona is tactful in replying to her father's question:

> *"Where most you owe obedience?"*

She admits her duty to her father but stresses her loyalty to her husband:

> *"I am hitherto your daughter: but here's my husband."*

She does not try to excuse her elopement but is firm in asserting her love for Othello:

> *"And so much duty as my mother show'd*
> *To you, preferring you before her father,*
> *So much I challenge that I may profess,*
> *Due to the Moor my lord."*

ROMANTIC

When Desdemona appeals to be allowed to go with Othello, she shows the romantic side of her character:

> *"... My heart's subdu'd*
> *Even to the very quality of my lord;*
> *I saw Othello's visage in his mind,*
> *And to his honours and his valiant parts*
> *Did I my soul and fortunes consecrate."*

This confirms the deep romantic relationship of Desdemona and Othello.

IAGO
PERSUASIVE

Early in the scene, Iago bides his time, as if assessing how he can turn the latest events to his own purposes.

Roderigo challenges Iago again, but Iago succeeds in persuading him to have courage and patience and to provide more money by selling his land:

> *"Thou art sure of me: go, make money. I have told thee*
> *often, and I re-tell thee again and again, I hate the Moor:*
> *my cause is hearted: thine hath no less reason. Let us*
> *be communicative in our revenge."*

Iago's plausible speeches win over the despairing Roderigo yet again:

> *"I am changed."*

COLD AND PASSIONLESS

Iago reveals some of his true nature in this scene. He is cold and deliberate in his manipulation of Roderigo and plots revenge on Othello for the sheer enjoyment of it:

> *"if thou canst cuckold him, thou dost thyself a pleasure, me a sport."*

He will continue to prey on the human weaknesses of others.

Iago seems incapable of any real feelings and is therefore repulsive to us. His advice to Roderigo is his own rule of life:

> *"We have reason to cool our raging motions, our carnal stings, our unbitted lusts, whereof I take this that you call love to be a sect or scion."*

His evil-doing is less forgiveable, since it is so cool and calculated – it is evil for evil's sake:

> *"The power and corrigible authority of this lies in our wills."*

THE DUKE
FIRM AND REASONABLE

The Duke deals with the national crisis with skill and competence. He listens to the conflicting reports, discusses them and then makes a firm decision:

> *"'Tis certain then, for Cyprus.*
> *Marcus Luccicos, is not he in town?...*
> *Write from us to him; post-post-haste dispatch."*

When Othello at last arrives, the Duke comes quickly to the point:

> *"Valiant Othello, we must straight employ you*
> *Against the general enemy Ottoman."*

The Duke listens patiently to Brabantio's complaints against Othello and Othello's defence, interrupting only to ensure fair play.

> *"'To vouch this, is no proof,*
> *Without more certain and more overt test."*

He advises Brabantio to leave well enough alone, showing sound common sense:

> *"Good Brabantio,*
> *Take up this mangled matter at the best;*
> *Men do their broken weapons rather use,*
> *Than their bare hands."*

In the end, he decides for Othello, for whom he has a high regard:

> *"Noble signior,*
> *If virtue no delighted beauty lack,*
> *Your son-in-law is far more fair than black."*

RODERIGO
A GULLIBLE FOOL

Roderigo begins his conversation with Iago, intending to commit suicide:

> *"'I will incontinently drown myself."*

At the end he is willing to sell his land, give more money to Iago and place total trust in him.

> *"'I'll be with thee betimes."*

A few persuasive speeches and the pathetic, degraded Roderigo is yet again hoping to buy love with the help of the underhanded Iago. Roderigo stoops low in this scene.

Act 2
Scene I

A Sea-port Town in Cyprus.
An open place near the Quay.
Enter Montano and two Gentlemen.

Montano   What from the cape can you discern at sea?
First Gentleman Nothing at all: it is a high-wrought[1] flood;
                     I cannot 'twixt the heaven and the main
                     Descry[2] a sail.
Montano   Methinks the wind hath spoke aloud at land;
                     A fuller blast ne'er shook our battlements;
                     If it hath ruffian'd[3] so upon the sea,
                     What ribs of oak, when mountains melt on them,
                     Can hold the mortise? what shall we hear of this?
Second Gentleman
                     A segregation[4] of the Turkish fleet;   10
                     For do but stand upon the foaming shore,
                     The chidden billow[5] seems to pelt the clouds;
                     The wind-shak'd surge[6], with high and
                          monstrous mane,
                     Seems to cast water on the burning bear[7]
                     And quench the guards[8] of the ever-fixed pole:
                     I never did like molestation[9] view
                     On the enchafed[10] flood.
Montano   If that the Turkish fleet
                     Be not enshelter'd and embay'd, they are drown'd;
                     It is impossible they bear it out[11].

                     Enter a third Gentleman.

Third Gentleman
                     News, lads! our wars are done.   20
                     The desperate tempest hath so bang'd the Turks
                     That their designment[12] halts; a noble ship of
                          Venice
                     Hath seen a grievous wrack and sufferance[13]
                     On most part of their fleet.
Montano   How! is this true?
Third Gentleman   The ship is here put in,
                     A Veronesa; Michael Cassio,
                     Lieutenant to the war-like Moor Othello,
                     Is come on shore: the Moor himself's at sea,
                     And is in full commission here for Cyprus.

1 rough

2 see

3 raged

4 scattering

5 noisy waves

6 swelling waves

7 The Little Bear – stars which guided sailors
8 The Guardian – stars which guided sailors
9 disturbance
10 raging

11 withstand it

12 plan

13 wrecking

Montano	I am glad on't; 'tis a worthy governor. *30*
Third Gentleman	But this same Cassio, though he speak of comfort
	Touching[14] the Turkish loss, yet he looks sadly
	And prays the Moor be safe; for they were parted
	With foul and violent tempest.
Montano	Pray heaven he be;
	For I have serv'd him, and the man commands
	Like a full soldier. Let's to the sea-side, ho!
	As well to see the vessel that's come in
	As to throw out our eyes for brave Othello,
	Even till we make the main and the aerial blue
	An indistinct regard[15]. *40*
Third Gentleman	Come, let's do so;
	For every minute is expectancy
	Of more arrivance.

Enter Cassio.

Cassio	Thanks, you the valiant of this war-like isle,
	That so approve the Moor. O! let the heavens
	Give him defence against the elements[16],
	For I have lost him on a dangerous sea.
Montano	Is he well shipp'd?
Cassio	His bark is stoutly timber'd, and his pilot
	Of very expert and approv'd allowance[17]
	Therefore my hopes, not surfeited[18] to death, *50*
	Stand in bold cure[19].
	[*Within*, 'A sail!–a sail!–a sail!'

Enter a Messenger.

Cassio	What noise?
Messenger	The town is empty; on the brow o' the sea
	Stand ranks of people, and they cry, 'A sail!'
Cassio	My hopes do shape him[20] for the governor.
	[*Guns heard.*
Second Gentleman	
	They do discharge their shot of courtesy;
	Our friends at least.
Cassio	I pray you, sir, go forth,
	And give us truth who 'tis that is arriv'd.
Second Gentleman	
	I shall. [*Exit.*
Montano	But, good lieutenant, is your general wiv'd[21]? *60*
Cassio	Most fortunately: he hath achiev'd a maid
	That paragons[22] description and wild fame;
	One that excels the quirks of blazoning pens[23],
	And in th' essential vesture of creation
	Does tire the ingener[24].

Footnotes (left margin):

[14] concerning

[15] until we make the sea and sky indistinguishable

[16] wind and sea

[17] reputation
[18] exaggerated
[19] healthy

[20] think it is

[21] married

[22] surpasses
[23] poetic descriptions of her
[24] is more beautiful than can be described by an artist

Re-enter second Gentleman.

How now! who has put in?

Second Gentleman
'Tis one Iago, ancient to the general.

Cassio
He has had most favourable and happy speed:
Tempests themselves, high seas, and howling
   winds,
The gutter'd[25] rocks, and congregated sands,
Traitors ensteep'd[26] to clog the guiltless keel[27],   *70*
As having sense of beauty, do omit
Their mortal[28] natures, letting go safely by
The divine Desdemona.

Montano
What is she?

Cassio
She that I spake of, our great captain's captain,
Left in the conduct of the bold Iago,
Whose footing here anticipates our thoughts
A se'nnight's[29] speed. Great Jove, Othello guard,
And swell his sail with thine own powerful
   breath,
That he may bless this bay with his tall ship,
Make love's quick pants in Desdemona's arms, *80*
Give renew'd fire to our extinct spirits,
And bring all Cyprus comfort!

Enter Desdemona, Emilia, Iago, Roderigo and Attendants.

O! behold,
The riches of the ship is come on shore.
Ye men of Cyprus, let her have your knees,
Hail to thee, lady! and the grace of heaven,
Before, behind thee, and on every hand,
Enwheel thee round!

Desdemona
I thank you, valiant Cassio.
What tidings can you tell me of my lord?

Cassio
He is not yet arriv'd; nor know I aught
But that he's well, and will be shortly here.   *90*

Desdemona
O! but I fear — How lost you company?

Cassio
The great contention[30] of the sea and skies
Parted our fellowship. But hark! a sail.
            [Cry within, 'A sail!–a sail!' *Guns heard.*

Second Gentleman They give their greeting to the citadel[31]:
This likewise is a friend.

Cassio
See for the news!
                  [Exit Gentleman.
Good ancient, you are welcome: — *[To Emilia]*
   welcome, mistress.

[25] jagged
[26] under water
[27] innocent ship

[28] deadly

[29] a week's

[30] conflict

[31] fortress

32 make you impatient

33 wish

34 criticise silently

35 beautiful

36 noisy

37 pretenders
38 grudging

39 try

40 hide

41 I am thinking about it
42 mind
43 with difficulty

44 I find it difficult to think
45 intelligence

46 clever

Let it not gall your patience³², good Iago,
That I extend my manners; 'tis my breeding
That gives me this bold show of courtesy.

[Kissing her.

Iago   Sir, would she give you so much of her lips   100
As of her tongue she oft bestows on me,
You'd have enough.

Desdemona   Alas! she has no speech.

Iago   In faith, too much;
I find it still when I have list³³ to sleep:
Marry, before your ladyship, I grant,
She puts her tongue a little in her heart,
And chides with thinking³⁴.

Emilia   You have little cause to say so.

Iago   Come on, come on; you are pictures³⁵ out of
doors,
Bells³⁶ in your parlours, wild cats in your
kitchens,   110
Saints in your injuries, devils being offended,
Players³⁷ in your housewifery, and housewives³⁸ in
your beds.

Desdemona   O! fie upon thee, slanderer.

Iago   Nay, it is true, or else I am a Turk:
You rise to play and go to bed to work.

Emilia   You shall not write my praise.

Iago   No, let me not.

Desdemona   What wouldst thou write of me, if thou shouldst
praise me?

Iago   O gentle lady, do not put me to't,
For I am nothing if not critical.

Desdemona   Come on; assay³⁹. There's one gone to the   120
harbour?

Iago   Ay, madam.

Desdemona   I am not merry, but I do beguile⁴⁰
The thing I am by seeming otherwise.
Come, how wouldst thou praise me?

Iago   I am about it⁴¹; but indeed my invention
Comes from my pate⁴² as birdlime does from
frize⁴³;
It plucks out brains and all: but my muse labours,
And thus she is deliver'd⁴⁴.
If she be fair and wise, fairness and wit⁴⁵,
The one's for use, the other useth it.   130

Desdemona   Well prais'd! How if she be black and witty⁴⁶?

Iago   If she be black, and thereto have a wit,
She'll find a white that shall her blackness fit.

Desdemona   Worse and worse.

Emilia	How if fair and foolish?
Iago	She never yet was foolish that was fair,
	For even her folly help'd her to an heir.
Desdemona	These are old fond paradoxes to make fools laugh
	i' the alehouse. What miserable praise hast thou
	for her that's foul and foolish? 140
Iago	There's none so foul and foolish thereunto
	But does foul pranks which fair and wise ones do.
Desdemona	O heavy ignorance! thou praisest the worst best.
	But what praise couldst thou bestow on a
	deserving woman indeed, one that, in the
	authority[47] of her merit, did justly put on the
	vouch[48] of very malice itself?
Iago	She that was ever fair and never proud,
	Had tongue at will and yet was never loud,
	Never lack'd gold and yet went never gay, 150
	Fled from her wish and yet said 'Now I may',
	She that being anger'd, her revenge being nigh,
	Bade her wrong stay and her displeasure fly,
	She that in wisdom never was so frail
	To change the cod's head for the salmon's tail,
	She that could think and ne'er disclose her mind,
	See suitors following and not look behind,
	She was a wight[49], if ever such wight were, –
Desdemona	To do what?
Iago	To suckle fools and chronicle small beer[50]. 160
Desdemona	O most lame and impotent conclusion! Do not
	learn of him, Emilia, though he be thy
	husband.
	How say you, Cassio? is he not a most profane
	and liberal[51] counsellor?
Cassio	He speaks home[52], madam: you may relish him
	more in the soldier than in the scholar.
Iago	[Aside] He takes her by the palm; ay, well said,
	whisper; with as little a web as this will I ensnare
	as great a fly as Cassio. Ay, smile upon her, do; I will
	gyve[53] thee in thine own courtship. You say
	true, 170
	'tis so, indeed. If such tricks as these strip you out
	of your lieutenantry, it had been better you
	had
	not kissed your three fingers so oft, which now
	again you are most apt to play the sir in.
	Very good; well kissed! an excellent courtesy! 'tis
	so, indeed. Yet again your fingers to your lips?
	would they were clyster-pipes[54] for your sake!
	[A trumpet heard.] The Moor! I know his trumpet.

[47] power
[48] win the approval of
[49] woman
[50] to be concerned with trivial matters
[51] coarse and immoral
[52] bluntly
[53] trap
[54] tubes for douches

Cassio	'Tis truly so.
Desdemona	Let's meet him and receive him.	*180*
Cassio	Lo! where he comes.

Enter Othello and Attendants.

Othello	O my fair warrior!
Desdemona	My dear Othello!
Othello	It gives me wonder great as my content

To see you here before me. O my soul's joy!
If after every tempest come such calms,
May the winds blow till they have waken'd
    death!
And let the labouring bark[55] climb hills of seas
Olympus-high[56], and duck again as low
As hell's from heaven! If it were now to die,
'Twere now to be most happy, for I fear   *190*
My soul hath her content so absolute
That not another comfort like to this
Succeeds in unknown fate.

| Desdemona | The heavens forbid |

But that our loves and comforts should increase
Even as our days do grow!

| Othello | Amen to that, sweet powers! |

I cannot speak enough of this content;
It stops me here; it is too much of joy:
And this, and this, the greatest discords be,
[Kissing her] That e'er our hearts shall make!

| Iago | *[Aside]* O! you are well tun'd now,   *200* |

But I'll set down the pegs[57] that make this music,
As honest as I am.

| Othello | Come, let us to the castle, |

News, friends; our wars are done, the Turks are
    drown'd.
How does my old acquaintance of this isle?
Honey, you shall be well desired in Cyprus;
I have found great love amongst them. O my
    sweet,
I prattle out of fashion, and I dote
In mine own comforts. I prithee, good Iago,
Go to the bay and disembark my coffers[58].
Bring thou the master to the citadel;   *210*
He is a good one, and his worthiness
Does challenge much respect. Come, Desdemona,
Once more well met at Cyprus.
      [Exeunt all except Iago and Roderigo.

[55] ship
[56] as high as Mount Olympus
[57] slacken the strings to produce disharmony
[58] luggage

Iago	Do thou meet me presently at the harbour. Come hither. If thou be'st valiant, as they say base men being in love have then a nobility in their natures more than is native to them, list me[59]. The lieutenant to-night watches on the court of guard[60]: first, I must tell thee this, Desdemona is directly in love with him. *220*
Roderigo	With him! why, 'tis not possible.
Iago	Lay thy finger thus[61], and let thy soul be instructed. Mark me with what violence she first loved the Moor but for bragging and telling her fantastical lies; and will she love him still for prating? let not thy discreet heart think it. Her eye must be fed; and what delight shall she have to look on the devil? When the blood is made dull with the act of sport[62], there should be, again to inflame it, and to give satiety a fresh appetite, *230* loveliness in favour[63], sympathy in years, manners, and beauties; all which the Moor is defective in. Now, for want of these required conveniences[64], her delicate tenderness will find itself abused, begin to heave the gorge[65], disrelish and abhor the Moor; very nature will instruct her in it, and compel her to some second choice. Now, sir, this granted, as it is a most pregnant and unforced position[66], who stands so eminently in the degree of[67] this fortune as Cassio *240* does? a knave very voluble[68], no further conscionable[69] than in putting on the mere form of civil and humane[70] seeming, for the better compassing of his salt and most hidden loose affection[71]? why, none; why, none: a slipper[72] and subtle knave, a finder-out of occasions, that has an eye can stamp and counterfeit advantages[73], though true advantage never present itself; a devilish knave! Besides, the knave is handsome, young, and hath all those requisites in him that *250* folly and green minds[74] look after; a pestilent complete knave! and the woman hath found him already.
Roderigo	I cannot believe that in her; she is full of most blessed condition[75].
Iago	Blessed fig's end[76]! the wine she drinks is made of grapes; if she had been blessed she would never

[59] listen to me

[60] guardroom

[61] Lay your finger on your lips

[62] sexual activity

[63] appearance

[64] advantages

[65] to become sick of it

[66] evident and natural conclusion
[67] suitable for
[68] eloquent
[69] conscientious
[70] polite
[71] to achieve his lustful and immoral desire
[72] slippery

[73] invent opportunities

[74] inexperienced

[75] qualities
[76] worthless!

77 stroke

78 notice

79 a pointer

80 intimacies
81 show

82 physical

83 upsetting

84 provide

85 anger
86 perhaps

87 remedy

88 advance

89 likely and credible

90 perhaps

have loved the Moor; blessed pudding! Didst
thou not see her paddle with[77] the palm of his
hand?
didst not mark[78] that?   260

Roderigo   Yes, that I did; but that was but courtesy.
Iago   Lechery, by this hand: an index and obscure
prologue[79] to the history of lust and foul thoughts
They met so near with their lips, that their breaths
embraced together. Villanous thoughts,
Roderigo!
when these mutualities[80] so marshal[81] the way,
hard at hand comes the master and main exercise,
the incorporate conclusion[82]. Pish! But, sir, be you
ruled by me: I have brought you from Venice. Watch
you to-night; for the command, I'll lay't upon
you: 270
Cassio knows you not. I'll not be far from you: do
you find some occasion to anger Cassio, either by
speaking too loud, or tainting[83] his discipline; or
from what other course you please, which the
time shall more favourably minister[84].

Roderigo   Well.
Iago   Sir, he is rash and very sudden in choler[85], and
haply[86] may strike at you: provoke him, that he
may; for even out of that will I cause these of
Cyprus to mutiny, whose qualification[87] shall
come   280
into no true taste again but by the displanting of
Cassio. So shall you have a shorter journey to your
desires by the means I shall then have to prefer[88]
them; and the impediment most profitably
removed, without the which there were no
expectation of our prosperity.

Roderigo   I will do this, if I can bring it to any opportunity.
Iago   I warrant thee. Meet me by and by at the citadel:
I must fetch his necessaries ashore. Farewell.
Roderigo   Adieu.   290
                                                        [Exit.

Iago   That Cassio loves her, I do well believe it;
That she loves him, 'tis apt, and of great credit:[89]
The Moor, howbeit that I endure him not,
Is of a constant, loving, noble nature;
And I dare think he'll prove to Desdemona
A most dear husband. Now, I do love her too;
Not out of absolute lust, – thought peradventure[90]
I stand accountant for as great a sin, –
But partly led to diet my revenge,
For that I do suspect the lusty Moor   300

Hath leap'd into my seat[91]; the thought whereof
Doth like a poisonous mineral gnaw my inwards;
And nothing can or shall content my soul
Till I am even'd with him, wife for wife;
Or failing so, yet that I put the Moor
At least into a jealousy so strong
That judgment cannot cure. Which thing to do,
If this poor trash of Venice, whom I trash[92]
For his quick hunting, stand the putting-on[93],
I'll have our Michael Cassio on the hip[94];   310
Abuse him to the Moor in the rank garb[95],
For I fear Cassio with my night-cap too[96],
Make the Moor thank me, love me, and reward
    me
For making him egregiously an ass
And practising[97] upon his peace and quiet
Even to madness. 'Tis here, but yet confus'd:
Knavery's[98] plain face is never seen till us'd.

[Exit.

[91] has made love to my wife

[92] keep in check
[93] follow my orders
[94] at my mercy
[95] coarsely
[96] with my wife

[97] interfering with

[98] villainy

The Plot (Day Two – After an Interval
A Seaport Town in Cyprus, on the Quay)

A FIERCE STORM AT SEA

A fierce storm rages and on the quay Montano and gentlemen anxiously try to see what is happening. The storm has scattered the Turkish fleet and Cassio's ship brings this good news. However, Othello's ship and Desdemona's have been delayed.

As the crowd excitedly await further ships, Cassio talks enthusiastically about Desdemona's marriage to Othello and her charming nature. Iago's ship arrives with Desdemona and Cassio speaks admiringly about her. Desdemona fears for her husband's safety but engages in light-hearted conversation with Iago about women's hypocrisy and infidelity. Othello's ship arrives and he greets Desdemona with great affection and kisses her.

IAGO CONTINUES TO PLOT

Iago is jealous of Othello and Desdemona's relationship. He sees an opportunity for mischief in the friendly relationship between Desdemona and Cassio. He intends to use Cassio to destroy Othello and Desdemona's love.

When unloading the baggage, Iago takes Roderigo aside and turns Roderigo's jealousy against Cassio, who, he claims, is in love with Desdemona. Roderigo is to annoy Cassio and provoke a fight, so that Cassio will be dismissed from his position.

Watch you to-night; for the command, I'll lay't upon you.

(Iago, Act 2, Scene 1)

IAGO'S TRUE INTENTIONS

Roderigo promises to carry out Iago's instructions and leaves. Then Iago reveals his further plans. He is now convinced that Cassio loves Desdemona but his difficulty is how to shake Othello's constant love of Desdemona. Iago suggests that he too loves Desdemona and that Cassio and even Othello may have made love to Emilia, his wife. Iago decides to play upon Othello's peace and quiet and to make him mad with jealousy, but as yet he has not worked out how to achieve this.

Dramatic Significance

A THREATENING STORM

The fierce storm in this scene gives the impression that time has passed, as we wait anxiously for Cassio, Iago, Desdemona and Othello to arrive. The anxiety with which all await Othello's safe arrival emphasises still further the high reputation and achievements of Othello as a commander. Montano exclaims:

> "Pray heaven he be [safe].
> For I have serv'd him, and the man commands
> Like a full soldier."

The storm also disposes of the political theme of the play, which is now insignificant to the drama. Nature has averted the Turkish threat by destroying their fleet. Othello is about to take command of Cyprus but he is now a general without a war to fight. He has been outstanding in many battles but his conduct in time of peace has still to be tested. It is the strange, unfamiliar world of Cyprus, cut off from the normality and assurance of the homeland, that will form an appropriate testing-ground for Othello, Desdemona, Cassio and Iago.

The storm too may be a symbol of the storm of passion, which will erupt later, through the connivance of Iago. The calm, which Othello and Desdemona enjoy when they are reunited after the storm, is really a calm before a new storm about to break:

> "O my soul's joy!
> If after every tempest come such calms,
> May the winds blow till they have waken'd death."

Othello's words ironically foretell the future.

A DEEP AND MUTUAL DEVOTION

Desdemona and Othello are parted by the storm but are eventually reunited in a scene of rapture. Their heartfelt joy makes clear that their love is not just romance, based on exciting tales of adventure and a swift midnight elopement. It is a deep and real affection for each other:

> *"The heavens forbid*
> *But that our loves and comforts should increase*
> *Even as our days do grow."*   Desdemona

> *"Amen to that, sweet powers!*
> *I cannot speak enough of this content,*
> *It stops me here; it is too much of joy:*
> *And this, and this, the greatest discords be,*
> *That e'er our hearts shall make!"*   Othello

Cassio greatly admires this love relationship and wishes:

> *"Great Jove, Othello guard,*
> *And swell his sail with thine own powerful breath,*
> *That he may bless this bay with his tall ship,*
> *Make love's quick pants in Desdemona's arms."*

We hope that this real love will be strong enough to withstand the attack already contemplated by Iago. Iago makes light of their obvious love to suit himself:

> *"O! you are well tun'd now,*
> *But I'll set down the pegs that make this music,*
> *As honest as I am."*

IAGO'S SCHEME BEGINS TO FORM

At the end of this scene, Iago tries to convince Roderigo that his chances of winning Desdemona are improving. He claims that Desdemona is probably in love with Cassio and that Cassio desires Desdemona. He sees lust in their innocent conversation:

> *"Lechery, by this hand: an index and obscure prologue to*
> *the history of lust and foul thoughts. They met so near*
> *with their lips, that their breaths embraced together."*

Iago will use this to work on Othello's *"peace and quiet, even to madness"* by putting him,

> *"... into a jealousy so strong*
> *That judgment cannot cure."*

Gradually Iago's plot begins to form and he instructs his dupe, Roderigo, to provoke a quarrel with Cassio. Cassio will be disgraced in public and dismissed from his post and Roderigo's rival for Desdemona will be out of their way.

> *"Sir, he is rash and very sudden in choler, and haply may strike at*
> *you: provoke him, that he may; for even out of that will I cause*
> *these of Cyprus to mutiny, whose qualification shall come into no*
> *true taste again but by the displanting of Cassio."*

IAGO'S MOTIVE-HUNTING

Left alone, Iago reveals the true state of his mind. His reasons for scheming against Othello are not really credible. He sees the real love of Othello for Desdemona and enviously accuses Othello of lechery with Emilia. He desires to get even with Othello, not for any secret affair with Emilia but simply because Othello has what Iago can never have, a relationship of deep and mutual love:

> "... I dare think he'll prove to Desdemona
> A most dear husband. Now, I do love her too;
> Not out of absolute lust, – though peradventure
> I stand accountant for as great a sin, –
> But partly led to diet my revenge."

Iago hates what Othello, Desdemona and Cassio are and have, out of all proportion to his actual grievances. He tries to work himself up to hate and revenge for their own sake. The outline of Iago's basic plan is complete and we realise that his main motivation is his sheer delight in villainy.

> "Knavery's plain face is never seen till us'd."

He improvises his schemes, as he gloats on the mischief of making:

> "... the Moor thank me, love me, and reward me
> For making him egregiously an ass."

Character Development

IAGO
CONTEMPT FOR GOODNESS

Iago shows open contempt for his own wife, Emilia, and more subtly for Desdemona.

> "You rise to play and go to bed to work."

He sees Cassio's innocent kissing of Desdemona as:

> "Lechery, by this hand: an index and obscure prologue
> to the history of lust and foul thoughts."

Othello's marriage he regards as mere sexual *"appetite"* or *"lust"*.

WISHFUL THINKING

While Iago shows contempt for goodness in others, he seems a little envious and indulges in wishful thinking. He admits to the goodness in others and envies them:

> "The Moor, howbeit that I endure him not,
> Is of a constant, loving, noble nature;
> And I dare think he'll prove to Desdemona

> *A most dear husband. Now, I do love her too;*
> *Not out of absolute lust."*

Iago imagines that both Othello and Cassio may have made love to Emilia, his wife. He is consumed with envy of others which,

> *"Doth like a poisonous mineral gnaw my inwards."*

This envy and wishful thinking he turns into a seething desire for revenge on all who are good:

> *"... nothing can nor shall content my soul*
> *Till I am even'd with him, wife for wife."*

Iago deserves our pity and contempt.

DIABOLIC CLEVERNESS

Iago continues to deceive Roderigo into believing that he is busy working on his behalf to win Desdemona. He convinces him that Desdemona and Cassio are in love and that this will undermine Desdemona's marriage to Roderigo's advantage. Skilfully he cons Roderigo into doing his dirty work for him in getting rid of Cassio:

> *"So shall you have a shorter journey to your desires by*
> *the means I shall then have to prefer them."*

All the gullible Roderigo has to do is to *"find some occasion to anger Cassio"* and provoke him to a quarrel. Iago will use this and Cassio's innocent courtesy to Desdemona to incriminate him. Roderigo is a mere pawn in Iago's clever and unscrupulous game.

A STRUGGLE TO CORRUPT GOODNESS

Iago, in his soliloquy, reveals his diseased mind, which casts an evil slant on the innocent encounters and relationships he has witnessed. He almost believes that his slanted view is a true one:

> *"I'll have our Michael Cassio on the hip;*
> *Abuse him to the Moor in the rank garb,*
> *For I fear Cassio with my night-cap too,*
> *Make the Moor thank me, love me, and reward me*
> *For making him egregiously an ass."*

Yet he realises that those he seeks to destroy are good and noble. He is obsessed with the thrill of devising evil schemes for the sheer pleasure of it:

> *"... 'Tis here but yet confus'd:*
> *Knavery's plain face is never seen till us'd."*

He is not a demon but he is diabolically clever and unscrupulous in his pursuit of evil, which is only beginning.

CASSIO

A SINCERE ADMIRER

Cassio anxiously awaits Othello's and Desdemona's arrival. He shows sincere admiration for Othello and a courteous regard for Desdemona:

> "O! behold,
> The riches of the ship is come on shore.
> Ye men of Cyprus, let her have your knees."

He has no ulterior motives in his affections for Desdemona.

A POLISHED GENTLEMAN

Cassio speaks in eloquent, polished language about the storm and Othello and Desdemona. He is courteous to Emilia and greets her with a kiss. Impetuously he kisses Desdemona's hand, showing his great admiration for her. He is not a show-off nor a lecher, as Iago insinuates, but a chivalrous gentleman, who treats all with respect and courtesy, especially ladies.

> "Let it not gall your patience, good Iago,
> That I extend my manners; 'tis my breeding
> That gives me this bold show of courtesy."

DESDEMONA

SELF-CONTROL

While Desdemona anxiously awaits the arrival of Othello, she hides her anxiety by engaging in witty banter with Iago. She is in full control of her own feelings:

> "I am not merry, but I do beguile
> The thing I am by seeming otherwise."

LOVE

When Othello arrives she is overjoyed, as they exchange loving greetings. She wishes that their love and happiness will continue to grow:

> "The heavens forbid
> But that our loves and comforts should increase
> Even as our days do grow."

OTHELLO

AN ECSTATIC LOVE

Othello too is overjoyed to be reunited with Desdemona. He feels that he has reached a peak of happiness, as he greets his *"soul's joy"* with kisses. His language is extravagant, reflecting the depths of his romantic love:

> *"If it were now to die,*
> *'Twere now to be most happy, for I fear*
> *My soul hath her content so absolute*
> *That not another comfort like to this*
> *Succeeds in unknown fate."*

He is overjoyed too that the wars are over, as he prepares to celebrate his marriage.

RODERIGO
CREDULOUS

Roderigo, as before, is easily taken in by Iago's cleverness. He agrees to seek an opportunity to provoke Cassio to an angry outburst, in order to disgrace him. He believes that this will advance his hopes of gaining Desdemona in marriage, since Iago has convinced him that Cassio and Desdemona are in love:

> *"I will do this, if I can bring it to any opportunity."*

Yet, Roderigo is not as blind to reality as Iago is. He cannot bring himself to doubt Desdemona's honour:

> *"I cannot believe that in her; she is full of most blessed condition."*

However, he succumbs to Iago's persuasion rather too easily to be forgivable. He is as credulous and gullible as ever.

MONTANO

We learn little of Montano's personality except that he admires Othello and looks forward to his safe arrival:

> *"Pray heaven he be [safe];*
> *For I have serv'd him, and the man commands*
> *Like a full soldier. Let's to the sea-side, ho!"*

EMILIA
A NAGGING WIFE?

Emilia has little to say in this scene except that she has little regard for her husband:

> *"You shall not write my praise."*

Cassio greets her with a kiss and seems to have respect for her. Yet Iago sees her as a nagging wife, who repeatedly tongue-lashes him.

> *"Sir, would she give you so much of her lips*
> *As of her tongue she oft bestows on me,*
> *You'd have enough.*

Perhaps Iago deserves all he gets.

Scene II

A Street
Enter a Herald with a proclamation; People following.

Herald   It is Othello's pleasure, our noble and valiant
general, that, upon certain tidings now arrived,
importing[1] the mere perdition[2] of the Turkish   [1] reporting
fleet, every man put himself into triumph; some to   [2] destruction
dance, some to make bonfires, each man to what
sport and revels his addiction leads him; for,
besides these beneficial news, it is the celebration
of his nuptial. So much was his pleasure should be
proclaimed. All offices[3] are open, and there is full   [3] kitchens
liberty of feasting from this present hour of
    five till   *10*
the bell have told eleven. Heaven bless the isle of
Cyprus and our noble general Othello!   *[Exeunt.*

The Plot (Day Two – A Street in Cyprus)

A DOUBLE CELEBRATION

A herald declares that night a holiday in celebration of the destruction of the Turkish fleet
and the marriage of Othello and Desdemona. There is to be feasting and revelry from five
o'clock until eleven to do honour to Othello and to Cyprus.

Dramatic Significance

AN INTERLUDE OF REVELRY

This short scene introduces the celebrations for the end of the war against the Turks.
Othello now governs Cyprus, a peaceful island once more. Nothing but good fortune seems
to lie ahead for the newly married couple, as they begin to enjoy their married life together.

Amidst the rejoicing, Iago's menacing schemes threaten this good fortune. The revelry will
provide a good opportunity for hidden mischief and villainy. Thus this scene is a brief
interlude of merriment before the tragic action is begun by Iago's contriving against Cassio
in the following scene.

> "Besides these beneficial news, it is the celebration of his
> nuptial. So much was his pleasure should be proclaimed. All
> offices are open, and there is full liberty of feasting from this
> present hour of five till the bell have told eleven."

Scene III

A Hall in the Castle.
Enter Othello, Desdemona, Cassio and Attendants.

Othello	Good Michael, look you to the guard to-night:
	Let's teach ourselves that honourable stop[1],
	Not to outsport discretion[2].
Cassio	Iago hath direction what to do;
	But notwithstanding, with my personal eye
	Will I look to't.
Othello	Iago is most honest.
	Michael, good night; to-morrow with your earliest
	Let me have speech with you. *[To Desdemona]*
	Come, my dear love,
	The purchase made, the fruits are to ensue[3];
	That profit's yet to come 'twixt me and you. *10*
	Good night.
	[Exeunt Othello, Desdemona and Attendants.

Enter Iago.

Cassio	Welcome, Iago; we must to the watch.
Iago	Not this hour, lieutenant; 'tis not yet ten o' the
	clock. Our general cast[4] us thus early for the love
	of his Desdemona, who let us not therefore
	blame; he hath not yet made wanton[5] the night
	with her, and she is sport for love.
Cassio	She's a most exquisite lady.
Iago	And, I'll warrant her, full of game[6].
Cassio	Indeed, she is a most fresh and delicate
	creature. *20*
Iago	What an eye she has! methinks it sounds a parley
	of provocation[7].
Cassio	An inviting eye; and yet methinks right modest.
Iago	And when she speaks, is it not an alarum[8] to love?
Cassio	She is indeed perfection.
Iago	Well, happiness to their sheets! Come, lieutenant,
	I have a stoup[9] of wine, and here without are a
	brace[10] of Cyprus gallants that would fain have a
	measure[11] to the health of black Othello.
Cassio	Not to-night, good Iago: I have very poor and *30*
	unhappy brains for drinking: I could well
	wish courtesy would invent some other custom
	of entertainment.
Iago	O! they are our friends; but one cup; I'll drink for you.
Cassio	I have drunk but one cup to-night, and that was

Side notes (left margin):

[1] decent restraint
[2] go beyond the limits of decency
[3] the consummation of marriage
[4] sent us away
[5] spent the night in sexual pleasure
[6] love-making
[7] signal for lust
[8] signal for
[9] jug
[10] two
[11] wish to drink

	craftily qualified[12] too, and, behold, what	[12] diluted
	innovation[13] it makes here: I am unfortunate in	[13] change
	the infirmity, and dare not task my weakness with	
	any more. 40	

Iago   What, man! 'tis a night of revels; the gallants
                desire it.

Cassio   Where are they?

Iago   Here at the door; I pray you, call them in.

Cassio   I'll do't; but it dislikes me.   [Exit.

Iago   If I can fasten but one cup upon him,

With that which he hath drunk to-night already,

He'll be as full of quarrel and offence

As my young mistress' dog. Now, my sick fool Roderigo,

Whom love has turn'd almost the wrong side out,   50

To Desdemona hath to-night carous'd

Potations pottle deep;[14] and he's to watch.   [14] has drunk to his fill

Three lads of Cyprus, noble swelling spirits,

That hold their honours in a wary distance[15],   [15] take offence easily

The very elements[16] of this war-like isle,   [16] typical

Have I to-night fluster'd with flowing cups,

And they watch too. Now, 'mongst this flock of drunkards,

Am I to put our Cassio in some action

That may offend the isle. But here they come.

If consequence[17] do but approve[18] my dream,   60   [17] what happens now

My boat sails freely, both with wind and stream.   [18] confirm

Re-enter Cassio, with him Montano and Gentlemen.
Servant following with wine.

Cassio   'Fore God, they have given me a rouse[19] already.   [19] a large drink

Montano   Good faith, a little one; not past a pint, as I am a
                soldier.

Iago   Some wine, ho!

       And let me the canakin[20] clink, clink;   [20] small tankard

       And let me the canakin clink:

         A soldier's a man;

      A life's but a span;

       Why then let a soldier drink.   70

Some wine, boys!

Cassio   'Fore God, an excellent song.

Iago   I learned it in England, where indeed they are

most potent in potting;[21] your Dane, your   [21] good at drinking

German, and your swag-bellied Hollander[22],   [22] fat Dutchman

– drink, ho! – are nothing to your English.

Cassio	Is your Englishman so expert in his drinking?
Iago	Why he drinks you with facility[23] your Dane dead
	drunk; he sweats not to overthrow your Almain[24];
	he gives your Hollander a vomit ere the next *80*
	pottle[25] can be filled.
Cassio	To the health of our general!
Montano	I am for it, lieutenant; and I'll do you justice.
Iago	O sweet England!
	King Stephen was a worthy peer,[26]
	His breeches cost him but a crown;
	He held them sixpence all too dear,
	With that he call'd the tailor lown[27].
	He was a wight[28] of high renown,
	And thou art but of low degree: *90*
	'Tis pride that pulls the country down,
	Then take thine auld cloak about thee.
	Some wine, ho!
Cassio	Why, this is a more exquisite song than the other.
Iago	Will you hear't again?
Cassio	No; for I hold him to be unworthy of his place that
	does those things. Well, God's above all; and there
	be souls must be saved, and there be souls must
	not be saved.
Iago	It's true, good lieutenant. *100*
Cassio	For mine own part, – no offence to the general, nor
	any man of quality, – I hope to be saved.
Iago	And so do I too, lieutenant.
Cassio	Ay; but, by your leave, not before me; the
	lieutenant is to be saved before the ancient.
	Let's have no more of this; let's to our affairs. God
	forgive us our sins! Gentlemen, let's look to our
	business. Do not think, gentlemen, I am drunk:
	this
	is my ancient; this is my right hand, and this is my
	left hand. I am not drunk now; I can stand well *110*
	enough, and speak well enough.
All	Excellent well.
Cassio	Why, very well, then; you must not think then that
	I am drunk. *[Exit.*
Montano	To the platform, masters; come, let's set the watch.
Iago	You see this fellow that is gone before;
	He is a soldier fit to stand by Caesar
	And give direction; and do but see his vice
	'Tis to his virtue a just equinox[29],
	The one as long as the other; 'tis pity of him. *120*
	I fear the trust Othello puts him in,

Margin glosses:

[23] easily
[24] German
[25] tankard
[26] nobleman
[27] foolish
[28] a man
[29] an exact opposite

	On some odd time of his infirmity[30],	[30] weakness
	Will shake this island.	
Montano	But is he often thus?	
Iago	'Tis evermore the prologue to his sleep:	[31] stay awake twice around the clock
	He'll watch the horologe a double set[31],	
	If drink rock not his cradle.	
Montano	It were well	
	The general were put in mind of it.	
	Perhaps he sees it not; or his good nature	
	Prizes the virtue that appears in Cassio,	
	And looks not on his evils. Is not this true? *130*	

Enter Roderigo.

Iago	[*Aside to him*] How now, Roderigo!	
	I pray you, after the lieutenant; go.	
	[*Exit Roderigo.*	
Montano	And 'tis great pity that the noble Moor	
	Should hazard such a place as his own second	
	With one of an ingraft infirmity;[32]	[32] inbred weakness
	It were an honest action to say	
	So to the Moor.	
Iago	Not I, for this fair island:	
	I do love Cassio well, and would do much	
	To cure him of this evil. But hark! what noise!	
	[*Cry within*, 'Help! Help!'	

Re-enter Cassio, driving in Roderigo.

Cassio	You rogue! you rascal! *140*	
Montano	What's the matter, lieutenant?	
Cassio	A knave teach me my duty!	
	I'll beat the knave into a twiggen bottle.[33]	[33] a bottle encased in wickerwork
Roderigo	Beat me!	
Cassio	Dost thou prate, rogue!	
	[*Striking Roderigo.*	
Montano	[*Staying him*] Nay, good lieutenant;	
	I pray you, sir, hold your hand.	
Cassio	Let me go, sir,	
	Or I'll knock you o'er the mazzard[34].	[34] head
Montano	Come, come; you're drunk.	
Cassio	Drunk! [*They fight.*	
Iago	[*Aside to Roderigo*] Away, I say! go out, and cry	
	a mutiny[35]. [*Exit Roderigo.*	[35] a riot
	Nay, good lieutenant! God's will, gentlemen!	
	Help, ho! Lieutenant! sir! Montano! sir! *150*	
	Help, masters! Here's a goodly watch indeed!	
	[*Bell rings.*	
	Who's that that rings the bell! Diablo[36], ho!	[36] the Devil

The town will rise: God's will! lieutenant, hold!
You will be sham'd for ever.

Re-enter Othello and Attendants.

Othello	What is the matter here?
Montano	'Zounds! I bleed still; I am hurt to the death.
Othello	Hold, for your lives!
Iago	Hold, ho, lieutenant! Sir! Montano! gentlemen!
	Have you forgot all sense of place and duty?
	Hold! the general speaks to you; hold for shame!
Othello	Why, how now, ho! from whence ariseth this? *160*
	Are we turn'd Turks, and to ourselves do that
	Which heaven hath forbid the Ottomites?
	For Christian shame put by this barbarous brawl;
	He that stirs next to carve[37] for his own rage
	Holds his soul light; he dies upon his motion.
	Silence that dreadful bell! it frights the isle
	From her propriety[38]. What is the matter, masters?
	Honest Iago, that look'st dead with grieving,
	Speak, who began this? on thy love, I charge thee.
Iago	I do not know; friends all but now, even now, *170*
	In quarter[39] and in terms[40] like bride and groom
	Devesting them for bed; and then, but now, –
	As if some planet had unwitted men, –
	Swords out, and tilting one at other's breast,
	In opposition bloody. I cannot speak
	Any beginning to this peevish odds[41],
	And would in action glorious I had lost
	Those legs that brought me to a part of it!
Othello	How comes it, Michael, you are thus forgot?
Cassio	I pray you, pardon me; I cannot speak. *180*
Othello	Worthy Montano, you were wont be civil;
	The gravity and stillness[42] of your youth
	The world hath noted, and your name is great
	In mouths of wisest censure[43]: what's the matter,
	That you unlace[44] your reputation thus
	And spend your rich opinion[45] for the name
	Of a night-brawler? give me answer to it.
Montano	Worthy Othello, I am hurt to danger;
	Your officer, Iago, can inform you,
	While I spare speech, which something now *190*
	offends[46] me,
	Of all that I do know; nor know I aught
	By me that's said or done amiss this night,
	Unless self-charity[47] be sometimes a vice,

[37] strike a blow

[38] proper rest

[39] in their proper positions
[40] circumstances

[41] foolish quarrel

[42] seriousness and sobriety

[43] judgement
[44] undo
[45] good reputation

[46] hurts

[47] self-indulgence

	And to defend ourselves it be a sin	
	When violence assails us.	
Othello	Now, by heaven,	
	My blood[48] begins my safer guides[49] to rule,	[48] passions
	And passion, having my best judgment collied[50],	[49] reason
	Assays[51] to lead the way. If I once stir,	[50] clouded
	Or do but lift this arm, the best of you	[51] tries
	Shall sink in my rebuke. Give me to know *200*	
	How this foul rout[52] began, who set it on;	[52] brawl
	And he that is approv'd[53] in this offence,	[53] proven guilty
	Though he had twinn'd with me – both at a birth –	
	Shall lose me. What! in a town of war,	
	Yet wild, the people's hearts brimful of fear,	
	To manage private and domestic quarrel,	
	In night, and on the court and guard of safety!	
	'Tis monstrous. Iago, who began't?	
Montano	If partially affin'd, or leagu'd in office[54],	[54] partial or loyal to a superior officer
	Thou dost deliver more or less than truth, *210*	
	Thou art no soldier.	
Iago	Touch me not so near;	
	I had rather have this tongue cut from my	
	mouth	
	Than it should do offence to Michael Cassio;	
	Yet, I persuade myself, to speak the truth	
	Shall nothing wrong him. Thus it is, general.	
	Montano and myself being in speech,	
	There comes a fellow crying out for help,	
	And Cassio following with determin'd sword	
	To execute upon[55] him. Sir, this gentleman	[55] kill
	Steps in to Cassio, and entreats his pause; *220*	
	Myself the crying fellow did pursue,	
	Lest by his clamour, as it so fell out,	
	The town might fall in fright; he, swift of foot,	
	Outran my purpose, and I return'd the rather[56]	[56] more quickly
	For that I heard the clink and fall of swords,	
	And Cassio high in oath, which till to-night	
	I ne'er might say before. When I came back, –	
	For this was brief, – I found them close together,	
	At blow and thrust, even as again they were	
	When you yourself did part them. *230*	
	More of this matter can I not report:	
	But men are men; the best sometimes forget:	
	Though Cassio did some little wrong to him,	
	As men in rage strike those that wish them best,	
	Yet, surely Cassio, I believe, receiv'd	
	From him that fled some strange indignity[57],	[57] insult
	Which patience could not pass[58].	[58] overlook

⁵⁹ minimise

Othello
I know, Iago,
Thy honesty and love doth mince⁵⁹ this matter,
Making it light to Cassio. Cassio, I love thee;
But never more be officer of mine.   *240*

Enter Desdemona, attended.

Look! if my gentle love be not rais'd up;
[To Cassio] I'll make thee an example.
Desdemona   What's the matter?
Othello
All's well now, sweeting; come away to bed,
Sir, for your hurts, myself will be your surgeon.
Lead him off.   *[Montano is led off.*
Iago, look with care about the town,
And silence those whom this vile brawl distracted.
Come, Desdemona; 'tis the soldiers' life,
⁶⁰ soothing
To have their balmy⁶⁰ slumbers wak'd with strife.
                 [Exeunt all but Iago and Cassio.
Iago   What! are you hurt, lieutenant?   *250*
Cassio   Ay; past all surgery.
⁶¹ By Mary
Iago   Marry⁶¹, heaven forbid!
Cassio
Reputation, reputation, reputation! O! I have lost
my reputation. I have lost the immortal part of
myself, and what remains is bestial. My reputation,
Iago, my reputation!
Iago
As I am an honest man, I thought you had received
some bodily wound; there is more offence in that
than in reputation. Reputation is an idle and most
false imposition; oft got without merit, and
            lost   *260*
without deserving: you have lost no reputation at
all, unless you repute yourself such a loser. What!
⁶² regain favour with
⁶³ dismissed
man; there are ways to recover⁶² the general
again; you are but now cast⁶³ in his mood, a
punishment more in policy than in malice; even so
as one would beat his offenceless dog to affright
⁶⁴ appeal
an imperious lion. Sue⁶⁴ to him again, and he is
            yours.
Cassio
I will rather sue to be despised than to deceive so
good a commander with so slight, so drunken, *270*
and so indiscreet an officer. Drunk! and speak
⁶⁵ talk nonsense
parrot⁶⁵! and squabble, swagger, swear, and
⁶⁶ talk rubbish
discourse fustian⁶⁶ with one's own shadow! O
thou invisible spirit of wine! if thou hast no
            name
to be known by, let us call thee devil!

Iago	What was he that you followed with your sword! What had he done to you?
Cassio	I know not.
Iago	Is't possible?
Cassio	I remember a mass of things, but nothing *280* distinctly; a quarrel, but nothing wherefore. O God! that men should put an enemy in their mouths to steal away their brains; that we should, with joy, pleasance, revel, and applause, transform ourselves into beasts.
Iago	Why, but you are now well enough; how came you thus recovered?
Cassio	It hath pleased the devil drunkenness to give place to the devil wrath; one unperfectness shows me another, to make me frankly despise myself. *290*
Iago	Come, you are too severe a moraler[67]. As the time, the place, and the condition of this country stands, I could heartily wish this had not befallen, but since it is as it is, mend it for your own good.
Cassio	I will ask him for my place again; he shall tell me I am a drunkard! Had I as many mouths as Hydra[68], such an answer would stop them all. To be now a sensible man, by and by a fool, and presently a beast! O strange! Every inordinate cup is unblessed and the ingredient is a devil. *300*
Iago	Come, come; good wine is a good familiar creature if it be well used; exclaim no more against it. And, good lieutenant, I think you think I love you.
Cassio	I have well approved it, sir. I drunk!
Iago	You or any man living may be drunk at some time, man. I'll tell you what you shall do. Our general's wife is now the general: I may say so in this respect, for that he hath devoted and given up himself to the contemplation, mark, and *310* denotement of her parts and graces[69]: confess yourself freely to her; importune her; she'll help to put you in your place again. She is of so free, so kind, so apt, so blessed a disposition, that she holds it a vice in her goodness not to do more than she is requested. This broken joint between you and her husband entreat her to splinter;[70] and my fortunes against any lay[71] worth naming, this crack of your love shall grow stronger than it was before. *320*
Cassio	You advise me well.
Iago	I protest, in the sincerity of love and honest kindness.

[67] moraliser

[68] The many-headed monster killed by Hercules

[69] has observed her good qualities

[70] remedy

[71] wager

Cassio	I think it freely; and betimes[72] in the morning
	I will beseech the virtuous Desdemona to
	undertake for me. I am desperate of my fortunes
	if they check me here.
Iago	You are in the right. Good night, lieutenant;
	I must to the watch.
Cassio	Good night, honest Iago! *330*
	[Exit.
Iago	And what's he then that says I play the villain?
	When this advice is free I give and honest,
	Probal[73] to thinking and indeed the course
	To win the Moor again? For 'tis most easy
	The inclining Desdemona to subdue[74]
	In any honest suit; she's fram'd as fruitful[75]
	As the free elements. And then for her
	To win the Moor, were't to renounce his baptism,
	All seals and symbols of redeemed sin,
	His soul is so enfetter'd to her love, *340*
	That she may make, unmake, do what she list[76],
	Even as her appetite shall play the god
	With his weak function[77]. How am I then a villain
	To counsel Cassio to this parallel[78] course,
	Directly to his good? Divinity of hell!
	When devils will the blackest sins put on[79],
	They do suggest[80] at first with heavenly shows,
	As I do now; for while this honest fool
	Plies Desdemona to repair his fortunes,
	And she for him pleads strongly to the Moor, *350*
	I'll pour this pestilence into his ear
	That she repeals[81] him for her body's lust;
	And, by how much she strives to do him good,
	She shall undo her credit[82] with the Moor.
	So will I turn her virtue into pitch,
	And out of her own goodness make the net
	That shall enmesh them all.
	Re-enter Roderigo.
	How now, Roderigo!
Roderigo	I do follow here in the chase, not like a hound that
	hunts, but one that fills up the cry[83]. My money is
	almost spent; I have been to-night exceedingly *360*
	well cudgelled[84]; and I think the issue will be, I
	shall have so much experience for my pains; and
	so, with no money at all and a little more wit[85],
	return again to Venice.

Notes in margin:

73 reasonable

74 persuade
75 generous

76 wishes

77 mental powers
78 convenient (to Iago)

79 wish to advance
80 tempt

81 desires his reinstatement

82 reputation

83 fills up the pack

84 beaten

85 sense

Iago   How poor are they that have not patience!
            What wound did ever heal but by degrees?
            Thou know'st we work by wit and not by
                witchcraft[86],   [86] by intellect and not by magic
            And wit depends on dilatory time[87].   [87] taking time
            Does't not go well? Cassio hath beaten thee,
            And thou by that small hurt hast cashiered[88] *370* [88] dismissed
                Cassio.
            Though other things grow fair against the sun,
            Yet fruits that blossom first will first be ripe:
            Content thyself awhile. By the mass, 'tis morning;
            Pleasure and action make the hours seem short.   [89] lodging
            Retire thee; go where thou are billeted[89]:
            Away, I say; thou shalt know more hereafter:
            Nay, get thee gone. *[Exit Roderigo.]* Two things are
                to be done,
            My wife must move for Cassio to her mistress;
            I'll set her on;
            Myself the while to draw the Moor apart,   *380* [90] at the exact time
            And bring him jump[90] when he may Cassio find
            Soliciting his wife: ay, that's the way: [91] scheming
            Dull not device[91] by coldness and delay.   *[Exit.*

The Plot (Day Two – A Hall in the Castle)

CASSIO'S DRINKING SESSION

Othello instructs Cassio to supervise the guard, so that the merry-making will not interfere with good order. Cassio agrees and Othello and Desdemona go to bed, leaving Iago and Cassio in charge.

Iago invites Cassio to drink to Othello's health. Cassio at first refuses but eventually joins in the drinking. They talk of Desdemona's virtues and Iago encourages Cassio to drink more with two men of Cyprus. As Cassio leaves, Iago reveals his plans to provoke Cassio into a brawl with Roderigo and some local men.

Cassio re-enters with Montano and they celebrate and drink too much wine, encouraged by Iago. Cassio protests that he is not drunk and goes out. As he leaves, Iago expresses concern about Cassio's weakness for drink. Montano is shocked and wishes to inform Othello.

A RIOTOUS SCENE

A cry of help is heard as Iago's plan proceeds. Cassio, provoked, rushes in, chasing Roderigo. Montano intervenes and Cassio attacks him. Iago begs Cassio to stop fighting but meanwhile Othello has been awakened by the brawling.

Othello reprimands the brawlers and Iago explains what happened, pretending to defend Cassio. When Cassio has no explanation for wounding Montano, Othello becomes angry and demands a full explanation, which Iago is persuaded to give. Iago describes the brawl, insinuating that Cassio should have behaved better. Othello, realising that Iago is making matters light for Cassio, dismisses Cassio as his officer and leaves with Desdemona and the wounded Montano.

THE DISGRACE OF CASSIO

Iago is left to restore order and pretends to be concerned about Cassio. Cassio cannot recall clearly what happened but laments the loss of his good reputation. Iago assures him that he can easily change Othello's mind. He advises Cassio to ask Desdemona to plead with Othello for his reinstatement as lieutenant. Cassio, unaware of Iago's scheming, agrees to approach Desdemona and leaves, grateful to Iago for his advice.

IAGO REFINES HIS SCHEMES

Alone, Iago enjoys the success so far of his schemes, while outwardly he seems honest. He looks forward to filling Othello's mind with suspicions, when Desdemona appeals to him on Cassio's behalf. He enjoys doing evil for evil's sake and will use Desdemona's goodness to create evil.

Roderigo comes in, disappointed that his money has been wasted without success. Iago persuades him to be patient since their plans are beginning to succeed. Finally, Iago decides to use Emilia to speak favourably to Desdemona, concerning Cassio, and to arrange that Othello will see Cassio pleading with Desdemona.

Dramatic Significance

IAGO'S INTRIGUE ADVANCES

The first major step in Iago's intrigue begins in a comic interlude in this scene. Iago persuades Cassio into drunken revelry, despite Othello's instructions to Cassio and Cassio's own better judgement. Having succeeded in making Cassio drunk, he convinces Montano that Cassio is prone to excessive drinking, so that Montano will inform Othello. When Cassio rushes in, provoked by Roderigo, the well-meaning Montano tries to intervene and is wounded. Iago raises a commotion to bring Othello on the scene.

When Othello tries to sort out the brawl, Iago puts himself beyond suspicion and pretends to be unwilling to incriminate Cassio:

> *"I had rather have this tongue cut from my mouth*
> *Than it should do offence to Michael Cassio;*
> *Yet, I persuade myself, to speak the truth*
> *Shall nothing wrong him."*

Cassio, I love thee;
But never more be officer of mine.

Iago's honesty is not in question and he has secured Cassio's dismissal:

> *"I know, Iago,*
> *Thy honesty and love doth mince this matter,*
> *Making it light to Cassio. Cassio, I love thee;*
> *But never more be officer of mine."*

In addition, he has given Othello further reasons to rely on Iago's advice, rather than on his own judgement (which has proved wrong in Cassio's case).

IAGO WEAVES HIS WEB

As Iago pretends to comfort Cassio for his loss of reputation and position, he turns Cassio's misfortune to his own advantage. Cassio gratefully accepts Iago's advice to plead with Desdemona to use her influence with Othello to restore him to favour:

> *"This broken joint between you and her husband entreat her to splinter;*
> *and my fortunes against any lay worth naming, this crack of your love*
> *shall grow stronger than it was before."*

Iago now has the means to make Othello jealous – he will contrive that Othello sees Cassio and Desdemona talking alone together:

> *"I'll pour this pestilence into his ear*
> *That she repeals him for her body's lust;*
> *And, by how much she strives to do him good,*
> *She shall undo her credit with the Moor."*

Othello can then judge for himself.

Having disgraced Cassio, Iago now turns his villainy on Desdemona, even though he has no personal quarrel with her:

> *"So will I turn her virtue into pitch,*
> *And out of her own goodness make the net*
> *That shall enmesh them all."*

He convinces the impatient Roderigo that he must not return to Venice, since their plan is almost complete.

Having successfully played on each of his victims' weaknesses in this scene, Iago is impressive and sure of himself. He is no longer hunting for motives but acknowledges evil for evil's sake:

> *"Divinity of hell!*
> *When devils will the blackest sins put on,*
> *They do suggest at first with heavenly shows,*
> *As I do now."*

So I will turn her virtue into pitch,
And out of her own goodness make the net
That shall enmesh them all.   (Iago, Act 2, Scene III)

THE DANGEROUS SIDE OF OTHELLO'S CHARACTER

This scene shows us not only Iago's skill in playing on his victims' weaknesses but also reveals some of Othello's weaknesses, which will help Iago to destroy him.

Othello's faith in his own judgement of people has been shattered by the gross misconduct of Cassio. In its place Othello has learned to rely on the advice of Iago, who provides fresh evidence of his *"honesty"* in this scene. Iago has, at great *"pain"* to himself, exposed the misconduct of his good friend, Cassio.

Othello is impetuous and cannot deal with uncertainty. Without proper enquiry he readily accepts Cassio's guilt and acts decisively in dismissing him. Othello is a man of action and takes matters as they seem at first glance.

Othello prides himself on firmness and fair play whatever his personal feelings. His punishment of Cassio is harsh, despite his obvious high regard for Cassio's qualities:

> *"... Cassio, I love thee;*
> *But never more be officer of mine."*

In a sense, Othello's own strengths will prove his undoing as Iago later uses them to ensnare Othello in his web of deceit.

Character Development

IAGO
HONESTY TO FIT THE OCCASION

Iago makes the most of every opportunity in this scene, while at the same time convincing everyone of his honesty and sincerity. Skilfully he makes Othello, Cassio, Roderigo and Montano his grateful dupes.

To Cassio, Iago is a sociable companion, who encourages him to drink in celebration of Othello's victory and marriage. When Cassio is in disgrace, Iago seems a shrewd and sympathetic comrade, who consoles Cassio and advises how to regain Othello's favour:

> *"This broken joint between you and her husband entreat*
> *her to splinter; and my fortunes against any lay worth naming,*
> *this crack of your love shall grow stronger than it was before."*

To Montano, Iago acts the disappointed friend, who laments Cassio's weakness for drink and to Othello he becomes the dutiful officer, who reports his colleague's misdemeanour. All the while Iago gains, at others' expense, further credit for his honesty.

> *"I know, Iago,*
> *Thy honesty and love doth mince this matter,*
> *Making it light to Cassio. Cassio, I love thee;*
> *But never more be officer of mine.*

Finally, Iago convinces the maligned Roderigo that, by this *"small hurt"*, he has secured the dismissal of Cassio and free access to the love of Desdemona. Roderigo is running out of patience but Iago's skilful persuasion convinces him yet again that success is at hand:

> *"Thou know'st we work by wit and not by witchcraft,*
> *And wit depends on dilatory time.*
> *Does't not go well?"*

A DIVINITY OF HELL

In his soliloquy, Iago, delighted with his success, attempts to justify his villainy. He suggests that his advice to Cassio will work for Cassio's own good, since Desdemona will easily succeed in pleading with Othello for Cassio's reinstatement:

> *"How am I then a villain*
> *To counsel Cassio to this parallel course,*
> *Directly to his good?"*

Iago then reveals his true sinister intentions: he will insinuate that Desdemona appeals for Cassio because of her lust for him. Thus he will discredit Desdemona as well as Cassio and will destroy Othello's peace of mind.

> *"I'll pour this pestilence into his ear*
> *That she repeals him for her body's lust;*
> *And, by how much she strives to do him good,*
> *She shall undo her credit with the Moor."*

Iago adopts the methods used by the *"divinities of hell"* – to make the blackest sins seem credible by an enticing show of goodness and to use the virtue in people to lead them to sin:

> *"So will I turn her virtue into pitch,*
> *And out of her own goodness make the net*
> *That shall enmesh them all."*

As he leads his dupes to their ruin, Iago coolly gloats on his devices like a Mephistopheles.

CASSIO
TOO EASY-GOING

Iago plays on Cassio's good nature and his desire to be sociable and to do honour to Othello's marriage and victory over the Turks. Cassio knows that he ought not to drink too much, especially since he is responsible for the good conduct of the watch on the Castle. He gives in too easily and this proves his undoing:

> *"I'll do't, but it dislikes me."*

GOOD INTENTIONS

Cassio at first attempts to be responsible to the trust Othello placed in him:

> *"Not to-night, good Iago: I have very poor and unhappy brains for drinking."*

When Othello demands an explanation for his behaviour, he is ashamed:

> *"I pray you, pardon me; I cannot speak."*

Later he laments the loss of his good standing with Othello.

> *"I will rather sue to be despised than to deceive so good a commander with so slight, so drunken, and so indiscreet an officer."*

What he desires most is to make up to Othello for betraying his trust in him. It is little wonder that he grasps at Iago's advice as a solution to his present misfortune.

OTHELLO

A STRONG SENSE OF DUTY

Othello wished that the celebration of his marriage would not interfere with his duty as commander. He is outraged at a brawl occurring on the watch, especially since Cassio, his lieutenant, seems to be the ringleader. He accepts *"honest"* Iago's account of the brawl without question. His sense of military authority and duty lead him to punish Cassio severely despite his affection for him:

> *"Cassio, I love thee;*
> *But never more be officer of mine."*

He wishes to reassure the people of Cyprus that all is safe and well:

> *"Iago, look with care about the town,*
> *And silence those whom this vile brawl distracted."*

He is responsible and diligent as Governor of Cyprus.

RODERIGO

AT THE END OF HIS TETHER

Roderigo still clings to his hope of winning Desdemona, but he is losing his money and his spirits.

> *"I think the issue will be, I shall have so much experience*
> *for my pains; and so, with no money at all and a little*
> *more wit, return again to Venice."*

Yet Iago persuades him to be patient, as his plans are beginning to succeed. Roderigo is not quite content with this. He has no other avenue of success besides Iago and so he persists in his self-delusion.

MONTANO
A RESPONSIBLE COMRADE

Montano is sociable but holds his drink better than Cassio. He reminds his comrades that they must return to the watch. When he realises the dangers of Cassio's weakness for drink, he believes that Othello should be informed. Such an action would be honest.

> *"It were well*
> *The general were put in mind of it."*

Montano is a worthy officer and comrade.

DESDEMONA
PERFECTION

We learn little directly of Desdemona in this scene, but conflicting opinions are expressed about her by others. Iago regards her as both *"full of game"* and:

> *"so free, so kind, so apt, so blessed a disposition, that she*
> *holds it a vice in her goodness not to do more than she*
> *is requested."*

Cassio sees her as *"a most exquisite lady"* and *"a most fresh and delicate creature."* Othello calls her *"my gentle love"* and *"sweeting"*. Obviously she is a paragon of virtue and goodness.

Act 3
Scene I

Cyprus. Before the Castle.
Enter Cassio, and some Musicians.

Cassio	Masters, play here, I will content your pains¹; Something that's brief; and bid 'Good morrow, general.' [*Music.*

Enter Clown.

Clown	Why, masters, have your instruments been in Naples, that they speak i' the nose² thus?
First Musician	How, sir, how?
Clown	Are these, I pray you, wind-instruments?
First Musician	Ay, marry, are they, sir.
Clown	O! thereby hangs a tail³.
First Musician	Whereby hangs a tale, sir? 10
Clown	Marry, sir, by many a wind-instrument that I know. But, masters, here's money for you; and the general so likes your music, that he desires you, for love's sake, to make no more noise with it.
First Musician	Well, sir, we will not.
Clown	If you have any music that may not be heard, to't again; but, as they say, to hear music the general does not greatly care.
First Musician	We have none such, sir.
Clown	Then put up your pipes in your bag, for I'll away. 20 Go; vanish into air; away!
	[*Exeunt Musicians.*
Cassio	Dost thou hear, mine honest friend?
Clown	No, I hear not your honest friend; I hear you.
Cassio	Prithee, keep up thy quillets⁴. There's a poor piece of gold for thee. If the gentlewoman that attends the general's wife be stirring, tell her there's one Cassio entreats her a little favour of speech: wilt thou do this?
Clown	She is stirring sir: if she will stir hither, I shall seem⁵ to notify unto her. 30
Cassio	Do, good my friend. [*Exit Clown.*

Enter Iago.

In happy time⁶, Iago.

---

¹ reward your efforts

² like a person whose nose was attacked by the pox (which was said to have originated in Naples)

³ genitals (a pun on 'tail' and 'tale')

⁴ quibbles

⁵ see fit to

⁶ well met!

Iago	You have not been a-bed, then?
Cassio	Why, no; the day had broke
	Before we parted. I have made bold, Iago,
	To send in to your wife; my suit to her
	Is, that she will to virtuous Desdemona
	Procure me some access.
Iago	I'll send her to you presently;
	And I'll devise a mean to draw the Moor
	Out of the way, that your converse⁷ and business
	May be more free.
Cassio	I humbly thank you for't.

⁷ conversation

40

Enter Emilia.

[Exit Iago.

I never knew
A Florentine more kind and honest.

Emilia	Good morrow, good lieutenant: I am sorry
	For your displeasure; but all will soon be well.
	The general and his wife are talking of it,
	And she speaks for you stoutly: the Moor replies
	That he you hurt is of great fame in Cyprus
	And great affinity⁸, and that in wholesome wisdom
	He might not but refuse you; but he protests he loves you,
	And needs no other suitor but his likings
	To take the saf'st occasion⁹ by the front
	To bring you in again¹⁰.
Cassio	Yet, I beseech you,
	If you think fit, or that it may be done,
	Give me advantage of some brief discourse
	With Desdemona alone.
Emilia	Pray you, come in:
	I will bestow you where you shall have time
	To speak your bosom¹¹ freely.
Cassio	I am much bound to you.

⁸ of noble family

50

⁹ best opportunity
¹⁰ reinstate you

¹¹ private thoughts

[Exeunt.

The Plot (Day Three – Before the Castle)

CASSIO APPEALS TO EMILIA

In the morning, Cassio has arranged for musicians to entertain Desdemona and Othello. Othello sends a clown to dismiss the musicians. Cassio tells the clown to send Emilia to him. Iago arrives and promises to send Emilia to Cassio and to keep Othello occupied.

Emilia enters and Cassio begs her to arrange a meeting between him and Desdemona. Emilia agrees but suggests that Cassio's own reputation is high with Othello and that he does not need Desdemona to appeal on his behalf.

Dramatic Significance

A STROKE OF GOOD FORTUNE FOR IAGO

Cassio has arranged musicians as a traditional greeting to the bridegroom general, Othello, but Othello sends a clown to dismiss them, providing a brief comic interlude in the play.

Cassio impatiently tries to arrange a meeting with Desdemona through Emilia. Iago arrives to find Cassio playing into his hands, by his impatience to meet Desdemona. Now Iago does not need to ask Emilia to arrange the meeting.

Cassio unwittingly advances Iago's scheme to convince Othello that Desdemona and Cassio are having a love affair.

> *"... I have made bold, Iago,*
> *To send in to your wife; my suit to her*
> *Is, that she will to virtuous Desdemona*
> *Procure me some access."*

Emilia tells Cassio that Othello is ready to forgive Cassio, if he could only have patience:

> *"... he protests he loves you,*
> *And needs no other suitor but his likings*
> *To take the saf'st occasion by the front*
> *To bring you in again."*

By arranging a meeting between Desdemona and Cassio alone, Emilia unwittingly helps Iago's plans to destroy Othello and Desdemona's happiness together.

Thus Iago's plan to have Othello eavesdrop on Cassio and Desdemona's solicitation is advanced by a stroke of good luck and we wait in suspense to see the outcome.

Character Development

CASSIO

IMPATIENT OF DISGRACE

Cassio's eagerness to enlist Desdemona's help in regaining Othello's favour leads him further into trouble. Cassio is tortured by his disgrace and cannot begin to live again until he is restored to his general's favour. He employs musicians to please Othello and arranges with Emilia to meet Desdemona.

> *"...I have made bold, Iago,*
> *To send in to your wife; my suit to her*
> *Is, that she will to virtuous Desdemona*
> *Procure me some access."*

Not once does he suspect that his adviser, Iago, is double-dealing him:

> *"I humbly thank you for't. I never knew*
> *A Florentine more kind and honest."*

IAGO

A HIDDEN SHREWDNESS

Iago's scheme works better than he expected due to Cassio's impatience to see Desdemona. Here is an ideal opportunity to arrange that Othello sees Desdemona and Cassio in close conversation together without danger of discovery:

> *"... I'll devise a mean to draw the Moor*
> *Out of the way, that your converse and business*
> *May be more free."*

EMILIA

A SYMPATHETIC HELPER

Emilia comforts Cassio and reassures him that all will soon be well and goes to arrange the meeting with Desdemona. She is helpful and considerate, unlike Iago's earlier view of her:

> *"Good morrow, good lieutenant; I am sorry*
> *For your displeasure, but all will soon be well.*
> *The general and his wife are talking of it,*
> *And she speaks for you stoutly."*

Scene II

A Room in the Castle.
Enter Othello, Iago and Gentlemen.

Othello	These letters give, Iago, to the pilot[1],
	And by him do my duties[2] to the senate;
	That done, I will be walking on the works[3];
	Repair[4] there to me.
Iago	Well, my good lord, I'll do't.
Othello	This fortification, gentlemen, shall we see't?
Gentlemen	We'll wait upon your lordship. [*Exeunt.*

[1] the pilot of the ships
[2] pay my respects
[3] fortifications
[4] return

The Plot (Day Three – a Room in the Castle)

IAGO WILL MEET OTHELLO

Othello is busy with military matters. He sends Iago with letters to the pilot and instructs him to meet him later. He then proceeds to inspect the fortifications to make sure all is safe against any possible attack.

Dramatic Significance

THE ENEMY WITHIN

Othello inspects the defences against any possible attack. He is a busy military man in command of the island of Cyprus and takes his duties seriously. Iago, on the other hand, has less responsibilities and more time to plot and scheme.

This scene prepares for the following scene and shows how Othello may be caught unawares by the coming attack on his own personality and marriage relationship. Ironically, Othello has little defence against the enemy within – the Iago within the walls, just as much as the Iago within his own personality. We await the coming meeting with Iago with anxiety for Othello.

Character Development

OTHELLO
A DILIGENT COMMANDER

Othello, in this short scene, attends to his duties as Governor of Cyprus. He is sending letters through the pilot of his fleet to the Senate and prepares to inspect the fortifications of the castle. He is diligent in his duties.

> *"This fortification, gentlemen, shall we see't?"*

IAGO
UNRELIABLE

Iago has promised to keep Othello away from the meeting of Desdemona and Cassio. Obviously he has no intention of preventing Othello from witnessing their conversation, as he leaves to deliver Othello's letters:

"Well, my good lord, I'll do't."

Scene III

Before the Castle.
Enter Desdemona, Cassio and Emilia.

Desdemona	Be thou assur'd, good Cassio, I will do
	All my abilities[1] in thy behalf.
Emilia	Good madam, do: I warrant it grieves my husband,
	As if the case[2] were his.
Desdemona	O! that's an honest fellow. Do not doubt, Cassio,
	But I will have my lord and you again
	As friendly as you were.
Cassio	Bounteous madam,
	Whatever shall become of Michael Cassio,
	He's never anything but your true servant.
Desdemona	I know't; I thank you. You do love my lord; *10*
	You have known him long; and be you well assur'd
	He shall in strangeness stand no further off
	Than in a politic distance[3].
Cassio	Ay, but, lady,
	That policy may either last so long,
	Or feed upon such nice and waterish diet[4],
	Or breed itself so out of circumstance[5],
	That, I being absent and my place supplied[6],
	My general will forget my love and service.
Desdemona	Do not doubt that; before Emilia here
	I give thee warrant[7] of thy place. Assure thee, *20*
	If I do vow a friendship, I'll perform it
	To the last article; my lord shall never rest;
	I'll watch him tame[8], and talk him out of patience;
	His bed shall seem a school, his board a shrift[9];
	I'll intermingle every thing he does
	With Cassio's suit. Therefore be merry, Cassio;
	For thy solicitor[10] shall rather die
	Than give thy cause away.

Enter Othello, and Iago at a distance.

[1] do my best

[2] matter

[3] expedient distance

[4] kept up for trivial reasons

[5] grow because of accidents

[6] filled

[7] guarantee

[8] prevent him from sleeping

[9] confessional

[10] advocate

Emilia	Madam, here comes my lord.
Cassio	Madam, I'll take my leave. 30
Desdemona	Why, stay, and hear me speak.
Cassio	Madam, not now; I am very ill at ease,
	Unfit for mine own purposes.
Desdemona	Well, do your discretion[11].

[Exit Cassio.

Iago	Ha! I like not that.
Othello	What dost thou say?
Iago	Nothing, my lord: or if – I know not what.
Othello	Was not that Cassio parted from my wife?
Iago	Cassio, my lord? No, sure, I cannot think it
	That he would steal away so guilty-like,
	Seeing you coming. 40
Othello	I do believe 'twas he.
Desdemona	How now, my lord!
	I have been talking with a suitor here,
	A man that languishes in your displeasure.
Othello	Who is't you mean?
Desdemona	Why, your lieutenant, Cassio. Good my lord,
	If I have any grace or power to move you,
	His present[12] reconciliation take;
	For if he be not one that truly loves you,
	That errs in ignorance and not in cunning,
	I have no judgment in an honest face. 50
	I prithee[13] call him back.
Othello	Went he hence now?
Desdemona	Ay, sooth[14] so humbled,
	That he hath left part of his grief with me,
	To suffer with him. Good love, call him back.
Othello	Not now, sweet Desdemona; some other time.
Desdemona	But shall't be shortly?
Othello	The sooner, sweet, for you.
Desdemona	Shall't be to-night at supper?
Othello	No, not to-night.
Desdemona	To-morrow dinner then?
Othello	I shall not dine at home;
	I meet the captains at the citadel.
Desdemona	Why then, to-morrow night; or Tuesday morn; 60
	On Tuesday noon, or night; or Wednesday morn:
	I prithee name the time, but let it not
	Exceed three days: in faith, he's penitent;
	And yet his trespass[15], in our common reason[16]–
	Save that they say, the wars must make examples
	Out of their best, – is not almost[17] a fault
	To incur a private check[18]. When shall he come?
	Tell me, Othello: I wonder in my soul,

[11] what you think fit

[12] immediate

[13] please

[14] indeed

[15] offence
[16] in our normal opinion

[17] is hardly

[18] reprimand

	What you could ask me that I should deny,	
	Or stand so mammering[19] on. What! Michael	*70*
	Cassio,	
	That came a wooing with you, and so many a time,	
	When I have spoke of you dispraisingly,	
	Hath ta'en your part; to have so much to do	
	To bring him in[20]! Trust me, I could do much. –	
Othello	Prithee, no more; let him come when he will;	
	I will deny thee nothing.	
Desdemona	Why, this is not a boon;[21]	
	'Tis as I should entreat you wear your gloves,	
	Or feed on nourishing dishes, or keep you warm,	
	Or sue to you to do a peculiar[22] profit	
	To your own person; nay, when I have a suit	*80*
	Wherein I mean to touch[23] your love indeed,	
	It shall be full of poise[24] and difficult weight,	
	And fearful to be granted.	
Othello	I will deny thee nothing:	
	Whereon[25], I do beseech thee, grant me this,	
	To leave me but a little to myself.	
Desdemona	Shall I deny you? no, farewell, my lord.	
Othello	Farewell, my Desdemona: I'll come to thee straight.	
Desdemona	Emilia, come. Be as your fancies teach you;	
	Whate'er you be, I am obedient.	

[Exit, with Emilia.

Othello	Excellent wretch! Perdition[26] catch my soul	*90*
	But I do love thee! and when I love thee not,	
	Chaos is come again.	
Iago	My noble lord, –	
Othello	What dost thou say, Iago?	
Iago	Did Michael Cassio, when you woo'd my lady,	
	Know of your love?	
Othello	He did, from first to last: why dost thou ask?	
Iago	But for a satisfaction of my thought;	
	No further harm.	
Othello	Why of thy thought, Iago?	
Iago	I did not think he had been acquainted with her.	
Othello	O! yes; and went between[27] us very oft.	*100*
Iago	Indeed!	
Othello	Indeed! ay, indeed; discern'st thou aught in that?	
	Is he not honest?	
Iago	Honest, my lord?	
Othello	Honest! ay, honest.	
Iago	My lord, for aught I know.	
Othello	What dost thou think?	

[19] hesitating

[20] reinstate

[21] favour

[22] particular

[23] test
[24] weight

[25] therefore

[26] damnation

[27] acted as a messenger

	Iago	Think, my lord!
	Othello	Think, my lord!

Iago   Think, my lord!

Othello   Think, my lord!
By heaven, he echoes me,
As if there were some monster in his thought
Too hideous to be shown. Thou dost mean
    something:
I heard thee say but now, thou lik'dst not that,
When Cassio left my wife; what didst not like? *110*
And when I told thee he was of my counsel[28]
In my whole course of wooing, thou criedst,
    'Indeed!'
And didst contract and purse thy brow together,
As if thou then hadst shut up in thy brain
Some horrible conceit[29]. If thou dost love me,
Show me thy thought.

Iago   My lord, you know I love you.

Othello   I think thou dost;
And, for I know thou art full of love and honesty,
And weigh'st thy words before thou giv'st them
    breath,
Therefore these stops of thine fright me the   *120*
    more;
For such things in a false disloyal knave
Are tricks of custom[30], but in a man that's just
They are close dilations[31], working from the heart
That passion cannot rule.

Iago   For Michael Cassio,
I dare be sworn I think that he is honest.

Othello   I think so too.

Iago   Men should be what they seem;
Or those that be not, would they might seem
    none[32]!

Othello   Certain, men should be what they seem.

Iago   Why then, I think Cassio's an honest man.

Othello   Nay, yet there's more in this.   *130*
I pray thee, speak to me as to thy thinkings,
As thou dost ruminate[33], and give thy worst of
    thoughts
The worst of words.

Iago   Good my lord, pardon me;
Though I am bound to every act of duty,
I am not bound to that all slaves are free to[34].
Utter my thoughts? Why, say they are vile and false;
As where's that palace whereinto foul things
Sometimes intrude not? who has a breast so pure
But some uncleanly apprehensions[35]

28 in my confidence

29 idea

30 customary behaviour

31 secret expressions

32 might seem not to be men

33 consider secretly

34 not bound to

35 unwholesome thoughts

	Keep leets and law days[36], and in session sit *140*
	With meditations lawful[37]?
Othello	Thou dost conspire against thy friend, Iago,
	If thou but think'st him wrong'd, and mak'st his ear
	A stranger to thy thoughts.
Iago	I do beseech you,
	Though I perchance am vicious[38] in my guess, –
	As, I confess, it is my nature's plague
	To spy into abuses, and oft my jealousy[39]
	Shapes faults that are not, – that your wisdom yet,
	From one that so imperfectly conceits[40],
	Would take no notice, nor build yourself a *150*
	trouble
	Out of his scattering and unsure observance[41].
	It were not for your quiet[42] nor your good,
	Nor for my manhood, honesty, or wisdom,
	To let you know my thoughts.
Othello	What dost thou mean?
Iago	Good name in man and woman, dear my lord,
	Is the immediate jewel[43] of their souls:
	Who steals my purse steals trash; 'tis something, nothing;
	'Twas mine, 'tis his, and has been slave to thousands;
	But he that filches from me my good name
	Robs me of that which not enriches him, *160*
	And makes me poor indeed.
Othello	By heaven, I'll know thy thoughts.
Iago	You cannot, if[44] my heart were in your hand;
	Nor shall not, whilst 'tis in my custody.
Othello	Ha!
Iago	O! beware, my lord, of jealousy;
	It is the green-ey'd monster which doth mock
	The meat it feeds on; that cuckold[45] lives in bliss
	Who, certain of his fate, loves not his wronger;
	But, O! what damned minutes tells he o'er
	Who dotes[46], yet doubts; suspects, yet *170*
	soundly loves!
Othello	O misery!
Iago	Poor and content is rich, and rich enough,
	But riches fineless[47] is as poor as winter
	To him that ever fears he shall be poor.
	Good heaven, the souls of all my tribe defend
	From jealousy!
Othello	Why, why is this?
	Think'st thou I'd make a life of jealousy,

[36] days on which local courts are held
[37] accompany innocent thoughts
[38] malicious
[39] suspicion
[40] guesses wrongly
[41] random guesses
[42] peace of mind
[43] most precious jewel
[44] even if
[45] deceived husband
[46] loves
[47] endless

⁴⁸ to grow in suspicion from
month to month
⁴⁹ once and for all

⁵⁰ silly and exaggerated guesses

⁵¹ allegation

⁵² open and eloquent

⁵³ infidelity

⁵⁴ generosity
⁵⁵ native habits

⁵⁶ sense of morality

⁵⁷ there you are

⁵⁸ pretence

⁵⁹ to deceive totally

To follow still the changes of the moon
With fresh suspicions⁴⁸? No; to be once in doubt
Is once⁴⁹ to be resolved. Exchange me for a
　　　goat　　　　　　　　　　　　　　　　　180
When I shall turn the business of my soul
To such exsufflicate and blown surmises⁵⁰,
Matching thy inference⁵¹. 'Tis not to make me
　　　jealous
To say my wife is fair, feeds well, loves company,
Is free⁵² of speech, sings, plays, and dances well;
Where virtue is, these are more virtuous:
Nor from mine own weak merits will I draw
The smallest fear, or doubt of her revolt⁵³;
For she had eyes, and chose me. No, Iago;
I'll see before I doubt; when I doubt, prove;　190
And, on the proof, there is no more but this,
Away at once with love or jealousy!

Iago　I am glad of it; for now I shall have reason
To show the love and duty that I bear you
With franker spirit; therefore, as I am bound,
Receive it from me; I speak not yet of proof.
Look to your wife; observe her well with Cassio;
Wear your eye thus, not jealous nor secure:
I would not have your free and noble nature
Out of self-bounty⁵⁴ be abus'd; look to't:　200
I know our country disposition⁵⁵ well;
In Venice they do let heaven see the pranks
They dare not show their husbands; their best
　　　conscience⁵⁶
Is not to leave't undone, but keep unknown.

Othello　Dost thou say so?

Iago　She did deceive her father, marrying you;
And when she seem'd to shake and fear your
　　　looks,
She lov'd them most.

Othello　　　And so she did.

Iago　　　　　Why, go to⁵⁷, then;
She that so young could give out such a seeming⁵⁸,
To seal her father's eyes up close as oak⁵⁹,　210
He thought 'twas witchcraft; but I am much to
　　　blame;
I humbly do beseech you of your pardon
For too much loving you.

Othello　　　I am bound to thee for ever.

Iago　I see, this hath a little dash'd your spirits.

Othello　Not a jot, not a jot.

Iago	I'faith, I fear it has.
	I hope you will consider what is spoke
	Comes from my love. But, I do see you're mov'd;
	I am to pray you not to strain my speech
	To grosser issues[60] nor to larger reach
	Than to suspicion. *220*
Othello	I will not.
Iago	Should you do so, my lord,
	My speech should fall into such vile success[61]
	As my thoughts aim not at. Cassio's my worthy friend
	– My lord, I see you're mov'd.
Othello	No, not much mov'd:
	I do not think but Desdemona's honest[62].
Iago	Long live she so! and long live you to think so!
Othello	And, yet, how nature erring from itself, –
Iago	Ay, there's the point: as, to be bold with you,
	Not to affect[63] many proposed matches
	Of her own clime, complexion, and degree[64], *230*
	Whereto, we see, in all things nature tends;
	Foh! one may smell in such, a will most rank[65],
	Foul disproportion[66], thoughts unnatural.
	But pardon me; I do not in position[67]
	Distinctly speak of her, though I may fear
	Her will, recoiling[68] to her better judgment,
	May fail to match you[69] with her country forms[70]
	And happily repent[71].
Othello	Farewell, farewell:
	If more thou dost perceive, let me know more;
	Set on thy wife to observe. Leave me, Iago. *240*
Iago	My lord, I take my leave. *[Going.*
Othello	Why did I marry? This honest creature, doubtless,
	Sees and knows more, much more, than he unfolds.
Iago	*[Returning]* My lord, I would I might entreat your honour
	To scan this thing no further; leave it to time.
	Although 'tis fit that Cassio have his place,
	For, sure he fills it up with great ability,
	Yet, if you please to hold him off awhile,
	You shall by that perceive him and his means[72]:
	Note if your lady strain his entertainment[73] *250*
	With any strong or vehement importunity[74];
	Much will be seen in that. In the mean time,
	Let me be thought too busy[75] in my fears,
	As worthy cause I have to fear I am,
	And hold her free[76], I do beseech your honour.

[60] broader implications

[61] result

[62] faithful

[63] desire
[64] country, skin-colour and rank

[65] foul
[66] abnormality
[67] in my argument

[68] going back
[69] may compare unfavourably
[70] her countrymen's appearance
[71] perhaps regret

[72] methods
[73] press hard for his reinstatement
[74] pleading

[75] exaggerating

[76] innocent of blame

⁷⁷ self-control	**Othello**	Fear not my government⁷⁷.
	Iago	I once more take my leave. [*Exit.*
	Othello	This fellow's of exceeding honesty,
		And knows all qualities, with a learned spirit,
		Of human dealings; if I do prove her
⁷⁸ wild		haggard⁷⁸, 260
⁷⁹ ties to me		Though that her jesses⁷⁹ were my dear heart-
		strings,
⁸⁰ send		I'd whistle⁸⁰ her off and let her down the wind,
⁸¹ to fend for herself		To prey at fortune⁸¹. Haply, for I am black,
		And have not those soft parts of conversation
⁸² seducers		That chamberers⁸² have, or, for I am declin'd
		Into the vale of years – yet that's not much –
		She's gone, I am abus'd; and my relief
		Must be to loathe her. O curse of marriage!
		That we can call these delicate creatures ours,
		And not their appetites. I had rather be a toad, 270
		And live upon the vapour of a dungeon,
		Than keep a corner in the thing I love
		For others' uses. Yet, 'tis the plague of great ones;
⁸³ privileged		Prerogativ'd⁸³ are they less than the base;
		'Tis destiny unshunnable, like death:
⁸⁴ cuckolding		Even then this forked plague⁸⁴ is fated to us
⁸⁵ are born		When we do quicken⁸⁵.
		Look! where she comes.
		If she be false, O! then heaven mocks itself.
		I'll not believe it.

Re-enter Desdemona and Emilia.

	Desdemona	How now, my dear Othello!
		Your dinner and the generous islanders 280
		By you invited, do attend your presence.
	Othello	I am to blame.
	Desdemona	Why do you speak so faintly?
		Are you not well?
	Othello	I have a pain upon my forehead here.
⁸⁶ lack of sleep	**Desdemona**	Faith, that's with watching⁸⁶; 'twill away again:
		Let me but bind it hard, within this hour
		It will be well.
	Othello	Your napkin is too little:
		[She drops her handkerchief.
		Let it alone. Come, I'll go in with you.
	Desdemona	I am very sorry that you are not well.
		[Exeunt Othello and Desdemona.
⁸⁷ handkerchief	**Emilia**	I am glad I have found this napkin⁸⁷; 290
		This was her first remembrance from the Moor;

My wayward husband hath a hundred times
Woo'd[88] me to steal it, but she so loves the token,
For he conjur'd[89] her she should ever keep it,
That she reserves[90] it evermore about her
To kiss and talk to. I'll have the work ta'en out[91],
And give't Iago:
What he will do with it heaven knows, not I;
I nothing but to please his fantasy.

Enter Iago.

Iago	How now! what do you here alone?	300
Emilia	Do not you chide; I have a thing for you.	
Iago	A thing for me? It is a common thing –	
Emilia	Ha!	
Iago	To have a foolish wife.	
Emilia	O! is that all? What will you give me now	
	For that same handkerchief?	
Iago	What handkerchief?	
Emilia	What handkerchief!	
	Why, that the Moor first gave to Desdemona:	
	That which so often you did bid me steal.	
Iago	Hast stol'n it from her?	310
Emilia	No, faith; she let it drop by negligence,	
	And, to the advantage, I, being there, took't up.	
	Look, here it is.	
Iago	A good wench[92]; give it to me.	
Emilia	What will you do with 't, that you have been so earnest	
	To have me filch it?	
Iago	Why, what's that to you?	

[Snatches it.

Emilia	If it be not for some purpose of import[93]	
	Give't me again; poor lady! she'll run mad	
	When she shall lack[94] it.	
Iago	Be not acknown[95] on't; I have use for it.	320
	Go, leave me.	

[Exit Emilia.

I will in Cassio's lodging lose this napkin,
And let him find it; trifles light as air
Are to the jealous confirmations strong
As proofs of holy writ; this may do something.
The Moor already changes with my poison:
Dangerous conceits[96] are in their natures poisons,
Which at the first are scarce found to distaste[97],
But with a little act upon the blood,
Burn like the mines of sulphur. I did say so: 330
Look! where he comes!

[88] enticed
[89] warned on oath
[90] keeps
[91] copied

[92] woman

[93] importance

[94] miss

[95] pretend ignorance of it

[96] thoughts
[97] be unpleasant to the taste

Enter Othello.

	Not poppy, nor mandragora[98]
	Nor all the drowsy syrups[99] of the world,
	Shall ever medicine thee to that sweet sleep
	Which thou ow'dst[100] yesterday.
Othello	Ha! ha! false to me!
Iago	Why, how now, general! no more of that.
Othello	Avaunt[101]! be gone! thou hast set me on the rack;
	I swear 'tis better to be much abus'd
	Than but to know't a little.
Iago	How now, my lord!
Othello	What sense had I of her stol'n hours of lust?
	I saw't not, thought it not, it harmed not me; *340*
	I slept the next night well, was free[102] and merry;
	I found not Cassio's kisses on her lips;
	He that is robb'd, not wanting[103] what is stol'n,
	Let him not know't and he's not robbed at all.
Iago	I am sorry to hear this.
Othello	I had been happy, if the general camp,
	Pioners[104] and all, had tasted her sweet body,
	So I had nothing known. O! now, for ever
	Farewell the tranquil mind; farewell content!
	Farewell the plumed troop and the big wars *350*
	To make ambition virtue! O, farewell!
	Farewell the neighing steed, and the shrill trump[105],
	The spirit-stirring drum, the ear-piercing fife[106],
	The royal banner, and all quality[107],
	Pride, pomp, and circumstance of glorious war!
	And, O you mortal engines[108], whose rude throats
	The immortal Jove's dread clamours counterfeit[109],
	Farewell! Othello's occupation's gone!
Iago	Is it possible, my lord?
Othello	Villain, be sure thou prove my love a whore, *360*
	Be sure of it; give me the ocular[110] proof;
	Or, by the worth of mine eternal soul,
	Thou hadst been better have been born a dog
	Than answer my wak'd wrath.
Iago	Is't come to this?
Othello	Make me to see't; or, at the least, so prove it,
	That the probation bear no hinge nor loop
	To hang a doubt on; or woe upon thy life!
Iago	My noble lord, –
Othello	If thou dost slander her and torture me,
	Never pray more; abandon all remorse; *370*
	On horror's head horrors accumulate;
	Do deeds to make heaven weep, all earth amaz'd;

Margin glosses:

[98] mandrake, a narcotic
[99] sleep-inducing drugs
[100] enjoyed
[101] Go away!
[102] carefree
[103] missing
[104] soldiers of lowest rank
[105] trumpet
[106] flute
[107] qualities
[108] deadly cannons
[109] thunder: Jove was the god of thunder
[110] visual

For nothing canst thou to damnation add
Greater than that.

Iago   O grace! O heaven forgive me!
Are you a man! have you a soul or sense?
God be wi' you; take mine office. O wretched fool!
That liv'st to make thine honesty a vice.
O monstrous world! Take note, take note, O world!
To be direct and honest is not safe.
I thank you for this profit[111], from hence   *380*   [111]profitable lesson
I'll love no friend, sith[112] love breeds such offence.   [112]since

Othello   Nay, stay; thou shouldst[113] be honest.   [113]seem to be

Iago   I should be wise; for honesty's a fool,
And loses that it works for.

Othello   By the world,
I think my wife be honest and think she is not;
I think that thou art just and think thou art not.
I'll have some proof. Her name, that was as fresh
As Dian's visage[114], is now begrim'd and black   [114]as chaste as Diana, goddess
As mine own face. If there be cords or knives,   of chastity
Poison or fire or suffocating streams,   *390*
I'll not endure it. Would I were satisfied!

Iago   I see, sir, you are eaten up with passion.
I do repent me that I put it to you.
You would be satisfied?

Othello   Would! nay, I will.

Iago   And may; but how? how satisfied, my lord?
Would you, the supervisor, grossly gape on;
Behold her tupp'd[115]?   [115]seduced

Othello   Death and damnation! O!

Iago   It were a tedious difficulty, I think,
To bring them to that prospect[116]; damn them   [116]situation
then,
If ever mortal eyes do see them bolster[117]   *400*   [117]go to bed
More than their own! What then? how then?
What shall I say? Where's satisfaction?
It is impossible you should see this,
Were they as prime[118] as goats, as hot[119] as   [118]lecherous
monkeys,   [119]sexually excited
As salt as wolves in pride[120], and fools as gross   [120]lecherous as wolves in heat
As ignorance made drunk; but yet, I say,
If imputation[121], and strong circumstances[122],   [121]opinion
Which lead directly to the door of truth,   [122]evidence from circumstances
Will give you satisfaction, you may have it.

Othello   Give me a living reason she's disloyal.   *410*

Iago   I do not like the office[123];   [123]duty
But, sith I am enter'd in this cause so far,
Prick'd[124] to't by foolish honesty and love,   [124]pushed

¹²⁵toothache

I will go on. I lay with Cassio lately;
And, being troubled with a raging tooth¹²⁵,
I could not sleep.
There are a kind of men so loose of soul
That in their sleeps will mutter their affairs;
One of this kind is Cassio.
In sleep I heard him say, 'Sweet Desdemona,   *420*
Let us be wary, let us hide our loves!'
And then, sir, would he gripe and wring my hand,
Cry, 'O, sweet creature!' and then kiss me hard,
As if he pluck'd up kisses by the roots,
That grew upon my lips; then laid his leg
Over my thigh, and sigh'd, and kiss'd; and then
Cried, 'Cursed fate, that gave thee to the Moor!'

Othello   O monstrous! monstrous!

Iago   Nay, this was but his dream.

¹²⁶previous action

¹²⁷strong suspicion

Othello   But this denoted a foregone conclusion¹²⁶:
'Tis a shrewd doubt¹²⁷, though it be but a
dream.   *430*

¹²⁸strengthen

Iago   And this may help to thicken¹²⁸ other proofs
That do demonstrate thinly.

Othello   I'll tear her all to pieces.

Iago   Nay, but be wise; yet we see nothing done;
She may be honest yet. Tell me but this:
Have you not sometimes seen a handkerchief
Spotted with strawberries in your wife's hand?

Othello   I gave her such a one; 'twas my first gift.

Iago   I know not that; but such a handkerchief –
I am sure it was your wife's – did I to-day
See Cassio wipe his beard with.   *440*

Othello   If it be that, –

Iago   If it be that, or any that was hers,
It speaks against her with the other proofs.

Othello   O! that the slave had forty thousand lives;
One is too poor, too weak for my revenge.
Now do I see 'tis true. Look here, Iago;

¹²⁹foolish

All my fond¹²⁹ love thus do I blow to heaven:
'Tis gone.
Arise, black vengeance, from the hollow hell!

¹³⁰in the heart

Yield up, O love! thy crown and hearted¹³⁰ throne
To tyrannous hate. Swell, bosom, with thy   *450*
fraught¹³¹,

¹³¹load

For 'tis of aspics'¹³² tongues!

¹³²asps, poisonous snakes

Iago   Yet be content¹³³.

¹³³calm

Othello   O! blood, blood, blood!

Iago   Patience, I say; your mind, perhaps, may change.

¹³⁴The Black Sea

Othello   Never, Iago. Like to the Pontic sea¹³⁴,

	Whose icy current and compulsive course[135]	[135]continuous course
	Ne'er feels retiring ebb, but keeps due on	
	To the Propontic[136] and the Hellespont[137],	[136]Sea of Marmora
		[137]Dardanelles
	Even so my bloody thoughts, with violent pace,	
	Shall ne'er look back, ne'er ebb to humble love,	
	Till that a capable and wide[138] revenge 460	[138]complete and far-reaching
	Swallow them up. [Kneels.	
	Now, by yond marble heaven,	
	In the due reverence of a sacred vow	
	I here engage[139] my words.	[139]pledge
Iago	Do not rise yet. [Kneels.	
	Witness, you ever-burning lights above!	
	You elements that clip[140] us round about!	[140]surround
	Witness, that here Iago doth give up	
	The execution[141] of his wit, hands, heart,	[141]full use of
	To wrong'd Othello's service! Let him command,	
	And to obey shall be in me remorse[142],	[142]in compassion (to Othello)
	What bloody business ever. 470	
Othello	I greet thy love,	
	Not with vain thanks, but with acceptance	
	bounteous,	
	And will upon the instant put thee to't:	
	Within these three days let me hear thee say	
	That Cassio's not alive.	
Iago	My friend is dead; 'tis done at your request:	
	But let her live.	
Othello	Damn her, lewd minx! O, damn her!	
	Come, go with me apart; I will withdraw	
	To furnish me with some swift means of death	
	For the fair devil. Now art thou my lieutenant.	
Iago	I am your own[143] for ever. 480	[143]your faithful servant

[Exeunt.

The Plot (Day Three – Before the Castle)

DESDEMONA REASSURES CASSIO

Cassio meets Desdemona as arranged and both she and Emilia assure him that Othello thinks highly of him and that he will soon be reinstated. Desdemona promises to keep Othello continually reminded of Cassio, until he is restored as lieutenant.

As Othello returns with Iago, Cassio leaves suddenly in embarrassment. Iago remarks on this to Othello and suggests that Cassio did not wish to be seen talking to Desdemona. However, Othello is not really sure about Cassio.

Come, go with me apart; I will withdraw
To furnish me with some swift means of death
For the fair devil.

(Othello, Act 3, Scene III)

DESDEMONA PLEADS FOR CASSIO

Desdemona tells Othello she has been talking to Cassio and asks him to forgive Cassio. Othello does not wish to see Cassio but Desdemona persists and tries to arrange a meeting between Cassio and Othello. He finally agrees but wishes to be left alone for now.

IAGO'S TEMPTATION OF OTHELLO

Alone with Othello, Iago gives the impression that he knows more about Desdemona's relationship with Cassio than he is prepared to tell Othello. This makes Othello curious and uneasy. Evasively, Iago plays on Cassio's involvement in wooing Desdemona for Othello and on Cassio's suspicious parting from her just now. He insinuates that Cassio's honesty may be in question, although he states that he believes Cassio is honest.

Then Iago warns of the danger of becoming jealous and how Venetian wives may deceive their husbands. Othello states that Desdemona chose him freely as a husband. Therefore he will require proof before he believes Iago's insinuations.

Now Iago becomes more direct in his hints. He suggests that he, a Venetian, knows well how women deceive their husbands. He warns Othello to watch his wife closely with Cassio, since she has already deceived her father by marrying Othello. Othello is anxious now and Iago pretends to regret that he has told Othello too much.

Seeing Othello's suspicions of Desdemona growing steadily, Iago suggests that Desdemona's choice of Othello was strange and she may have other strange tendencies. Confused and anxious, Othello wonders why he married Desdemona.

As Iago leaves, Othello requests him to continue to spy on Desdemona and to report to him. Iago returns to suggest that Othello refuses to see Cassio for a while, so that he may observe Desdemona's behaviour with Cassio.

Left alone, Othello still believes in Iago's honesty. He looks within himself for reasons why Desdemona should be unfaithful to him. He thinks the cause may be his colour or his age. He is torn between love and his belief that Iago's insinuations are true.

THE HANDKERCHIEF

Desdemona comes, with Emilia, to remind Othello to greet the guests he has invited to dinner. Othello says he has a headache and Desdemona tries to bind his head with her handkerchief, which was a love token from Othello. It is too small and it drops on the ground, unnoticed. Emilia picks it up, intending to have it copied, since Iago would like it. Iago comes and grabs the handkerchief and orders Emilia to keep the whole incident secret. Iago intends to plant the handkerchief in Cassio's lodgings to confirm Othello's suspicions.

IAGO'S SECOND TEMPTATION OF OTHELLO

Othello returns, raving, convinced of Desdemona's infidelity. He grieves that he has lost all that he valued, even his career. He appeals to Iago to find him positive proof of Desdemona's falseness and warns that the proof must be absolute. Iago pretends to be offended that Othello doubts his honesty, and feigns concern for his part in causing Othello's distress.

Now Iago offers Othello the proof he is seeking. Firstly, he tells Othello, in graphic terms, of hearing Cassio talk in his sleep about making love to Desdemona. Secondly, he claims that he has often seen Cassio wiping his beard with Desdemona's handkerchief.

Othello is now convinced and swears to have revenge. Iago promises to help him in this. Immediately Othello instructs Iago to kill Cassio within three days and decides to kill Desdemona himself. Iago now becomes Othello's lieutenant in Cassio's place.

Dramatic Significance

IAGO'S STEP-BY-STEP TEMPTATION OF OTHELLO

In this pivotal scene in the tragedy, Iago tempts Othello to enter his web of suspicion and mistrust, jealousy and confusion. Iago attacks Othello's judgement and emotions and eventually gains control of his mind one step at a time.

Iago's temptation of Othello consists of the following main stages:

(a)   Exploitation of the evidence against Cassio, casting suspicion on both Cassio and Desdemona.

(b)   Darker hints that he knows more than he is telling about Othello's good name, his reasons to be jealous and Desdemona's possible "cuckolding" of him.

(c)   More direct indications of reasons for Othello to be jealous of Desdemona, since she has been deceitful already and her choice of Othello was unnatural.

(d)   The circumstantial evidence of Cassio's dream and the handkerchief.

(A) THE EVIDENCE AGAINST CASSIO

First Iago returns with Othello from the fortifications, just in time to see the end of Cassio's appeal to Desdemona, which Iago had engineered. Cassio's embarrassment in leaving so suddenly is a stroke of good luck, which advances Iago's scheme. Iago insinuates that Cassio's sudden departure warrants suspicion:

> *"... No, sure, I cannot think it,*
> *That he would steal away so guilty-like,*
> *Seeing you coming."*

Then Desdemona appeals to Othello on Cassio's behalf, as arranged by Cassio on Iago's advice. Othello is already predisposed by Iago to believe that Desdemona is appealing for her lover, Cassio, and so Othello is preoccupied and evasive with Desdemona:

> *"I will deny thee nothing."*

Next Iago suggests that, since Cassio was involved in Othello's wooing of Desdemona, he may be playing a double game and that his honesty may be in question:

> *"For Michael Cassio,*
> *I dare be sworn I think that he is honest."*

(B) DESDEMONA'S INFIDELITY

Then Iago feigns unwillingness to betray his friend but hints that the loss of one's good name is a very great loss. As Othello continues to question him, Iago warns of the danger of jealousy and suggests that it is better not to be in love with a wife who is having an affair with another man:

> *"... O! what damned minutes tells he o'er*
> *Who dotes, yet doubts; suspects, yet fondly loves!"*

When Othello refuses to doubt his wife, Iago suggests that Othello watch Desdemona closely with Cassio. He is not to be jealous but open-minded:

> *"Look to your wife; observe her well with Cassio;*
> *Wear your eye thus, not jealous nor secure."*

(C) REASONS FOR JEALOUSY

Iago insinuates that Venetian women are inclined to deceive their husbands:

> *"I know our country disposition well."*

To clinch his temptations, Iago suggests that Desdemona has already shown herself capable of deception:

> *"She did deceive her father, marrying you."*

Next Iago apologises for worrying Othello, by saying more than he intended, and for betraying Cassio, his friend. He appeals to Othello not to ask him to say more:

> *"I am to pray you not to strain my speech*
> *To grosser issues nor to larger reach*
> *Than to suspicion."*

Then Iago hints that Desdemona may have unnatural tendencies:

> *"Not to affect many proposed matches*
> *Of her own clime, complexion, and degree,*
> *Whereto, we see, in all things nature tends:*
> *Foh! one may smell in such, a will most rank,*
> *Foul disproportion, thoughts unnatural."*

When Iago leaves he returns to advise Othello to put Cassio off and to note if Desdemona makes any strong appeals on Cassio's behalf. In the meantime, Othello is to disregard Iago's fears:

> *"Note if your lady strain his entertainment*
> *With any strong or vehement importunity;*
> *Much will be seen in that."*

(D) CIRCUMSTANTIAL EVIDENCE

Later in the scene when Othello returns, Iago sympathises with him and tries to calm his wrath. Othello desires proof and Iago provides it. He pretends he overheard Cassio in his sleep, dreaming of making love to Desdemona:

> *"And then, sir, would he gripe and wring my hand,*
> *Cry, 'O, sweet creature!' and then kiss me hard."*

Lastly Iago claims that he saw Cassio wiping his beard with Desdemona's handkerchief, a love-token from Othello:

> *"... such a handkerchief –*
> *I am sure it was your wife's – did I to-day*
> *See Cassio wipe his beard with."*

IAGO'S SKILL IN MANIPULATING OTHELLO

Iago's temptations succeed in shaking Othello to the core, since Iago is so skilful in seeing his victim's weaknesses and preying upon them. Iago devises his methods of entrapment to answer the needs of his victim from moment to moment. His keen observation of Othello's character traits and his ability to react to the mood of the moment display an understanding of human motivation, which is unsurpassed by any other character in literature. He is a master of the arts of manipulation and of improvisation. Hence it is that Othello is so swiftly and decisively trapped in Iago's web.

First Iago attacks Othello's reason and judgement by innuendo and insinuation and by reiterating certain key words. When Cassio leaves suddenly in embarrassment, Iago does not state directly that something is amiss. He merely hints, *"Ha, I like not that"* and plants the words *"steal"* and *"guilty"* in Othello's mind. Othello forms his own conclusion that Cassio was up to something underhand. Iago has said nothing so he cannot be blamed for the consequences. Yet Othello believes exactly what Iago intends him to believe.

Other examples of insinuation and reiteration of words or ideas are used to make Othello believe that Iago is honest and Cassio dishonest and that Desdemona is false to Othello. Key words include: *honest, think, deceive, know, jealous,* etc.

Secondly, Iago manipulates Othello's reactions to what he tells him, by planting in his mind images or references, designed to make Othello feel as Iago wishes him to feel:

> *"O, beware, my lord, of jealousy!"*

This is intended to make Othello jealous of Cassio and Desdemona.

> *"I see, this hath a little dash'd your spirits."*

This is designed to make Othello feel anxious to know if Desdemona is deceiving him. Sometimes Iago uses a roundabout method to draw out Othello's thoughts and fears. When Iago says,

> *"Good name in man or woman, dear my lord,*
> *Is the immediate jewel of their souls"*

he makes Othello anxious to know if his own good name is being undermined by Desdemona's relationship with Cassio. Iago pretends to be glad when Othello expresses his faith in Desdemona. Then he advises him to observe his wife with Cassio, thus increasing Othello's doubts. Thus Othello feels as Iago wishes him to feel – anxious, but grateful to Iago for letting him know.

Last but not least, it is the cumulative effect of Iago's skilful insinuations that weakens Othello's confidence in his own judgements and confuses his emotions. Towards the end of this scene, Othello is totally confused and shattered:

> *"By the world,*
> *I think my wife be honest and think she is not;*
> *I think that thou art just and think thou art not."*

He is at a loss what to believe or do. He cannot cope with uncertainty and looks to Iago for proof. When Iago suggests his proof was but a dream, it is Othello himself who says:

> *"But this denoted a foregone conclusion."*

Othello has become a pawn in Iago's malevolent power game.

OTHELLO'S VULNERABILITY TO ATTACK

It might seem incredible that an outstanding man of Othello's stature should so easily fall prey to Iago's manipulations, however skilful. Yet Othello's outstanding qualities of character make him vulnerable to attack.

Othello has a natural curiosity to know the truth. He cannot stand uncertainty. So he is an easy prey to doubts about Cassio's sudden departure, Desdemona's strong appeal for Cassio, his own marriage to Desdemona and her possible infidelity.

> *"What dost thou say, Iago?"*

Othello prides himself on being firm and decisive, even when he is dealing with friends.

He has a natural sense of justice. So he must find out if Desdemona and Cassio have committed a crime together and must punish them appropriately.

> *"O! that the slave had forty thousand lives;*
> *One is too poor, too weak for my revenge."*

Othello is an outsider to Venetian society. He does not know how Venetian women behave and so he accepts Iago's assertions that they cheat on their husbands.

> *"Dost thou say so?"*

Othello lacks self-knowledge. He does not really understand his own feelings for Desdemona. So it is easy for Iago to make Othello feel jealous of Desdemona, since he does not really understand how she feels about him or he about her.

> *"By the world,*
> *I think my wife be honest and think she is not."*

Othello is used to the masculine world of action. He tries to deal with the complex world of sentiment and emotion in the same terms as he would a battle or an army.

> *"If there be cords or knives,*
> *Poison or fire or suffocating streams,*
> *I'll not endure it. Would I were satisfied!"*

Othello is egoistic and is proud of himself and his achievements. In particular he is proud of his own wife's choice of him above all other suitors. He feels he is a worthy choice and cannot accept that Desdemona could possibly have any reason to reject him for Cassio:

> *"Nor from mine own weak merits will I draw*
> *The smallest fear, or doubt of her revolt,*
> *For she had eyes, and chose me."*

Othello is inexperienced in sexual matters. His sensuality has just been awakened through his recent marriage. He is easily prone to sexual jealousy, which can come in a flash for little real reason:

> *"She lov'd them most."* – Iago

> *"And so she did."* – Othello

Othello is unable to rationalise logically. He can only talk in generalisations, copying Iago's manner of thought in his pathetic efforts to rationalise his position.

Othello has a vivid imagination which comes, perhaps, from his exotic background of romance and adventure. When Iago plays on his imagination by planting images in it, it begins to run riot.

Thus it is a combination of Iago's manipulative skills and Othello's character traits, which make credible Iago's degradation of Othello from a happy loving husband to a tormented vengeful wretch. These, and some measure of good fortune on Iago's part, contribute to the breakdown of Othello's character, which occurs in this scene.

THE BEGINNING OF THE END FOR OTHELLO

Othello loses his trust of his friend, Cassio, and his belief in his wife's fidelity:

> *"Now do I see 'tis true. Look here, Iago;*
> *All my fond love thus do I blow to heaven:*
> *'Tis gone."*

He casts away as worthless his career as a soldier:

> *"Farewell the tranquil mind; farewell content!*
> *Farewell the plumed troops and the big wars*
> *That make ambition virtue! O, farewell!"*

He has lost his sense of what is reality:

> *"Make me to see't; or, at the least, so prove it,*
> *That the probation bear no hinge nor loop,*
> *To hang a doubt on."*

He is torn between love, jealousy and a desire for vengeance:

> *"Arise, black vengeance, from the hollow hell!*
> *Yield up, O love! thy crown and hearted throne*
> *To tyrannous hate. Swell, bosom, with thy fraught,*
> *For 'tis of aspics' tongues!"*

He orders Cassio's death, decides to kill Desdemona himself and appoints Iago his lieutenant:

> *"... I will withdraw*
> *To furnish me with some swift means of death*
> *For the fair devil. Now art thou my lieutenant."*

This scene is a turning point in Othello's character and is the beginning of the disintegration of his nobility of character. While he does not challenge the universe, like King Lear, Othello is becoming the typical tragic hero. His world is beginning to fall down around him. He is brought very low in this scene but he will fight bravely against his misfortunes.

> *"Never, Iago. Like to the Pontic sea,*
> *Whose icy current and compulsive course*
> *Ne'er feels retiring ebb, but keeps due on*
> *To the Propontic and the Hellespont,*
> *Even so my bloody thoughts, with violent pace,*
> *Shall ne'er look back, ne'er ebb to humble love,*
> *Till that a capable and wide revenge*
> *Swallow them up."*

Othello's jealousy begins to assume gigantic proportion – all the more tragic, since it is built on an illusion created by Iago's web of deceit. At the end of the scene, Othello and Iago join together in a demonic ceremony of ritual vengeance:

> *"Now, by yond marble heaven,*
> *In the due reverence of a sacred vow*
> *I here engage my words."*

THE HANDKERCHIEF – A CORRUPTED LOVE-TOKEN

In this scene, Iago takes a chance and finally convinces Othello of his wife's infidelity by claiming falsely:

> *"... such a handkerchief –*
> *I am sure it was your wife's – did I to-day*
> *See Cassio wipe his beard with."*

Thus Iago uses the innocent first love-token of Othello to corrupt and degrade Othello and Desdemona's real and mutual love for each other:

> *"Now do I see 'tis true. Look here, Iago;*
> *All my fond love thus do I blow to heaven:*
> *'Tis gone."*

Desdemona accidentally drops the handkerchief, attempting to comfort Othello. Emilia unwittingly picks it up to give to Iago. This prepares us for Iago's next degradation of Othello in Act 4 Scene I, where the handkerchief will be used to effect yet again. The handkerchief device will help to hasten the tragic action towards disaster and make the catastrophe all the more inevitable and tragic.

Character Development

OTHELLO
A PREY TO UNCERTAINTY

As Cassio leaves Desdemona, Iago sows the seeds of doubt in Othello's mind with the casual remark:

> *"Ha! I like not that."*

Iago's evasiveness arouses Othello's curiosity to know what Iago really means and Othello becomes preoccupied. Desdemona's earnest plea for Cassio makes Othello all the more uncertain and evasive:

> *"I will deny thee nothing:*
> *Whereon, I do beseech thee, grant me this,*
> *To leave me but a little to myself."*

Alone with the evasive Iago, Othello wrestles with his uncertainty about Cassio and Desdemona. The more Iago hesitates to speak his mind, the more Othello's vivid imagination is stimulated to imagine the worst.

> *"Nay, yet there's more in this.*
> *I pray thee, speak to me as to thy thinkings,*
> *As thou dost ruminate, and give the worst of thoughts*
> *The worst of words."*

Thus Othello's natural inability to cope with uncertainty allows Iago to plant doubts and jealousy in Othello's mind:

> *"No, not much mov'd:*
> *I do not think but Desdemona's honest ...*
> *And, yet, how nature erring from itself –"*

UNDER STRESS

Alone, Othello wrestles with his conflicting feelings of love and loathing for Desdemona and loses his self-confidence:

> *"She's gone, I am abus'd; and my relief*
> *Must be to loathe her: O curse of marriage!*
> *That we can call these delicate creatures ours,*
> *And not their appetites. I had rather be a toad."*

For a moment he seems to recover himself:

> *"If she be false, O! then heaven mocks itself.*
> *I'll not believe it."*

Then Desdemona soothes and comforts him and perhaps he will regain his senses.

> *"Let me but bind it hard, within this hour*
> *It will be well."*

CONFLICTING EMOTIONS

Alone again with the persistent Iago, Othello is furious with Iago for causing him such torture:

> *"Avaunt! be gone! thou hast set me on the rack;*
> *I swear 'tis better to be much abus'd*
> *Than but to know't a little."*

Othello wavers between doubt and trust in Desdemona's fidelity:

> *"I think my wife be honest and think she is not."*

He craves certainty:

> *"I'll not endure it. Would I were satisfied!"*

Momentarily he seems about to recover his senses.

A FIXED OBSESSION

When Iago provides the evidence of Cassio's lustful dream and the handkerchief, Othello obtains the certainty he craves:

> *"Now do I see 'tis true. Look here, Iago;*
> *All my fond love thus do I blow to heaven:*
> *'Tis gone."*

He is distraught and furiously resolves on revenge for Desdemona's infidelity:

> *"Arise, black vengeance, from the hollow hell!*
> *Yield up, O love! thy crown and hearted throne*
> *To tyrannous hate. Swell, bosom, with thy fraught,*
> *For 'tis of aspics' tongues!"*

He declares that his purpose is firmly fixed forever and will not falter:

> *"Even so my bloody thoughts, with violent pace,*
> *Shall ne'er look back, ne'er ebb to humble love,*
> *Till that a capable and wide revenge*
> *Swallow them up."*

His firm assertions of confidence hide his insecurity and vulnerability.

CORRUPTED NOBILITY

Iago has succeeded in corrupting Othello's nobility of character and better nature. He has poisoned Othello's mind with half-truths and insinuations and has worked him up to a frenzy of overwrought passions. Early in the scene, Othello asserted of Desdemona:

> *"But I do love thee! and when I love thee not,*
> *Chaos is come again."*

Later he raves:

> *"I'll tear her all to pieces."*

The Othello who was happily married now wonders,

> *"Why did I marry?"*

and asserts:

> *"Damn her, lewd minx! O, damn her!"*

He has been caught in Iago's poisonous web and now forms a demonic alliance with his tormentor:

> *"I greet thy love."*

IAGO
INGENUITY

Iago displays extraordinary insight into Othello's character and remarkable skill in corrupting Othello's noble personality. He matches his techniques to the psychological needs of Othello at each given moment and progressively takes control of Othello's mind and soul. He preys on Othello's uncertainty and inexperience of love and Venetian society:

> *"I know our country disposition well;*
> *In Venice they do let heaven see the pranks*
> *They dare not show their husbands."*

He manipulates Othello's firmness and fairness and converts it into a furious desire for revenge:

> *"'Tis a shrewd doubt, though it be but a dream". – Othello*

> *"And this may help to thicken other proofs*
> *That do demonstrate thinly." – Iago*

Othello's natural human weaknesses are turned by Iago into deadly weapons of destruction.

EVIL GENIUS

Iago's talent for evil and mischief knows no bounds. All the while he revels in Othello's gratitude, while he destroys him:

> *"I am bound to thee forever."*

He is heartless and cold-blooded in his persistent destruction of the noble Othello. He gloats sadistically on his success, as he witnesses Othello's personality disintegrating before him in agony and fury:

> *"Look! where he comes! Not poppy, nor mandragora*
> *Nor all the drowsy syrups of the world,*
> *Shall ever medicine thee to that sweet sleep*
> *Which thou ow'dst yesterday."*

Othello cannot imagine a fit punishment for Iago should his accusations prove false:

> *"Never pray more; abandon all remorse;*
> *On horror's head horrors accumulate."*

Iago's blasphemous humour, at the end of the scene, identifies him as not far off a demon, who belongs in hell:

> *"Witness, you ever-burning lights above!*
> *You elements that clip us round about!*
> *Witness, that here Iago doth give up*
> *The execution of his wit, hands, heart,*
> *To wrong'd Othello's service."*

DESDEMONA
REASSURING AND RELIABLE

Desdemona is really concerned to console Cassio and to see that he is restored to her husband's favour, as soon as possible.

> *"I know't; I thank you. You do love my lord;*
> *You have known him long; and be you well assur'd*
> *He shall in strangeness stand no further off*
> *Than in a politic distance."*

She assures Cassio that he may rely on her friendship and that she will not give up her efforts:

> *"I give thee warrant of thy place. Assure thee,*
> *If I do vow a friendship, I'll perform it*
> *To the last article."*

She is both determined and obliging.

LOVING KINDNESS

When Othello is under stress later, Desdemona tries hard to console and comfort him. She is affectionate and kind towards him:

> *"Let me but bind it hard, within this hour*
> *It will be well."*

She cannot understand Othello's mood but makes allowances for him. Her consideration brings him a brief moment of relief from his confusion. Perhaps her good nature makes her a little indiscreet. She is after all interfering in Othello's business as commander by advising him to reinstate Cassio.

CASSIO
OVER-ANXIOUS

Cassio is ashamed and self-conscious. He is humble and cannot believe that Othello will forgive him:

> *"Ay, but, lady,*
> *That policy may either last so long,*
> *Or feed upon such nice and waterish diet,*
> *Or breed itself so out of circumstance,*
> *That, I being absent and my place supplied,*
> *My general will forget my love and service."*

He is grateful to Desdemona for her efforts but is too self-conscious to meet Othello directly:

> *"Madam, not now; I am very ill at ease,*
> *Unfit for mine own purposes."*

His humility makes it easier for Iago to cause further mischief as he slips away quickly from Desdemona.

EMILIA
LOYALTY

We learn little new of Emilia except that she seems to believe that her husband is genuinely concerned about Cassio:

"Good madam, do: I warrant it grieves my husband,
As if the case were his."

She seems to have some faith in her husband and is taken in by his honest exterior.

Scene IV

Before the Castle.
Enter Desdemona, Emilia, and Clown.

Desdemona	Do you know, sirrah, where Lieutenant Cassio lies[1]?
Clown	I dare not say he lies[2] any where.
Desdemona	Why, man?
Clown	He is a soldier; and for one to say a soldier lies, is stabbing.
Desdemona	Go to; where lodges he?
Clown	To tell you where he lodges is to tell you where I lie.
Desdemona	Can anything be made of this?
Clown	I know not where he lodges, and for me to devise[3] a lodging, and say he lies here or he lies there, were to lie in mine own throat.
Desdemona	Can you inquire him out, and be edified[4] by report?
Clown	I will catechize[5] the world for him; that is, make questions, and by them answer.
Desdemona	Seek him, bid him come hither; tell him I have moved[6] my lord in his behalf, and hope all will be well.
Clown	To do this is within the compass of man's wit, and therefore I will attempt the doing it. *[Exit.*
Desdemona	Where should I lose that handkerchief, Emilia?
Emilia	I know not, madam.
Desdemona	Believe me, I had rather lost my purse Full of cruzadoes[7]; and, but my noble Moor Is true of mind, and made of no such baseness As jealous creatures are, it were enough To put him to ill thinking.
Emilia	Is he not jealous?
Desdemona	Who! he? I think the sun where he was born Drew all such humours[8] from him.

1 lives

2 tells a lie

3 invent

4 informed

5 question

6 pleaded with

7 Portuguese coins

8 moods

10

20

30

111

Emilia	Look! where he comes.
Desdemona	I will not leave him now till Cassio
	Be call'd to him.

Enter Othello.

	How is't with you, my lord?
Othello	Well, my good lady. *[Aside]* O! hardness to
	dissemble.
	How do you, Desdemona?
Desdemona	Well, my good lord.
Othello	Give me your hand. This hand is moist, my lady.
Desdemona	It yet has felt no age nor known no sorrow.
Othello	This argues fruitfulness[9] and liberal[10] heart;
	Hot, hot, and moist; this hand of yours requires
	A sequester[11] from liberty, fasting and prayer, 40
	Much castigation[12], exercise devout[13];
	For here's a young and sweating devil here,
	That commonly rebels. 'Tis a good hand,
	A frank[14] one.
Desdemona	You may, indeed, say so;
	For 'twas that hand that gave away my heart.
Othello	A liberal hand; the hearts of old gave hands,
	But our new heraldry[15] is hands not hearts.
Desdemona	I cannot speak of this. Come now, your promise.
Othello	What promise, chuck[16]?
Desdemona	I have sent to bid Cassio come speak with you. 50
Othello	I have a salt and sorry rheum[17] offends me.
	Lend me thy handkerchief.
Desdemona	Here, my lord.
Othello	That which I gave you.
Desdemona	I have it not about me.
Othello	Not?
Desdemona	No, indeed, my lord.
Othello	That is a fault.
	That handkerchief
	Did an Egyptian to my mother give;
	She was a charmer[18], and could almost read
	The thoughts of people; she told her, while she
	kept it,
	'Twould make her amiable[19] and subdue my
	father
	Entirely to her love, but if she lost it 60
	Or made a gift of it, my father's eye
	Should hold her loathed, and his spirits should
	hunt
	After new fancies. She dying gave it me;

[9] generosity or amorousness
[10] free or lustful
[11] separation
[12] discipline
[13] religious exercise

[14] generous or licentious

[15] convention

[16] love

[17] a running cold

[18] magician

[19] loveable

	And bid me, when my fate would have me wive[20],	[20] marry
	To give it her. I did so: and take heed on't;	
	Make it a darling like your precious eye;	
	To lose't or give't away, were such perdition[21]	[21] destruction
	As nothing else could match.	
Desdemona	Is't possible?	
Othello	'Tis true; there's magic in the web[22] of it;	[22] weaving
	A sibyl[23], that had number'd in the world 70	[23] prophetess
	The sun to course two hundred compasses[24],	[24] two hundred years
	In her prophetic fury[25] sew'd the work;	[25] inspiration
	The worms were hallow'd that did breed the silk,	
	And it was dy'd in mummy[26] which the skilful	[26] liquid from embalmed bodies
	Conserv'd[27] of maidens' hearts.	[27] preserved
Desdemona	Indeed! is't true?	
Othello	Most veritable; therefore look to't well.	
Desdemona	Then would to heaven that I had never seen it!	
Othello	Ha! wherefore?	
Desdemona	Why do you speak so startingly and rash?	
Othello	Is't lost? is't gone? speak, is it out o' the way? 80	
Desdemona	Heaven bless us!	
Othello	Say you?	
Desdemona	It is not lost: but what an if it were?	
Othello	How!	
Desdemona	I say, it is not lost.	
Othello	Fetch't, let me see't.	
Desdemona	Why, so I can, sir, but I will not now.	
	This is a trick to put me from my suit:	
	Pray you let Cassio be receiv'd again.	
Othello	Fetch me the handkerchief; my mind misgives[28].	[28] is suspicious
Desdemona	Come, come;	
	You'll never meet a more sufficient[29] man. 90	[29] capable
Othello	The handkerchief!	
Desdemona	I pray, talk me of Cassio.	
Othello	The handkerchief!	
Desdemona	A man that all his time	
	Hath founded his good fortunes on your love,	
	Shar'd dangers with you, –	
Othello	The handkerchief!	
Desdemona	In sooth you are to blame.	
Othello	Away! [Exit.	
Emilia	Is not this man jealous?	
Desdemona	I ne'er saw this before.	
	Sure, there's some wonder[30] in this handkerchief;	[30] magic
	I am most unhappy in the loss of it. 100	
Emilia	'Tis not a year or two shows us a man;	
	They are all but stomachs, and we all but food;	

³¹hungrily

³²coincidence

³³share in

³⁴intended good conduct
³⁵restore

³⁶trusting to fortune

³⁷appearance

³⁸as a target for

³⁹soldiers

⁴⁰blown up
⁴¹importance

⁴²uncovered plot

They eat us hungerly[31], and when they are full
They belch us. Look you! Cassio and my husband.

Enter Iago and Cassio.

Iago There is no other way; 'tis she must do't:
And, lo! the happiness[32]: go and importune her.

Desdemona How now, good Cassio! what's the news with
            you?

Cassio Madam, my former suit: I do beseech you
That by your virtuous means I may again
Exist, and be a member of[33] his love   110
Whom I with all the office of my heart
Entirely honour; I would not be delay'd.
If my offence be of such mortal kind
That nor my service past, nor present sorrows,
Nor purpos'd merit in futurity[34],
Can ransom[35] me into his love again,
But to know so must be in my benefit;
So shall I clothe me in a forc'd content,
And shut myself up in some other course
To fortune's alms[36].   120

Desdemona   Alas! thrice-gentle Cassio!
My advocation is not now in tune;
My lord is not my lord; nor should I know him,
Were he in favour[37] as in humour alter'd.
So help me every spirit sanctified,
As I have spoken for you all my best
And stood within the blank of[38] his displeasure
For my free speech. You must awhile be patient;
What I can do I will, and more I will
Than for myself I dare: let that suffice you.

Iago Is my lord angry?   130

Emilia   He went hence but now,
And, certainly in strange unquietness.

Iago Can he be angry? I have seen the cannon,
When it hath blown his ranks[39] into the air,
And, like the devil, from his very arm
Puff'd[40] his own brother; and can he be angry?
Something of moment[41] then; I will go meet him;
There's matter in't indeed, if he be angry.

Desdemona I prithee, do so. *[Exit Iago.]* Something, sure, of
            state,
Either from Venice, or some unhatch'd practice[42]
Made demonstrable here in Cyprus to him,   140
Hath puddled his clear spirit; and, in such cases
Men's natures wrangle with inferior things,

	Though great ones are their object. 'Tis even so;	
	For let our finger ache, and it indues[43]	[43] brings
	Our other healthful members ev'n to that sense	
	Of pain. Nay, we must think men are not gods,	
	Nor of them look for such observancy[44]	[44] respect
	As fits the bridal[45]. Beshrew me[46] much, Emilia,	[45] wedding day
		[46] Damn!
	I was – unhandsome warrior as I am –	
	Arraigning[47] his unkindness with my soul; 150	[47] accusing
	But now I find I had suborn'd the witness[48],	[48] misinterpreted
	And he's indicted[49] falsely.	[49] accused
Emilia	Pray heaven it be state-matters, as you think,	
	And no conception[50], nor no jealous toy[51]	[50] supposition
	Concerning you.	[51] fancy
Desdemona	Alas the day! I never gave him cause.	
Emilia	But jealous souls will not be answer'd so;	
	They are not ever jealous for the cause,	
	But jealous for they are jealous; 'tis a monster	
	Begot upon itself, born on itself. 160	
Desdemona	Heaven keep that monster from Othello's mind!	
Emilia	Lady, amen.	
Desdemona	I will go seek him. Cassio, walk here-about;	
	If I do find him fit[52], I'll move your suit	[52] in a good humour
	And seek to effect it to my uttermost.	
Cassio	I humbly thank your ladyship.	

                        [Exeunt Desdemona and Emilia.

          Enter Bianca.

Bianca	Save you[53], friend Cassio!	[53] God save you!
Cassio	What make[54] you from home?	[54] What are you doing?
	How is it with you, my most fair Bianca?	
	I'faith, sweet love, I was coming to your house.	
Bianca	And I was going to your lodging, Cassio. 170	
	What! keep a week away? seven days and nights?	
	Eight score eight hours? and lovers' absent hours,	
	More tedious than the dial[55] eight score times?	[55] clock
	O weary reckoning!	
Cassio	Pardon me, Bianca,	
	I have this while with leaden thoughts been	
	press'd[56],	[56] oppressed with sorrow
	But I shall, in a more continuate[57] time,	[57] uninterrupted
	Strike off this score[58] of absence. Sweet Bianca.	[58] make up for

                   [Giving her Desdemona's handkerchief.

	Take me this work out[59].	[59] copy this work
Bianca	O Cassio! whence came this?	
	This is some token from a newer friend;	
	To the felt[60] absence now I feel a cause; 180	[60] heartfelt
	Is't come to this? Well, well.	

⁶¹Go away!	**Cassio**	Go to⁶¹, woman!

Cassio   Go to⁶¹, woman!

[marginal note: ⁶¹Go away!]

         Throw your vile guesses in the devil's teeth,
From whence you have them. You are jealous now
That this is from some mistress, some
       remembrance:

[marginal note: ⁶²truly]

         No, in good troth⁶², Bianca.

Bianca   Why, whose is it?

Cassio   I know not, sweet; I found it in my chamber.
I like the work well; ere it be demanded, –
As like enough it will, – I'd have it copied;
Take it and do't; and leave me for this time.

Bianca   Leave you! wherefore?   *190*

Cassio   I do attend here on the general,

[marginal notes: ⁶³credit; ⁶⁴with a woman]

         And think it no addition⁶³ nor my wish
To have him see me woman'd⁶⁴.

Bianca   Why, I pray you?

Cassio   Not that I love you not.

Bianca   But that you do not love me
I pray you, bring me on the way a little
And say if I shall see you soon at night.

Cassio   'Tis but a little way that I can bring you,
For I attend here; but I'll see you soon.

[marginal note: ⁶⁵yield to circumstances]

Bianca   'Tis very good; I must be circumstance⁶⁵.

[Exeunt.

The Plot (Day Three – Before the Castle)

DESDEMONA SEEKS HER HANDKERCHIEF

Desdemona tells the clown to find Cassio. She is sure she has persuaded Othello to forgive Cassio. Desdemona tries to find the handkerchief she lost but Emilia denies any knowledge of it. Desdemona says she is sure the loss of the handkerchief will not make Othello jealous, since he is open and trusting.

OTHELLO QUESTIONS DESDEMONA

Othello comes and asks Desdemona for her handkerchief, telling her that his mother gave it to him when she was dying. He is perturbed when Desdemona admits that she has not got it with her and he warns that its loss will bring disaster.

When Othello asks if she has lost it, she evades his questions. She claims that, while she can produce it, she will not do so now, since she wants to discuss Cassio's plea. Othello becomes angry and continues to demand the handkerchief. Finally he storms off in a fit of anger and jealousy.

If I do find him fit, I'll move your suit
And seek to effect it to my uttermost. (Desdemona, Act 3, Scene III)

CASSIO AND THE HANDKERCHIEF

Cassio enters with Iago and asks Desdemona to appeal again to Othello on his behalf. Desdemona explains that something has confused Othello. She does not accept that Othello is jealous but believes that he is under pressure from state matters. However, she will go to speak to him again on Cassio's behalf.

Left alone, Cassio is approached by Bianca, his mistress, who criticises him for not visiting her for so long. Cassio gives her Desdemona's handkerchief, which he has found. Bianca calms down and Cassio promises to see her soon.

Dramatic Significance

A SCENE OF SUSPENSE

This scene opens with the light-hearted conversation of Desdemona with the clown. This provides "comic" relief from the intensity of the previous scene and a brief interlude before the disasters to come in the following scene.

It is also a scene of mounting tension as Desdemona frantically searches for her missing handkerchief. We hope that there may still be a chance of finding the handkerchief, before Iago uses it for further mischief. Desdemona's false sense of security, that her husband is not prone to jealousy and that he looks favourably on Cassio, increases the tension. Ironically we are already aware that Othello has been wrought to a high pitch of jealousy and revenge by Iago's temptations in the previous scene:

> "... my noble Moor
> Is true of mind, and made of no such baseness
> As jealous creatures are."

The tension rises further as Othello struggles with his conflicting feelings of love for Desdemona and shock and despair at her guilt. He demands the handkerchief from her, in an impulsive desire to know the worst, while she impulsively appeals for Cassio. We wait anxiously to learn how his conflicting emotions will resolve themselves.

Desdemona is taken aback by Othello's change of character. Innocently and lovingly she tries to understand this new side of Othello's character:

> "My advocation is not now in tune;
> My lord is not my lord; nor should I know him,
> Were he in favour as in humour alter'd.
> So help me every spirit sanctified."

She earns our sympathy and we hope she will escape Othello's coming fury.

THE HANDKERCHIEF – A TEST OF FIDELITY

The handkerchief assumes a new significance in this scene. To Desdemona the handkerchief is just a sentimental token of love; to Othello it represents his roots and the success or failure of his love and marriage:

> *"Make it a darling like your precious eye;*
> *To lose't or give't away, were such perdition*
> *As nothing else could match."*

To Iago it is a device to seal Desdemona's doom.

This scene merges the two strands of Iago's plot. Cassio's disgrace and Desdemona's pleading for his restoration to favour become linked to the mysterious disappearance of the handkerchief. Othello's fierce demands for the handkerchief turn it into a test and symbol of Desdemona's fidelity. Othello's impetuous drive to find out the worst is matched by Desdemona's equally impulsive desire to help Cassio:

> *"Pray you let Cassio be receiv'd again"* – Desdemona

> *"Fetch me the handkerchief; my mind misgives."* – Othello

Thus her pleas for Cassio and the loss of the handkerchief become firmly linked together in Othello's mind, as proof of her infidelity. When Cassio innocently gives the handkerchief to his mistress, Bianca, to copy, it becomes a potentially deadly weapon for Iago to use. Desdemona's doom is now sealed.

Character Development

OTHELLO
CONFLICTING PASSIONS

Othello is tortured by conflicting emotions of love for Desdemona and the feeling that she has betrayed him. He tries to pretend nothing is amiss but tests Desdemona's fidelity by questioning her about the handkerchief.

> *"I have a salt and sorry rheum offends me.*
> *Lend me thy handkerchief."*

He is imaginative in his description of the magic of the handkerchief, which becomes a symbol of his love:

> *"'Tis true; there's magic in the web of it;*
> *A sibyl.... sew'd the work."*

When Desdemona is evasive about the whereabouts of the handkerchief and persists in pleading for Cassio, Othello becomes angry and loses control of his emotions:

"Fetch me the handkerchief; my mind misgives."

His mind is fixed in an obsession that he has been betrayed. He leaves in torment, muttering repeatedly:

"The handkerchief!"

DESDEMONA
INNOCENT

Desdemona does not understand the importance of the handkerchief as a symbol of Othello's love and her fidelity to him. She innocently tries to save him from hurt by concealing the loss of the handkerchief:

"It is not lost: but what an if it were?"

She does not realise that she is unwise to plead for Cassio at this time, since she has no knowledge of the perturbed state of Othello's mind.

FORGIVENESS

Desdemona is guiltless and at a loss to understand Othello's reactions:

"Alas the day! I never gave him cause!"

However, yet again, she makes allowances for him and forgives his outbursts:

> *"Something, sure, of state ...*
> *Hath puddled his clear spirit ...*
> *Men's natures wrangle with inferior things,*
> *Though great ones are their object. 'Tis even so."*

IAGO
SECRET DELIGHT

Iago takes further pleasure in seeing Othello at last shaken from his usual firmness and resolution.

> *"Can he be angry? I have seen the cannon,*
> *When it hath blown his ranks into the air,*
> *And, like the devil, from his very arm*
> *Puff'd his own brother; and can he be angry?"*

CASSIO
LOYAL AND GENTLE

Cassio reminds Desdemona again to plead with Othello for him. She has tried unsuccessfully and will continue to try.

Cassio finds life unbearable without his general's favour:

> "Madam, my former suit: I do beseech you
> That by your virtuous means I may again
> Exist, and be a member of his love."

He remains loyal to Othello despite his loss of favour:

> "[Othello] I with all the office of my heart
> Entirely honour; I would not be delay'd."

Cassio is kind and gentle to Bianca, a lady of questionable reputation. He treats her politely and with respect:

> "How is it with you, my most fair Bianca?
> I' faith, sweet love, I was coming to your house."

He is a gentleman as always.

EMILIA
DECEITFUL AND MISGUIDED

Emilia seizes the opportunity of doing her husband a favour by keeping Desdemona's handkerchief, which she has found. She lies to Desdemona about the handkerchief:

> "I know not, madam."

Her misguided loyalty to Iago will advance his plans.

Emilia has a low idea of men and jumps to the conclusion that Othello is jealous:

> "Is not this man jealous?"

She intends no harm to Desdemona by her deceitfulness:

> "Pray heaven it be state-matters, as you think,
> And no conception, nor no jealous toy
> Concerning you."

She is somewhat heedless but later she redeems herself.

BIANCA
PETTY JEALOUSY

Bianca, Cassio's mistress, is jealous over a trivial matter. Yet she seems to love Cassio:

> "This is some token from a newer friend;
> To the felt absence now I feel a cause;
> Is't come to this? Well, well."

Her jealousy is forgivable, since Cassio has been absent frequently of late.

O Cassio! whence came this?

(Bianca, Act 3, Scene IV)

Act 4

Scene I

Cyprus. Before the Castle.
Enter Othello and Iago.

Iago	Will you think so?
Othello	Think so, Iago!
Iago	What!
	To kiss in private?
Othello	An unauthoriz'd[1] kiss.
Iago	Or to be naked with her friend a-bed
	An hour or more, not meaning any harm?
Othello	Naked a-bed, Iago, and not mean harm?
	It is hypocrisy against the devil[2]:
	They that mean virtuously, and yet do so,
	The devil their virtue tempts, and they tempt[3] heaven.
Iago	If they do nothing, 'tis a venial slip[4];
	But if I give my wife a handkerchief, –
Othello	What then?
Iago	Why, then, 'tis hers, my lord; and being hers,
	She may, I think, bestow't on any man.
Othello	She is protectress of her honour[5] too;
	May she give that?
Iago	Her honour is an essence[6] that's not seen;
	They have it very oft that have it not:
	But for the handkerchief, –
Othello	By heaven, I would most gladly have forgot it: –
	Thou said'st, – O! it comes o'er my memory,
	As doth the raven o'er the infected house,
	Boding[7] to all, – he had my handkerchief.
Iago	Ay, what of that?
Othello	That's not so good now.
Iago	What,
	If I had said I had seen him do you wrong?
	Or heard him say, as knaves be such abroad[8],
	Who having, by their own importunate suit[9],
	Or voluntary dotage[10] of some mistress,
	Convinced or supplied them[11], cannot choose
	But they must blab.
Othello	Hath he said any thing?
Iago	He hath, my lord; but be you well assur'd,
	No more than he'll unswear.
Othello	What hath he said?

10

20

30

[1] immoral

[2] pretending to sin

[3] provoke

[4] forgiveable misconduct

[5] chastity

[6] entity

[7] threatening

[8] as there are such knaves in the world
[9] ardent wooing
[10] willing infatuation
[11] satisfied their desires

Iago	Faith, that he did – I know not what he did.
Othello	What? what?
Iago	Lie –
Othello	With her?
Iago	With her, on her; what you will.
Othello	Lie with her! lie on her! We say, lie on her, when they belie[12] her. Lie with her! that's fulsome[13]. Handkerchief, – confessions, – handkerchief. To confess, and be hanged for his labour. First, to be hanged, and then to confess: I tremble at it. Nature would not invest herself in such shadowing[14] 40 passion without some instruction[15]. It is not words that shake me thus. Pish! Noses, ears, and lips. Is it possible? – Confess! – Handkerchief! – O devil!

[Falls in a trance.

Iago	Work on,
	My medicine, work! Thus credulous fools are caught;
	And many worthy and chaste dames even thus,
	All guiltless, meet reproach. What, ho! my lord!
	My lord, I say! Othello!

Enter Cassio.

	How now, Cassio!
Cassio	What's the matter? 50
Iago	My lord is fallen into an epilepsy;
	This is his second fit; he had one yesterday.
Cassio	Rub him about the temples.
Iago	No, forbear;
	The lethargy[16] must have its quiet course[17],
	If not he foams at mouth, and by and by
	Breaks out to savage madness. Look! he stirs;
	Do you withdraw yourself a little while,
	He will recover straight; when he is gone,
	I would on great occasion[18] speak with you.

[Exit Cassio.

	How is it, general? have you not hurt your 60 head?
Othello	Dost thou mock me?
Iago	I mock you! no, by heaven.
	Would you would bear your fortune like a man!
Othello	A horned man's[19] a monster and a beast.
Iago	There's many a beast then, in a populous city,
	And many a civil[20] monster.
Othello	Did he confess it?

[12] slander
[13] foul

[14] overwhelming

[15] reason

[16] fit
[17] undisturbed course

[18] an important matter

[19] a cuckold (deceived husband)

[20] civilised

124

Iago	Good sir, be a man;	
	Think every bearded fellow that's but yok'd[21]	[21] married
	May draw with you[22]; there's millions now alive	[22] be in your situation
	That nightly lie in those unproper[23] beds	[23] not their own
	Which they dare swear peculiar[24]; your case 70	[24] their own
	is better.	
	O! 'tis the spite of hell, the fiend's arch-mock,	
	To lip[25] a wanton[26] in a secure couch[27],	[25] kiss
	And to suppose her chaste. No, let me know;	[26] wanton woman
	And knowing what I am I know what she shall be.	[27] unsuspected
Othello	O! thou art wise; 'tis certain.	
Iago	Stand you awhile apart;	
	Confine yourself but in a patient list[28].	[28] limit
	Whilst you were here o'erwhelmed with	
	your grief, –	
	A passion most unsuiting such a man, –	
	Cassio came hither; I shifted him away,	
	And laid good 'scuse upon your ecstasy[29]; 80	[29] fit
	Bade him anon return and here speak with me;	
	The which he promis'd. Do but encave[30] yourself,	[30] hide
	And mark the fleers[31], the gibes, and notable[32]	[31] sneers
	scorns,	[32] obvious
	That dwell in every region of his face;	
	For I will make him tell the tale anew,	
	Where, how, how oft, how long ago, and when	
	He hath, and is again to cope[33] your wife:	[33] meet
	I say, but mark his gesture. Marry, patience;	
	Or I shall say you are all in all in spleen[34],	[34] full of anger
	And nothing of a man. 90	
Othello	Dost thou hear, Iago?	
	I will be found most cunning in my patience;	
	But – dost thou hear? – most bloody.	
Iago	That's not amiss;	
	But yet keep time[35] in all. Will you withdraw?	[35] control yourself
	[Othello goes apart.	
	Now will I question Cassio of Bianca,	
	A housewife that by selling her desires	
	Buys herself bread and clothes; it is a creature	
	That dotes on Cassio; as 'tis the strumpet's	
	plague	
	To beguile many and be beguil'd by one.	
	He, when he hears of her, cannot refrain	
	From the excess of laughter. Here he comes: 100	

    Re-enter Cassio.

As he shall smile, Othello shall go mad;

³⁶ inexperienced
³⁷ interpret

³⁸ title
³⁹ lack

⁴⁰ wretch

⁴¹ prostitute

⁴² unsound

⁴³ injured

⁴⁴ playtoy
⁴⁵ falls at me

⁴⁶ shows

⁴⁷ shakes

⁴⁸ God before me!

	And his unbookish[36] jealousy must construe[37]
	Poor Cassio's smiles, gestures, and light behaviour
	Quite in the wrong. How do you now, lieutenant?
Cassio	The worser that you give me the addition[38]
	Whose want[39] even kills me.
Iago	Ply Desdemona well, and you are sure on't.
	[Speaking lower.] Now, if this suit lay in Bianca's power,
	How quickly should you speed!
Cassio	Alas! poor caitiff![40]
Othello	Look! how he laughs already!
Iago	I never knew woman love man so.
Cassio	Alas! poor rogue, I think, i' faith, she loves me.
Othello	Now he denies it faintly, and laughs it out.
Iago	Do you hear, Cassio?
Othello	Now he importunes him
	To tell it o'er: go to; well said, well said.
Iago	She gives it out that you shall marry her;
	Do you intend it?
Cassio	Ha, ha, ha!
Othello	Do you triumph, Roman? do you triumph?
Cassio	I marry her! what a customer[41]? I prithee, bear some charity to my wit; do not think it so unwholesome[42]. Ha, ha, ha!
Othello	So, so, so, so. They laugh that win.
Iago	Faith, the cry goes that you shall marry her.
Cassio	Prithee, say true.
Iago	I am a very villain else.
Othello	Have you scored[43] me? Well.
Cassio	This is the monkey's own giving out: she is persuaded I will marry her, out of her own love and flattery, not out of my promise.
Othello	Iago beckons me; now he begins the story.
Cassio	She was here even now; she haunts me in every place. I was the other day talking on the sea bank with certain Venetians, and thither comes the bauble[44], and, by this hand, she falls[45] me thus about my neck; –
Othello	Crying, 'O dear Cassio!' as it were; his gesture imports[46] it.
Cassio	So hangs and lolls and weeps upon me; so hales[47] and pulls me; ha, ha, ha!
Othello	Now he tells how she plucked him to my chamber. O! I see that nose of yours, but not the dog I shall throw it to.
Cassio	Well, I must leave her company.
Iago	Before me[48]! look, where she comes.

110

120

130

140

Cassio	'Tis such another fitchew[49]! marry, a perfumed one.

Enter Bianca.

Bianca	What do you mean by this haunting of me? Let the devil and his dam[50] haunt you! What did you mean by that same handkerchief you gave me even now? I was a fine fool to take it. I must take 150 out the work! A likely piece of work, that you should find it in your chamber, and not know who left it there! This is some minx's[51] token, and I must take out the work! There, give it your hobby-horse[52]; wheresoever you had it I'll take out no work on't.
Cassio	How now, my sweet Bianca! how now, how now!
Othello	By heaven, that should be my handkerchief!
Bianca	An[53] you'll come to supper to-night, you may; an you will not, come when you are next 160 prepared for[54]. *[Exit.*
Iago	After her, after her.
Cassio	Faith, I must; she'll rail[55] in the street else.
Iago	Will you sup there?
Cassio	Faith, I intend so.
Iago	Well, I may chance to see you, for I would very fain[56] speak with you.
Cassio	Prithee, come; will you?
Iago	Go to; say no more. *[Exit Cassio.*
Othello	*[Advancing]* How shall I murder him, Iago? 170
Iago	Did you perceive how he laughed at his vice?
Othello	O! Iago!
Iago	And did you see the handkerchief?
Othello	Was that mine?
Iago	Yours, by this hand; and to see how he prizes[57] the foolish woman your wife! she gave it him, and he hath given it his whore.
Othello	I would have him nine years a-killing. A fine woman! a fair woman! a sweet woman!
Iago	Nay, you must forget that. 180
Othello	Ay, let her rot, and perish, and be damned to-night; for she shall not live. No, my heart is turned to stone; I strike it, and it hurts my hand. O! the world hath not a sweeter creature; she might lie by an emperor's side and command him tasks.

[49] lecherous polecat

[50] mother

[51] whore

[52] loose woman

[53] if

[54] never

[55] shout

[56] like to

[57] values

Iago	Nay, that's not your way.
Othello	Hang her! I do but say what she is. So delicate with her needle! An admirable musician! O, she will sing the savageness out of a bear. Of so high and plenteous wit[58] and invention! 190
Iago	She's the worse for all this.
Othello	O! a thousand, a thousand times. And then, of so gentle a condition[59]!
Iago	Ay, too gentle.
Othello	Nay, that's certain; – but yet the pity of it, Iago! O! Iago, the pity of it, Iago!
Iago	If you are so fond[60] over her iniquity, give her patent[61] to offend; for, if it touch not you, it comes near nobody.
Othello	I will chop her into messes[62]. Cuckold me! 200
Iago	O! 'tis foul in her.
Othello	With mine officer!
Iago	That's fouler.
Othello	Get me some poison, Iago; this night: I'll not expostulate[63] with her, lest her body and beauty unprovide my mind[64] again. This night, Iago.
Iago	Do it not with poison, strangle her in her bed, even the bed she hath contaminated.
Othello	Good, good; the justice of it pleases; very good.
Iago	And for Cassio, let me be his undertaker[65]; you 210 shall hear more by midnight.
Othello	Excellent good. *[A trumpet within.]* What trumpet is that same?
Iago	Something from Venice, sure. 'Tis Lodovico, Come from the duke; and see, your wife is with him.

Enter Lodovico, Desdemona, and Attendants.

Lodovico	God save you, worthy general!
Othello	With all my heart, sir.
Lodovico	The duke and senators of Venice greet you. *[Gives him a packet.*
Othello	I kiss the instrument of their pleasures[66]. *[Opens the packet, and reads.*
Desdemona	And what's the news, good cousin Lodovico?
Iago	I am very glad to see you, signior; 220 Welcome to Cyprus.
Lodovico	I thank you. How does Lieutenant Cassio?
Iago	Lives, sir.
Desdemona	Cousin, there's fallen between him and my lord An unkind[67] breach; but you shall make all well.

Footnotes:

[58] intelligence
[59] nature
[60] foolish
[61] permission
[62] small pieces
[63] argue
[64] weaken my resolve
[65] killer
[66] reason why they require me (the letters)
[67] unnatural

Othello	Are you sure of that?
Desdemona	My lord?
Othello	This fail you not to do, as you will –
Lodovico	He did not call; he's busy in the paper.
	Is there division 'twixt my lord and Cassio? 230
Desdemona	A most unhappy one; I would do much
	To atone[68] them, for the love I bear to Cassio.
Othello	Fire and brimstone!
Desdemona	My lord?
Othello	Are you wise[69]?
Desdemona	What! is he angry?
Lodovico	May be the letter moved him;
	For, as I think, they do command him home,
	Deputing Cassio in his government.
Desdemona	Trust me[70], I am glad on't.
Othello	Indeed!
Desdemona	My lord?
Othello	I am glad to see you mad[71].
Desdemona	Why, sweet Othello?
Othello	Devil!

                                                                        [Strikes her.

Desdemona	I have not deserved this.
Lodovico	My lord, this would not be believ'd in Venice, 240
	Though I should swear I saw't: 'tis very much[72];
	Make her amends, she weeps.
Othello	O devil, devil!
	If that the earth could teem with woman's tears,
	Each drop she falls would prove a crocodile[73].
	Out of my sight!
Desdemona	I will not stay to offend you.

                                                                            [Going.

Lodovico	Truly, an obedient lady;
	I do beseech your lordship, call her back.
Othello	Mistress!
Desdemona	My lord?
Othello	What would[74] you with her, sir?
Lodovico	Who, I, my lord?
Othello	Ay; you did wish that I would make her turn[75]: 250
	Sir, she can turn, and turn, and yet go on,
	And turn again; and she can weep, sir, weep;
	And she's obedient, as you say, obedient,
	Very obedient. Proceed you in your tears.
	Concerning this, sir, – O well-painted[76] passion!
	I am commanded home. Get you away;
	I'll send for you anon. Sir, I obey the mandate,
	And will return to Venice. Hence! avaunt[77]!

                                                                   [Exit Desdemona.

[68] reconcile

[69] in your right senses (sane)

[70] truly

[71] moved

[72] too much

[73] hypocritical

[74] want

[75] return, be false

[76] feigned

[77] be gone

	Cassio shall have my place. And, sir, to-night,
	I do entreat that we may sup together; *260*
	You are welcome, sir, to Cyprus. Goats and
	monkeys!
	[Exit.
Lodovico	Is this the noble Moor whom our full senate
	Call all-in-all sufficient[78]? is this the noble nature
	Whom passion could not shake? whose solid
	virtue
	The shot of accident nor dart of chance
	Could neither graze nor pierce?
Iago	He is much chang'd.
Lodovico	Are his wits safe[79]? is he not light of brain?
Iago	He's that he is; I may not breathe my censure[80].
	What he might be, if, what he might, he is not,
	I would to heaven he were! *270*
Lodovico	What! strike his wife!
Iago	Faith, that was not so well; yet would I knew
	That stroke would prove the worst!
Lodovico	Is it his use[81]?
	Or did the letters work upon his blood[82],
	And new-create this fault?
Iago	Alas, alas!
	It is not honesty[83] in me to speak
	What I have seen and known. You shall observe
	him,
	And his own courses[84] will denote[85] him so
	That I may save my speech. Do but go after
	And mark[86] how he continues.
Lodovico	I am sorry that I am deceived in him. *280*
	[Exeunt.

[78] able in every way
[79] sane
[80] criticism
[81] habit
[82] passions
[83] honour
[84] actions
[85] show
[86] watch

The Plot (Day Three – Before The Castle)

IAGO DEGRADES OTHELLO

Iago continues to poison Othello's mind against Desdemona and Cassio. He forces Othello to face up to the implications of Cassio's previous "confession" of adultery with Desdemona and the loss of the handkerchief. Then Iago reveals that he overheard Cassio actually boasting of his love affair with Desdemona. Othello, confused and overcome, falls into a trance, much to Iago's delight. Cassio enters and wishes to revive Othello but Iago advises that Othello is best left to recover.

OTHELLO EAVESDROPS ON CASSIO

Othello recovers, but is obsessed with what Iago has revealed. Iago suggests that other men have been deceived by their wives. He advises that Othello should hide and listen to a conversation that he will arrange with Cassio, so that Othello can judge for himself. Iago intends to question Cassio about Bianca, leaving Othello to believe that the conversation concerns Desdemona.

Othello thinks that Cassio's disrespectful remarks about Bianca refer to Desdemona and goes into a jealous rage. Bianca enters and scolds Cassio for giving her the handkerchief; some other woman's love token. She rushes off and Cassio follows her. Othello is now sure that Desdemona gave Cassio the handkerchief and asks Iago how shall he kill Cassio.

OTHELLO IN AGONY

Iago then torments Othello with the implications of the conversation he has just witnessed. Othello, torn between love and jealousy, decides to poison Desdemona that night, before her beauty weakens his resolve. Iago suggests that Othello strangle her in the bed she has contaminated and undertakes to kill Cassio himself.

OTHELLO INSULTS DESDEMONA

Desdemona enters with Lodovico, who has letters for Othello from the Duke. As Othello reads, Desdemona explains to Lodovico that there has been trouble between Othello and Cassio, and that she wishes to reconcile them. Othello overhears and, in a rage, strikes Desdemona. Lodovico is shocked and begs Othello to apologise. Othello insults her further in public and taunts her with her obedience to him.

OTHELLO'S STRANGE BEHAVIOUR

Othello announces that he will return to Venice, as commanded by the Duke's letters. He invites Lodovico to supper and leaves, muttering to himself.

Lodovico expresses his shock to Iago about Othello's strange behaviour. Iago gives the impression that Othello is much changed in his behaviour lately and advises Lodovico to watch Othello. Lodovico is convinced that Othello has lost his sanity.

Dramatic Significance

THE FINAL PHASE IN IAGO'S DEADLY SCHEME

This scene portrays the final phase in Iago's plot to destroy Desdemona and Othello. Iago forces Othello to confront the full implications of the loss of the handkerchief and of Cassio's alleged "confession" of guilt.

To Iago's insinuations about the handkerchief, Othello reacts:

> *"She is protectress of her honour too;*
> *May she give that?"*

Hearing the report of Cassio's alleged boasting about making love to Desdemona, Othello collapses in incoherence:

> *"Pish! Noses, ears, and lips. Is it possible? – Confess! –*
> *Handkerchief! – O devil!"*

Next Iago sadistically mocks Othello with images of monsters and devils. He arranges that Othello overhears him questioning Cassio about Bianca and leads Othello to believe that they are talking about Desdemona. Othello sees concrete evidence that Cassio is having an affair with Desdemona:

> *"Now he tells how she plucked him to my chamber."*

Now Iago has a stroke of good luck as Bianca enters to return Othello's handkerchief to Cassio.

> *"By heaven, that should be my handkerchief!"*

Finally convinced of Desdemona's infidelity, Othello makes definite plans for her just execution by strangling her in her bed:

> *"Do it not with poison, strangle her in her bed, even the bed she hath contaminated."*
> – Iago

> *"Good, good; the justice of it pleases; very good."* – Othello

The final catastrophe is now inevitable.

THE TRAGIC CLIMAX

Othello is already overwrought by Iago's insistent evidence, when Desdemona and Lodovico enter the scene. As he reads the letter recalling him to Venice, Othello hears Desdemona innocently declare her love for Cassio and her hope of his reinstatement:

> *"A most unhappy* [division]; *I would do much*
> *To atone them, for the love I bear to Cassio."*

Othello reacts furiously and strikes Desdemona in public, taunting her with her obedience to him:

> *"Sir, she can turn, and turn, and yet go on,*
> *And turn again; and she can weep, sir, weep;*
> *And she's obedient, as you say, obedient."*

This forms a turning point in the tragic action, as Othello is provoked to a jealous frenzy by Desdemona's frank and well-intentioned expression of concern for Cassio.

Images of Desdemona's betrayal have become fixed in obsession in his mind and he has reached a final stage of suffering and agony:

> *"O devil, devil!*
> *If that the earth could teem with woman's tears,*
> *Each drop she falls would prove a crocodile.*
> *Out of my sight!"*

Love and hate, attraction and repulsion exist together in his mind.

> *"O well-painted passion!... Get you away!"*

He oscillates tragically between conflicting feelings:

> *"Hang her! I do but say what she is. So delicate with her*
> *needle! An admirable musician! O, she will sing the*
> *savageness out of a bear!"*

His noble mind has been poisoned by Iago and he struggles to endure his agony:

> *"O! Iago, the pity of it, Iago!"*

IAGO COVERS HIS TRACKS

Iago has had good fortune on his side in carrying out his destruction of Othello. Bianca's timely entrance with Othello's handkerchief and Othello's striking of Desdemona in public contribute to the success of Iago's devilish schemes. The impatience of Cassio and the innocent helpfulness of Desdemona also play into Iago's hands.

However, Iago makes doubly sure that suspicion will not fall on himself, by suggesting to Lodovico that Othello is much changed and is no longer the great man that he was. He even suggests, in confidence, that Othello has lost his wits and that he is worried about what he might do:

> *"Faith, that was not so well; yet would I knew*
> *That stroke would prove the worst!"*

Iago is shrewd in covering his tracks here, but in the next scene he underestimates the real threat to him, Emilia, his own wife, who will eventually expose him:

> *"I will be hanged, if some eternal villain,*
> *... Have not devis'd this slander."*   *(Act 4, scene II)*

Character Development

OTHELLO
UNDER IAGO'S SPELL

Othello tries to examine objectively Cassio and Desdemona's behaviour but falls down unconscious, convinced by Iago that Cassio has confessed to infidelity:

"Confess! – Handkerchief! – O devil!"

Iago then arranges for Othello to overhear Cassio seeming to speak insultingly about how he used Desdemona for his own pleasure. Bianca interrupts to return Desdemona's handkerchief to Cassio. Othello is torn between love and vengeance, grief and rage:

"Ay, let her rot, and perish, and be damned to-night; for
she shall not live. No, my heart is turned to stone."

Reluctantly he decides that Desdemona and Cassio must die:

"O! Iago, the pity of it, Iago!"

Othello is completely in Iago's power.

A PERSONALITY BREAKDOWN

Othello's personality begins to break down, as he reads the letter from Venice and hears Desdemona declare her affection for Cassio:

"Fire and brimstone!"

He strikes the loving Desdemona and calls her, *"Mistress!"* He taunts her with her obedience to him:

"Sir, she can turn, and turn, and yet go on,
And turn again; and she can weep, sir, weep."

Othello's broken speech reflects the breakdown of his noble, loving mind, which has been poisoned by Iago's venomous schemes:

"Concerning this, sir – O well-painted passion! –
I am commanded home. Get you away;
I'll send for you anon. Sir, I obey the mandate,
And will return to Venice. Hence, avaunt!"

His language begins to echo Iago's:

"Goats and monkeys!"

Othello has become a thwarted lover who has lost his dignity and reputation through Desdemona's betrayal.

IAGO
TRIUMPHANT POWER

Iago is at the height of his success and enjoys absolute power over Othello:

"Work on,
My medicine, work! Thus credulous fools are caught;
And many worthy and chaste dames even thus,
All guiltless, meet reproach."

He is secure from threat of exposure since Othello's mind is now under his own control. He openly insults Desdemona and even advises Othello how to obtain revenge:

> *"Do it not with poison, strangle her in her*
> *bed, even the bed she hath contaminated."*

He revels in the security of his power of evil.

INSATIABLE EVIL

Iago is not content with his destruction of Othello's personality so far – he turns the screws still further for sheer pleasure. First he forces Othello to confront the full implications of Cassio's behaviour and the handkerchief. Then he orchestrates a conversation with Cassio, which Othello overhears.

Good luck is on his side too and he capitalises on its potential for further mischief. He uses Bianca's entrance with the handkerchief to torture Othello still further:

> *"Yours, by this hand: and to see how he prizes the foolish*
> *woman your wife! she gave it him, and he hath given it his whore."*

Iago uses Othello's blow to Desdemona to insinuate to Lodovico that Othello's mad behaviour is typical:

> *"It is not honesty in me to speak*
> *What I have seen and known."*

Iago's insatiable thirst to do more and more evil must prove his own undoing.

DESDEMONA
A SELFLESS PEACEMAKER

Desdemona's frank declaration of affection for Cassio and her eagerness to reconcile him with Othello maddens Othello even more. She is surprised and shocked at Othello's violent treatment of her:

> *"I have not deserved this."*

Yet she shows no resentment or desire for revenge. She is docile even when Othello makes fun of her obedience. She considers others before herself:

> *"A most unhappy [division]; I would do much*
> *To atone them, for the love I bear to Cassio."*

CASSIO
TRUSTFUL AND PATIENT

Unwittingly Cassio becomes the instrument of Iago's scheme. He trusts Iago implicitly and is frank and open when questioned by Iago:

*"I marry her! what a customer? I prithee, bear some
charity to my wit; do not think it so unwholesome. Ha, ha, ha!"*

With Bianca he is a little annoyed but patient. He does not wish to be embarrassed in public:

"Faith, I must; she'll rail in the street else."

Yet he seems to care for Bianca:

"How now, my sweet Bianca! how now, how now!"

LODOVICO
COMMON SENSE

Lodovico represents the ordinary man. He is shocked at Othello's violent treatment of Desdemona and tries to get Othello to make amends to her. He is concerned at Othello's seeming madness and will try to remedy the situation for Desdemona's sake:

"I am sorry that I am deceived in him."

Scene II

*A Room in the Castle.
Enter Othello and Emilia.*

Othello	You have seen nothing, then?
Emilia	Nor ever heard, nor ever did suspect.
Othello	Yes, you have seen Cassio and her together.
Emilia	But then I saw no harm, and then I heard Each syllable that breath made up between them.
Othello	What! did they never whisper?
Emilia	Never, my lord.
Othello	Nor send you out o' the way?
Emilia	Never.
Othello	To fetch her fan, her gloves, her mask[1], nor nothing?
Emilia	Never, my lord.
Othello	That's strange.
Emilia	I durst[2], my lord, to wager she is honest[3], Lay down my soul at stake: if you think other, Remove your thought; it doth abuse[4] your bosom. If any wretch have put this in your head, Let heaven requite[5] it with the serpent's curse[6]! For, if she be not honest, chaste, and true, There's no man happy; the purest of their wives Is foul as slander.

10

[1] facemask

[2] dare
[3] chaste

[4] deceive

[5] repay
[6] damnation

| Othello | Bid her come hither; go. |
| | [*Exit Emilia.* |

	She says enough; yet she's a simple bawd[7]		[7] naive brothel-keeper
	That cannot say as much. This[8] is a subtle[9] 20		[8] Desdemona
	whore,		[9] secret
	A closet[10] lock and key of[11] villanous secrets;		[10] cupboard
	And yet she'll kneel and pray; I have seen her do't.		[11] concealer

Re-enter Emilia with Desdemona.

Desdemona	My lord, what is your will?
Othello	Pray, chuck[12], come hither.		[12] dear
Desdemona	What is your pleasure?
Othello	Let me see your eyes;
	Look in my face.
Desdemona	What horrible fancy's this?
Othello	[*To Emilia.* Some of your function[13], mistress;		[13] Get about your business!
	Leave procreants[14] alone and shut the door;		[14] those engaged in procreation
	Cough or cry 'hem' if any body come;
	Your mystery[15], your mystery; nay, dispatch[16].		[15] trade
	[*Exit Emilia.*		[16] get going
Desdemona	Upon my knees, what doth your speech 30
	import[17]?		[17] mean
	I understand a fury in your words,
	But not the words.
Othello	Why, what art thou?
Desdemona	Your wife, my lord; your true
	And loyal wife.
Othello	Come, swear it, damn thyself;
	Lest, being like one of heaven[18], the devils		[18] an angel
	themselves
	Should fear to seize thee; therefore be double-
	damn'd;
	Swear thou art honest.
Desdemona	Heaven doth truly know it.
Othello	Heaven truly knows that thou art false as hell.
Desdemona	To whom, my lord? with whom? how am I false?
Othello	Ah! Desdemona; away, away, away! 40
Desdemona	Alas, the heavy day! — Why do you weep?
	Am I the motive of these tears, my lord?
	If haply[19] you my father do suspect		[19] perhaps
	An instrument of this your calling back,
	Lay not your blame on me; if you have lost him,
	Why, I have lost him too.
Othello	Had it pleas'd heaven
	To try me with affliction[20], had he rain'd		[20] to test me with suffering

All kinds of sores, and shames, on my bare head,
Steep'd me in poverty to the very lips,
Given to captivity me and my utmost hopes,   *50*
I should have found in some part of my soul
A drop of patience; but, alas! to make me
The fixed figure for the time of scorn
To point his slow and moving finger at;
Yet could I bear that too; well, very well:
But there, where I have garner'd[21] up my heart,
Where either I must live or bear no life,
The fountain[22] from the which my current[23] runs
Or else dries up; to be discarded thence!
Or keep it as a cistern[24] for foul toads   *60*
To knot and gender in[25]! Turn thy complexion[26]
   there,
Patience, thou young and rose-lipp'd cherubin[27]
Ay, there, look grim as hell!

Desdemona   I hope my noble lord esteems[28] me honest.
Othello   O! ay; as summer flies are in the shambles[29],
That quicken[30] even with blowing[31]. O thou
   weed!
Who art so lovely fair and smell'st so sweet
That the sense aches at thee, would thou hadst
   ne'er been born.

Desdemona   Alas! what ignorant[32] sin have I committed?
Othello   Was this fair paper, this most goodly book,   *70*
Made to write 'whore' upon? What committed!
Committed! O thou public commoner[33]!
I should make very forges[34] of my cheeks,
That would to cinders burn up modesty,
Did I but speak thy deeds. What committed!
Heaven stops the nose at it and the moon winks[35],
The bawdy wind that kisses all it meets
Is hush'd within the hollow mine[36] of earth,
And will not hear it. What committed!
Impudent strumpet[37]!   *80*

Desdemona   By heaven, you do me wrong.
Othello   Are not you a strumpet?
Desdemona   No, as I am a Christian.
If to preserve this vessel[38] for my lord
From any other foul unlawful touch
Be not to be a strumpet, I am none.
Othello   What! not a whore?
Desdemona   No, as I shall be saved.
Othello   Is it possible?
Desdemona   O! heaven forgive us.
Othello   I cry you mercy, then;

---

[21] stored

[22] source
[23] life

[24] pool
[25] copulate
[26] fair face

[27] angel

[28] believes

[29] slaughter-house
[30] increase
[31] laying eggs

[32] unintentional

[33] prostitute
[34] make fiery (like a forge)

[35] Diana, goddess of the moon, shuts her eyes

[36] the cave of the winds

[37] prostitute

[38] body

I took you for that cunning whore of Venice
That married with Othello. You, mistress,
That have the office opposite to Saint Peter[39],   90
And keep the gate of hell!

Re-enter Emilia.

You, you, ay, you!
We have done our course[40]; there's money for
    your pains.
I pray you, turn the key and keep our counsel[41].
                                                          [*Exit.*

Emilia	Alas! what does this gentleman conceive[42]?
	How do you, madam? how do you, my good lady?
Desdemona	Faith, half asleep.
Emilia	Good madam, what's the matter with my lord?
Desdemona	With who?
Emilia	Why, with my lord, madam.
Desdemona	Who is thy lord? 100
Emilia	He that is yours, sweet lady.
Desdemona	I have none; do not talk to me, Emilia;
	I cannot weep, nor answer have I none.
	But what should go by water[43]. Prithee, to-night
	Lay on my bed my wedding sheets: remember:
	And call thy husband hither.
Emilia	Here's a change indeed!

                                                          [*Exit.*

Desdemona	'Tis meet[44] I should be us'd so, very meet.
	How have I been behav'd, that he might stick
	The small'st opinion[45] on my least misuse[46]?

Re-enter Emilia, with Iago.

Iago	What is your pleasure, madam? How is it with you?
Desdemona	I cannot tell. Those that do teach young babes 110
	Do it with gentle means and easy tasks;
	He might have chid[47] me so; for, in good faith,
	I am a child to chiding.
Iago	What's the matter, lady?
Emilia	Alas! Iago, my lord hath so bewhor'd her[48],
	Thrown such despite[49] and heavy terms upon her,
	As true hearts cannot bear.
Desdemona	Am I that name, Iago?
Iago	What name, fair lady?

[39] who guards the gates of heaven

[40] finished our business

[41] keep our secret

[42] imagine

[43] be expressed in tears

[44] fair

[45] criticism
[46] misconduct

[47] criticised

[48] accused her of being a whore
[49] abuse

50 slut

Desdemona	Such as she says my lord did say I was.
Emilia	He call'd her whore; a beggar in his drink
	Could not have laid such terms upon his
	callat⁵⁰. 120
Iago	Why did he so?
Desdemona	I do not know; I am sure I am none such.
Iago	Do not weep, do not weep. Alas the day!
Emilia	Has she forsook so many noble matches,
	Her father and her country and her friends,
	To be call'd whore? would it not make one weep?
Desdemona	It is my wretched fortune.

51 curse him
52 deception

Iago	Beshrew him for it⁵¹!
	How comes this trick⁵² upon him?
Desdemona	Nay, heaven doth know.
Emilia	I will be hang'd, if some eternal villain,

53 two-faced
54 cheating and deceiving

	Some busy and insinuating⁵³ rogue, 130
	Some cogging cozening⁵⁴ slave, to get some
	office,
	Have not devis'd this slander; I'll be hang'd else.
Iago	Fie! there is no such man; it is impossible.
Desdemona	If any such there be, heaven pardon him!

55 hangman's noose

Emilia	A halter⁵⁵ pardon him, and hell gnaw his bones!
	Why should he call her whore? who keeps her
	company?

56 opportunity

	What place? what time? what form⁵⁶? what
	likelihood?
	The Moor's abused by some most villanous
	knave,
	Some base notorious knave, some scurvy fellow.

57 villains
58 reveal

	O heaven! that such companions⁵⁷ thou'dst 140
	unfold⁵⁸,
	And put in every honest hand a whip
	To lash the rascals naked through the world,
	Even from the east to the west!
Iago	Speak within door.

59 fellow
60 confused your common sense

Emilia	O! fie upon them. Some such squire⁵⁹ he was
	That turn'd your wit the seamy side⁶⁰ without,
	And made you to suspect me with the Moor.

61 be quiet

Iago	You are a fool; go to⁶¹.
Desdemona	O good Iago,
	What shall I do to win my lord again?
	Good friend, go to him; for, by this light of
	heaven,
	I know not how I lost him. Here I kneel: 150
	If e'er my will did trespass 'gainst his love,

62 while I was thinking

	Either in discourse of thought⁶² or actual deed,

Or that mine eyes, mine ears, or any sense,
Delighted them[63] in any other form[64]
Or that I do not yet, and ever did,
And ever will, though he do shake me off[65]
To beggarly divorcement[66], love him dearly,
Comfort forswear[67] me! Unkindness may do
   much;
And his unkindness may defeat[68] my life,
But never taint my love. I cannot say 'whore':   *160*
It does abhor me now I speak the word;
To do the act that might the addition[69] earn
Not the world's mass of vanity could make me.

Iago   I pray you be content, 'tis but his humour[70];
The business of the state does him offence[71],
And he does chide with you.

Desdemona   If 'twere no other, –

Iago   'Tis but so, I warrant.   *[Trumpets.*

Hark! how these instruments summon to supper;
The messengers of Venice stay the meat[72]:
Go in, and weep not; all things shall be well.   *170*
      [Exeunt Desdemona and Emilia.

     Enter Roderigo.

How now, Roderigo!

Roderigo   I do not find that thou dealest justly[73] with me.

Iago   What in the contrary?

Roderigo   Every day thou daffest[74] me with some device[75],
Iago; and rather, as it seems to me now, keepest
from me all conveniency[76], than suppliest me with
the least advantage of hope. I will indeed no
longer endure it, nor am I yet persuaded to put up
in peace what already I have foolishly suffered.

Iago   Will you hear me, Roderigo?   *180*

Roderigo   Faith, I have heard too much, for your words and
performances are no kin together[77].

Iago   You charge me most unjustly.

Roderigo   With nought but truth. I have wasted myself out of
my means[78]. The jewels you have had from me to
deliver to Desdemona would half have corrupted
a votarist[79]; you have told me she has received
them, and returned me expectations and comforts
of sudden respect[80] and acquaintance, but I find
none.   *190*

Iago   Well; go to; very well.

Roderigo   Very well! go to! I cannot go to[81], man; nor 'tis not

[63] themselves
[64] in any other way

[65] throw me

[66] rejection

[67] may joy forsake me

[68] destroy

[69] title

[70] mood

[71] worries him

[72] for a meal

[73] fairly

[74] put me off
[75] excuse

[76] opportunity

[77] do not match each other

[78] money

[79] nun

[80] immediate attention

[81] will not be put off

82 fooled

very well: by this hand. I say, it is very scurvy, and
begin to find myself fobbed82 in it.

Iago   Very well.

Roderigo   I tell you 'tis not very well. I will make myself
known to Desdemona; if she will return me my
jewels, I will give over my suit and repent83 my
83 reconsider, give up
84 illicit request
85 repayment
unlawful solicitation84; if not, assure yourself I will
seek satisfaction85 of you.   *200*

Iago   You have said now.

Roderigo   Ay, and I have said nothing, but what I protest
86 intention
intendment86 of doing.

87 spirit
Iago   Why, now I see there's mettle87 in thee, and even
from this instant do build on thee a better
opinion than ever before. Give me thy hand,
Roderigo; thou hast taken against me a most just
88 grievance
exception88; but yet, I protest, I have dealt most
89 honestly
directly89 in thy affair.

Roderigo   It hath not appeared.   *210*

Iago   I grant indeed it hath not appeared, and your
suspicion is not without wit90 and judgement.
90 sense
But, Roderigo, if thou hast that in thee indeed,
which I have greater reason to believe now than
ever, I mean purpose, courage, and valour, this
night show it: if thou the next night following
enjoy not Desdemona, take me from this world
91 plots against
with treachery and devise engines91 for my life.

Roderigo   Well, what is it? is it within reason and
92 reasonable and possible
compass92?   *220*

Iago   Sir, there is especial commission come from
Venice to depute Cassio in Othello's place.

Roderigo   Is that true? why, then Othello and Desdemona
return again to Venice.

Iago   O, no! he goes into Mauritania, and takes away
with him the fair Desdemona, unless his abode be
93 unless his stay is prolonged
lingered93 here by some accident; wherein none
94 decisive
can be so determinate94 as the removing of
Cassio.

Roderigo   How do you mean, removing of him?   *230*

Iago   Why, by making him uncapable of Othello's place;
knocking out his brains.

Roderigo   And that you would have me do?

Iago   Ay; if you dare do yourself a profit and a right. He
95 prostitute
sups to-night with a harlotry95, and thither will I
go to him; he knows not yet of his honourable
96 good fortune
fortune96. If you will watch his going thence,
97 arrange
which I will fashion97 to fall out98 between
98 happen
twelve and one, — you may take him at your

	pleasure; I will be near to second[99] your attempt,	*240*	[99] support
	and he shall fall between us. Come, stand not		
	amazed at it, but go along with me; I will show you		
	such a necessity in his death that you shall think		
	yourself bound to put it on him. It is now high[100]		
	supper-time, and the night grows to waste;		[100] fully
	about it.		
Roderigo	I will hear further reason for this.		
Iago	And you shall be satisfied. *[Exeunt.*		

The Plot (Day Three – A Room in the Castle)

OTHELLO QUESTIONS EMILIA

Othello questions Emilia about Desdemona's conduct with Cassio. Emilia protests that Desdemona is honest and is innocent of any wrongdoing with Cassio. Othello thinks she is protecting Desdemona and orders Emilia to bring Desdemona to him.

OTHELLO ACCUSES DESDEMONA

When Desdemona comes, Emilia is sent out to guard the door. Desdemona kneels before Othello and begs him to explain why he is angry with her. He orders her to swear that she is true to him. He now believes that she swears falsely and feels justified in killing her. Othello weeps and Desdemona tries to find out why he is so depressed.

Then Othello accuses her of being a whore but she asks what sin she has committed. Tortured by her beauty, Othello refuses to believe her protests of innocence and leaves in contempt.

DESDEMONA APPEALS TO IAGO

Emilia is shocked and tries to console Desdemona. Desdemona tells her to make her bed with her wedding sheets and to send Iago to her. She cannot understand Othello's treatment of her.

Emilia is angry at Othello's treatment of Desdemona. Desdemona begs Iago to speak to Othello and convince him of her love and fidelity for her husband. Iago assures her that all will be well and the women leave.

IAGO PLACATES RODERIGO

Roderigo enters, upset at the loss of his jewels, which he gave Iago to win Desdemona's love. Iago claims he has sent them to Desdemona but that there has been no response.

I took you for that cunning whore of Venice
That married with Othello.   (Othello, Act 4, Scene II)

Roderigo threatens to demand the jewels back from Desdemona or seek satisfaction from Iago.

Iago reassures Roderigo that he will soon win Desdemona's love. He explains that Othello is leaving for Cyprus and that Cassio is to replace him. If Roderigo is brave enough to kill Cassio, then Othello and Desdemona will have to remain in Cyprus and Roderigo will surely win Desdemona. Iago arranges with Roderigo to kill Cassio in a brawl that night after supper. Roderigo is dubious but agrees.

Dramatic Significance

TRAGIC HERO AND TRAGIC VICTIM

Iago has reached the height of his power over Othello. Othello questions Emilia about Desdemona's infidelity, as he enters his imagined brothel. He refuses to believe in Desdemona's innocence. He treats Desdemona as a prostitute and questions her, demanding that she swears her fidelity:

> "... therefore be double-damn'd;
> Swear thou art honest."

He concludes that his wronged, innocent wife is a whore, who has betrayed him:

> "I took you for that cunning whore of Venice
> That married with Othello. You, mistress."

Othello is in an agony of frustrated passion, caught between love of Desdemona's beauty and loathing of her foulness:

> "O thou weed!
> Who art so lovely fair and smell'st so sweet
> That the sense aches at thee, would thou hadst ne'er been born."

He struggles vainly to endure his conflicting emotions and becomes a truly tragic figure:

> "But there, where I have garner'd up my heart,
> Where either I must live or bear no life,
> The fountain from the which my current runs
> Or else dries up: to be discarded thence!
> Or keep it as a cistern for foul toads
> To knot and gender in! Turn thy complexion there,
> Patience, thou young and rose-lipp'd cherubin;
> Ay, there, look grim as hell!"

The blow delivered to Desdemona is overwhelming and she is dazed and speechless:

> "I cannot weep, nor answer have I none.
> But what should go by water."

I pray you be content, 'tis but his humour.

(Iago, Act 4, Scene II)

She wonders how she may have offended Othello by her innocent behaviour. When Iago enters, she appeals for help to the last person likely to help her:

> *"Good friend, go to him; for, by this light of heaven,*
> *I know not how I lost him. Here I kneel."*

Iago promises that all will be well but has no intention of abandoning his schemes:

> *"Go in, and weep not; all things shall be well."*

Desdemona is at his mercy but he has too much at stake to abandon his evil schemes.

IAGO'S FALSE SECURITY

Up to now, Iago has managed to keep his plot closely guarded from the other characters. Cassio is to die. Desdemona is discredited and Othello is demoralised. Hence Iago feels relatively safe from discovery.

However in this scene Iago underestimates the chance of his wife, Emilia, exposing his villainy. She has seen Othello's jealousy and his collapse in a frenzy and might link Iago's presence to these events. She is also aware of the true facts about the missing handkerchief. Yet Iago does not see her as a threat, since up to now she has followed his instructions heedlessly.

In this scene Emilia, for the first time, confronts the consequences of her earlier thoughtlessness, when she sees Desdemona humiliated by Othello. In the previous scene, she lied about not seeing the handkerchief. Now she realises:

> *"The Moor's abused by some most villanous knave."*

She does not yet suspect that Iago is that very knave, but her concern for Desdemona may encourage her to enquire further. Thus she is a danger to Iago but he thinks he can command her silence:

> *"Speak within door."*
> *"You are a fool, go to."*

His low regard for his wife will soon prove his undoing.

At the end of the scene, Iago is making plans to avert the danger to him from Cassio by arranging the brawl. Othello's recall by the Duke makes action all the more urgent. Roderigo stands to lose Desdemona finally at Othello's departure for Mauritania, and so would be likely to talk too much and perhaps expose Iago. Later we learn of Iago's true intentions – that both Cassio and Roderigo should die. At this stage Iago is at the height of his power and does not fear discovery, whether from Emilia or Roderigo.

Character Development

OTHELLO
PERVERTED PRINCIPLES

Othello is now immune to Emilia's evidence of Desdemona's innocence, as he enters to confront Desdemona with her infidelity. Judiciously he questions Desdemona, making her swear that she is honest, but bitterly concludes that she is false:

> *"Heaven truly knows that thou art false as hell."*

He scorns her protestations of innocence and is firmly convinced that she is a whore:

> *"I took you for that cunning whore of Venice,*
> *That married with Othello. You, mistress."*

Othello's semblance of fair play in examining the evidence is a gross perversion of justice, as he has already pronounced sentence of death on Desdemona. His great love has become corrupted:

> *"O thou weed!*
> *Who art so lovely fair and smell'st so sweet*
> *That the sense aches at thee, would thou hadst ne'er been born."*

A STRUGGLE TO ENDURE

Othello writhes in agony, as he confronts Desdemona. Loathing and passion contend within him, as he believes Desdemona's beauty hides the corruption of her soul:

> *"O thou public commoner!*
> *I should make very forges of my cheeks,*
> *That would to cinders burn up modesty,*
> *Did I but speak thy deeds. What committed!"*

He could endure all other afflictions but the loss of his love:

> *"But there, where I have garner'd up my heart,*
> *Where either I must live or bear no life,*
> *... Turn thy complexion there,*
> *Patience, thou young and rose-lipp'd cherubin;*
> *Ay, there, look grim as hell!"*

His noble mind struggles to endure its torment and degradation.

IAGO
OVER-CONFIDENCE

Iago, secure in his power over others, underestimates the threat of exposure from his wife, Emilia. He despises her so much that he sees her as no danger to him:

> *"Speak within door."*
> *"You are a fool, go to."*

As he callously gives false comfort to Desdemona, he underestimates the depths of Emilia's anger against the injustice done to Desdemona:

> *"Fie! there is no such man; it is impossible."*

Iago's over-confidence is a fatal flaw, since it makes him careless of danger.

DESDEMONA
A HELPLESS VICTIM

Desdemona is shocked at Othello's cruel inquisition and accusations. She does not understand why he treats her so coldly, and protests her innocence:

> *"I hope my noble lord esteems me honest."*

She is hurt and at a loss what to do:

> *"I cannot weep, nor answer have I none.*
> *But what should go by water."*

In desperation Desdemona appeals to Iago for help but he gives false comfort:

> *"I pray you be content, 'tis but his humour."*

She still cherishes her love for Othello, despite his cruelty:

> *"Unkindness may do much;*
> *And his unkindness may defeat my life,*
> *But never taint my love."*

She is the victim of Othello's corrupted love and Iago's callous schemes.

EMILIA
RIGHTEOUS INDIGNATION

Emilia is loyal and devoted to Desdemona. She protests Desdemona's innocence to Othello and tries to console her when she is rejected:

> *"Alas! what does this gentleman conceive?*
> *How do you, madam? how do you, my good lady?"*

Emilia is furious at Othello's treatment of Desdemona:

> *"He call'd her whore; a beggar in his drink*
> *Could not have laid such terms upon his callat."*

She feels that Othello has been abused by some *"base notorious knave"* and is determined to do her utmost to vindicate Desdemona's good name:

> *"A halter pardon him, and hell gnaw his bones!*
> *Why should he call her whore? who keeps her company?"*

Emilia begins to emerge as a less heedless person in this scene.

Alas! what ignorant sin have I committed?   *(Desdemona, Act 4, Scene II)*

RODERIGO
A TEMPORARY REVOLT

Roderigo begins to show some common sense at last. He shows more spirit than before, in confronting Iago with fruitlessly wasting his money and fobbing him off with useless advice:

> "Faith, I have heard too much, for your words and
> performances are no kin together".

Roderigo poses an immediate danger to Iago:

> "I tell you 'tis not very well. I will make myself known
> to Desdemona ... assure yourself I will seek satisfaction of you."

Yet the skilful Iago manages to persuade him to kill Cassio. Roderigo is led to believe that the death of Cassio will ensure that Desdemona and Othello cannot leave Cyprus for Mauritania. True to form, Roderigo falls in with Iago's plans.

Scene III

Another Room in the Castle.
Enter Othello, Lodovico, Desdemona, Emilia, and Attendants.

Lodovico	I do beseech you, sir, trouble yourself no further.
Othello	O! pardon me; 'twill do me good to walk.
Lodovico	Madam, good night; I humbly thank your ladyship.
Desdemona	Your honour is most welcome.
Othello	Will you walk, sir?
	O! Desdemona, –
Desdemona	My lord?
Othello	Get you to bed on the instant; I will be returned forthwith; dismiss your attendant there; look it be done.
Desdemona	I will, my lord. 10
	[Exeunt Othello, Lodovico, and Attendants.
Emilia	How goes it now? he looks gentler than he did.
Desdemona	He says he will return incontinent[1];
	He hath commanded me to go to bed,
	And bade me to dismiss you.
Emilia	Dismiss me!
Desdemona	It was his bidding; therefore, good Emilia,
	Give me my nightly wearing, and adieu:
	We must not now displease him.
Emilia	I would you had never seen him.
Desdemona	So would not I; my love doth so approve[2] him,

[1] immediately

[2] admire

³ harshness
⁴ criticism

⁵ attractiveness

⁶ no matter

⁷ you talk foolishly

⁸ I find it hard not to be sad

⁹ hurry and go

¹⁰ handsome

¹¹ lower

¹² hurry
¹³ soon

¹⁴ accept

¹⁵ more
¹⁶ sleep with

¹⁷ forebode

That even his stubbornness³, his checks⁴ and   20
   frowns, –
Prithee, unpin me, – have grace and favour⁵ in
   them.

Emilia I have laid those sheets you bade me on the bed.
Desdemona All's one⁶. Good faith! how foolish are our minds!
If I do die before thee, prithee, shroud me
In one of those same sheets.
Emilia   Come, come, you talk⁷.
Desdemona My mother had a maid call'd Barbara;
She was in love, and he she lov'd prov'd mad
And did forsake her; she had a song of 'willow;'
An old thing 'twas, but it expressed her fortune,
And she died singing it; that song to-night   30
Will not go from my mind; I have much to do
But to go hang my head all at one side⁸,
And sing it like poor Barbara. Prithee, dispatch⁹.
Emilia Shall I go fetch your night-gown?
Desdemona   No, unpin me here.
This Lodovico is a proper¹⁰ man.
Emilia A very handsome man.
Desdemona He speaks well.
Emilia I know a lady in Venice would have walked
barefoot to Palestine for a touch of his nether¹¹
   lip.   40
Desdemona *The poor soul sat sighing by a sycamore tree,*
   Sing all a green willow;
Her hand on her bosom, her head on her knee,
   Sing willow, willow, willow:
The fresh streams ran by her, and murmur'd her
   moans;
   Sing willow, willow, willow:
Her salt tears fell from her, and soften'd the
   stones; –
Lay by these: –
   Sing willow, willow, willow:
Prithee, hie¹² thee; he'll come anon¹³. –   50
Sing all a green willow must be my garland.
Let nobody blame him, his scorn I approve¹⁴, –
Nay, that's not next. Hark! who is it that knocks?
Emilia It is the wind.
Desdemona *I call'd my love false love; but what said he then?*
   Sing willow, willow, willow:
If I court moe¹⁵ women, you'll couch with¹⁶ moe
   men.
So, get thee gone; good night. Mine eyes do itch;
Doth that bode¹⁷ weeping?
Emilia   'Tis neither here nor there.

152

Desdemona	I have heard it said so. O! these men, these *60* men! Dost thou in conscience[18] think, tell me, Emilia, That there be women do abuse[19] their husbands In such gross kind[20]?
Emilia	There be some such, no question.
Desdemona	Wouldst thou do such a deed for all the world?
Emilia	Why, would not you?
Desdemona	No, by this heavenly light!
Emilia	Nor I neither by this heavenly light; I might do't as well i' the dark.
Desdemona	Wouldst thou do such a deed for all the world?
Emilia	The world is a huge thing; 'tis a great price[21] For a small vice. *70*
Desdemona	In troth[22], I think thou wouldst not.
Emilia	In troth, I think I should, and undo't when I had done. Marry, I would not do such a thing for a joint ring[23], nor measures of lawn[24], nor for gowns, petticoats, nor caps, nor any petty exhibition[25]; but for the whole world, who would not make her husband a cuckold to make him a monarch[26]? I should venture[27] purgatory for't.
Desdemona	Beshrew me[28], if I would do such a wrong For the whole world.
Emilia	Why, the wrong is but a wrong i' the world; and *80* having the world for your labour[29], 'tis a wrong in your own world, and you might quickly make it right.
Desdemona	I do not think there is any such woman.

Emilia	Yes, a dozen; and as many to the vantage[30], as
	 would store[31] the world they play'd for.
	 But I do think it is their husbands' faults
	 If wives do fall. Say that they slack their duties[32],
	 And pour our treasures into foreign[33] laps,
	 Or else break out in peevish[34] jealousies, *90*
	 Throwing restraint upon us; or, say they strike us,
	 Or scant our former having[35] in despite[36];
	 Why, we have galls[37], and though we have some
	      grace,
	 Yet have we some revenge. Let husbands know
	 Their wives have sense[38] like them; they see and
	      smell,
	 And have their palates both for sweet and sour,
	 As husbands have. What is it that they do
	 When they change us for others? Is it sport?

[18] honestly
[19] deceive
[20] so crudely

[21] reward

[22] truly

[23] ring made of two halves
[24] lengths of fine linen
[25] trivial gift

[26] rich or powerful
[27] risk
[28] curse me

[29] effort

[30] in addition
[31] populate

[32] sexual duties
[33] other women's
[34] senseless

[35] reduce our previous allowance
[36] for spite
[37] grudges

[38] senses, feelings

[39] does desire cause it

I think it is; and doth affection breed[39] it?
I think it doth; is't frailty that thus errs?   100
It is so too; and have not we affections,
Desires for sport, and frailty, as men have?

[40] treat

Then, let them use[40] us well; else let them know,
The ills we do, their ills instruct us so.

Desdemona

[41] treatment; habit
[42] follow example of bad treatment
[43] learn from bad treatment

Good night, good night; heaven me such
    usage[41] send,
Not to pick bad from bad[42], but by bad mend[43]!

                                            [Exeunt.

The Plot (Day Three – Another Room in the Castle)
DESDEMONA SADLY WAITS FOR OTHELLO

After supper, Lodovico, Desdemona and Othello are talking. Othello orders Desdemona to go to bed and to send Emilia away. Othello walks with Lodovico.

As she undresses, Desdemona sadly reflects on her love for Othello. She sings a sad song of false love and discusses with Emilia whether there are women who are false to their husbands. Emilia says that there are such women and that even she would betray her own husband, Iago, because of his inconsiderate treatment of her.

Desdemona does not wish to repay one evil with another. She would prefer to learn from her mistakes through suffering. She is left alone to await her husband.

Dramatic Significance
DESDEMONA – A TRAGIC VICTIM

As Othello sends Desdemona to prepare for bed and dismisses Emilia, we anxiously await the events of the coming night.

Desdemona is anxious too. She wishes to please Othello and obeys him, instructing Emilia to lay out her wedding sheets on the bed. She does not blame Othello for his stubbornness:

> "... My love doth so approve him,
> That even his stubbornness, his checks and frowns, –
> Prithee, unpin me, – have grace and favour in them."

Desdemona doesn't question Emilia about the handkerchief. A vague dread of unknown disaster haunts her. She tries to express it in singing the "willow" song – a song of love cruelly betrayed.

> "I call'd my love false love; but what said he then?
>   Sing willow, willow, willow:
> If I court moe women, you'll couch me moe men."

Wouldst thou do such a deed for all the world?

(Desdemona, Act 4, Scene III)

Then the women talk of women who betray their husbands. We realise that Desdemona is so pure and innocent that unlike Emilia, she could not be unfaithful in love for whatever reason:

> "Beshrew me, if I would do such a wrong
> For the whole world."

She could not repay evil with evil and has no thought of spite or vengeance on anyone for whatever cause:

> "Heaven me such usage send,
> Not to pick bad from bad, but by bad mend!"

Desdemona becomes the tragic victim of Iago's contriving and Othello's vengeance, but remains pure and untarnished to the end and so gains our admiration and sympathy.

Character Development
DESDEMONA
A PURE SOUL

Desdemona unquestioningly obeys Othello's curt order to go to bed. She loves and forgives Othello for his unkindness:

> "My love doth so approve him,
> That even his stubbornness, his checks and frowns, –
> Prithee, unpin me, – have grace and favour in them."

A vague fear takes hold of her as she sings the "willow" song. She is innocent and guiltless and sees no evil.

Desdemona is pure and selfless and cannot understand infidelity in marriage. She would not repay wrong with wrong but would seek to learn from mistakes or offences:

> "Good night, good night: Heaven me such usage send,
> Not to pick bad from bad, but by bad mend!"

She is almost saintlike in her innocent selflessness.

EMILIA
WORLDLY-WISE

In contrast to Desdemona, Emilia is experienced in the ways of the world. She would cheat on her husband, if the advantage was great enough. Since men use women, she feels women should also make use of men:

> "Then, let them use us well; else let them know,
> The ills we do, their ills instruct us so."

She seems a decent woman, who is embittered by her unhappy marriage to Iago:

> "But I do think it is their husbands' faults
> If wives do fall. Say that they slack their duties,
> And pour our treasures into foreign laps."

Act 5
Scene 1

Cyprus. A Street.
Enter Iago and Roderigo.

Iago   Here, stand behind this bulk[1]; straight will he
         come:
     Wear thy good rapier bare[2], and put it home.
     Quick, quick; fear nothing; I'll be at thy elbow.
     It makes us, or it mars[3] us; think on that,
     And fix most firm thy resolution.

Roderigo   Be near at hand; I may miscarry[4] in't.

Iago   Here, at thy hand: be bold, and take thy stand.
                              [Retires.

Roderigo   I have no great devotion to[5] the deed;
     And yet he has given me satisfying reasons:
     'Tis but a man gone: forth, my sword; he dies.   *10*

Iago   I have rubb'd this young quat[6] almost to the sense[7],
     And he grows angry. Now, whether he kill Cassio,
     Or Cassio him, or each do kill the other,
     Every way makes my gain: live[8] Roderigo,
     He calls me to a restitution[9] large
     Of gold and jewels that I bobb'd[10] from him,
     As gifts to Desdemona;
     It must not be: if Cassio do remain,
     He hath a daily beauty in his life
     That makes me ugly; and, besides, the Moor   *20*
     May unfold[11] me to him; there stand I in much
         peril.
     No, he must die. But so; I hear him coming.

Enter Cassio.

Roderigo   I know his gait; 'tis he. Villain, thou diest!
                  [Makes a pass at Cassio.

Cassio   That thrust had been mine enemy indeed
     But that my coat is better than thou know'st;
     I will make proof[12] of thine.
            [Draws, and wounds Roderigo.

Roderigo   O! I am slain.

[Iago from behind wounds Cassio in the leg, and exit.

Cassio   I am maim'd for ever. Help, ho! murder! murder!
                        [Falls.

---

[1] projecting building

[2] unsheathed

[3] ruins

[4] fail

[5] enthusiasm for

[6] pimple
[7] until it hurts

[8] if Roderigo lives
[9] restoration
[10] cheated

[11] reveal

[12] test

Enter Othello, at a distance.

Othello	The voice of Cassio: Iago keeps his word.
Roderigo	O! villain that I am!
Othello	It is e'en so.
Cassio	O, help, ho! light! a surgeon! 30
Othello	'Tis he: O brave Iago, honest and just!
	That hast such noble sense of thy friend's wrong;
	Thou teachest me. Minion[13], your dear[14] lies dead,
	And your unblest fate hies[15]; strumpet, I come!
	Forth of[16] my heart those charms, thine eyes, are blotted;
	Thy bed lust-stain'd shall with lust's blood be spotted.

                                   [Exit.

Enter Lodovico and Gratiano, at a distance.

Cassio	What ho! no watch? no passage[17]? murder! murder!
Gratiano	'Tis some mischance[18]; the cry is very direful[19].
Cassio	O, help!
Lodovico	Hark!
Roderigo	O wretched villain! 40
Lodovico	Two or three groan: it is a heavy[20] night;
	These may be counterfeits[21]; let's think't unsafe
	To come in to the cry without more help.
Roderigo	Nobody come? then shall I bleed to death.
Lodovico	Hark!

Re-enter Iago, with a light.

Gratiano	Here's one comes in his shirt, with light and weapons.
Iago	Who's there? whose noise is this that cries on murder?
Lodovico	We do not know.
Iago	Did not you hear a cry?
Cassio	Here, here! for heaven's sake, help me. 50
Iago	What's the matter?
Gratiano	This is Othello's ancient, as I take it.
Lodovico	The same indeed; a very valiant fellow.
Iago	What are you here that cry so grievously?
Cassio	Iago? O! I am spoil'd[22], undone by villains!
	Give me some help.
Iago	O me, lieutenant! what villains have done this?
Cassio	I think that one of them is hereabout,
	And cannot make away[23].

[13] slave
[14] darling
[15] wretched fate approaches quickly
[16] banish from
[17] passers-by
[18] misfortune
[19] distressing
[20] gloomy, violent
[21] a trap (false cries)
[22] injured
[23] get away

Iago	O treacherous villains!
	[*To Lodovico and Gratiano.*] What are you
	there? come in, and give some help.
Roderigo	O! help me here. 60
Cassio	That's one of them.
Iago	O murderous slave! O villain!
	[*Stabs Roderigo.*
Roderigo	O damn'd Iago! O inhuman dog!
Iago	Kill men i' the dark! Where be these bloody
	thieves?
	How silent is this town! Ho! murder! murder!
	What may you be? are you of good or evil?
Lodovico	As you shall prove us[24], praise us[25].
Iago	Signior Lodovico?
Lodovico	He, sir.
Iago	I cry you mercy. Here's Cassio hurt by villains.
Gratiano	Cassio! 70
Iago	How is it, brother?
Cassio	My leg is cut in two.
Iago	Marry, heaven forbid,
	Light, gentlemen; I'll bind it with my shirt.

Enter Bianca.

Bianca	What is the matter, ho? who is't that cried?
Iago	Who is't that cried!
Bianca	O my dear Cassio! my sweet Cassio!
	O Cassio, Cassio, Cassio!
Iago	O notable[26] strumpet! Cassio, may you suspect
	Who they should be that have thus mangled you?
Cassio	No. 80
Gratiano	I am sorry to find you thus; I have been to seek
	you.
Iago	Lend me a garter[27]. So. O! for a chair,
	To bear him easily hence!
Bianca	Alas! he faints! O Cassio, Cassio, Cassio!
Iago	Gentlemen all, I do suspect this trash[28]
	To be a party in this injury.
	Patience awhile, good Cassio. Come, come.
	Lend me a light. Know we this face, or no?
	Alas! my friend and my dear countryman,
	Roderigo? no: yes, sure, O heaven! Roderigo. 90
Gratiano	What! of Venice?
Iago	Even he, sir: did you know him?
Gratiano	Know him! ay.
Iago	Signior Gratiano? I cry[29] you gentle pardon:

[24] as you find us (good or evil)
[25] judge us

[26] well-known

[27] binding material

[28] Bianca

[29] beg

30 unfortunate events

31 stop your efforts

32 fear
33 watch

34 alas!

35 result

36 order

37 bandaged
38 tell us

39 happened

40 ruins

	These bloody accidents30 must excuse my manners,
	That so neglected you.
Gratiano	I am glad to see you.
Iago	How do you, Cassio? O! a chair, a chair!
Gratiano	Roderigo! *[A chair brought in.*
Iago	He, he, 'tis he. – O! that's well said; the chair:
	Some good men bear him carefully from hence;
	I'll fetch the general's surgeon. *100*
	[To Bianca]
	For you, mistress,
	Save you your labour31. He that lies slain here,
	Cassio,
	Was my dear friend. What malice was between
	you?
Cassio	None in the world; nor do I know the man.
Iago	*[To Bianca]* What! look you pale? O! bear him out
	o'the air –
	[Cassio and Roderigo are borne off.
	Stay you, good gentlemen. Look you pale,
	mistress? –
	Do you perceive the gastness32 of her eye?
	Nay, if you stare33, we shall hear more anon.
	Behold her well; I pray you, look upon her:
	Do you see, gentlemen? nay, guiltiness will speak
	Though tongues were out of use. *110*

Enter Emilia.

Emilia	'Las34! what's the matter, husband?
Iago	Cassio hath here been set on in the dark
	By Roderigo and fellows that are 'scaped:
	He's almost slain, and Roderigo dead.
Emilia	Alas! good gentleman; alas! good Cassio!
Iago	This is the fruit35 of whoring. Prithee, Emilia,
	Go know of Cassio where he supp'd to-night.
	What! do you shake at that?
Bianca	He supp'd at my house; but I therefore shake not.
Iago	O! did he so? I charge36 you, go with me. *120*
Emilia	Fie, fie upon thee, strumpet!
Bianca	I am no strumpet, but of life as honest
	As you that thus abuse me.
Emilia	As I! foh! fie upon thee!
Iago	Kind gentlemen, let's go see poor Cassio dress'd37.
	Come, mistress, you must tell's38 another tale.
	Emilia, run you to the citadel,
	And tell my lord and lady what hath happ'd39.
	Will you go on afore? *[Aside]* This is the night
	That either makes me or fordoes40 me quite.
	[Exeunt.

*Cassio hath here been set on in the dark
By Roderigo and fellows that are 'scaped.
He's almost slain, and Roderigo dead.*

(Iago, Act 5, Scene I)

The Plot (Day Three – A Street in Cyprus)

CASSIO IS WOUNDED

Iago and Roderigo wait in the darkness for Cassio. Iago hopes that both Cassio and Roderigo will be killed, since both might betray him.

As Cassio enters, Roderigo stabs him and Roderigo is wounded. Iago, from behind, wounds Cassio in the leg and runs away.

Othello hears Cassio's cries but ignores them. Delighted that Iago's plan is working, Othello goes to kill Desdemona.

IAGO AVERTS SUSPICION

Lodovico and Gratiano hear the commotion but believe it is a trick to lure them into an ambush.

Iago enters with a light and Cassio and Roderigo appeal to him for help. Cassio accuses Roderigo of being one of his attackers. Iago quickly stabs Roderigo, pretending to avenge Cassio.

Bianca comes and Iago casts suspicion on her, since she had supper with Cassio that night. She is arrested.

Iago pretends to be surprised when he recognises Roderigo. He enquires of Cassio what grudge was between them but Cassio has no knowledge of it.

Iago and Emilia accuse Bianca of treachery and Emilia is sent to inform Othello and Desdemona of what has happened. Iago hopes that he will escape suspicion.

Dramatic Significance

"THE NIGHT THAT FORDOES IAGO QUITE"

This dramatic scene is the turning point in Iago's fortunes and marks the beginning of the end for his malevolent schemes. Roderigo can no longer be fooled. Cassio too is a danger to the success of Iago's schemes. Both must die. In a daring move, Iago decides to make sure that Roderigo dies too.

> "... Whether he kill Cassio,
> Or Cassio him, or each do kill the other,
> Every way makes my gain."

Thus far Iago has been successful, and has managed not only to avoid discovery but also to gain great credit for his actions. Nobody has been killed yet nor has Iago had to take an active part in his own schemes. This time he intends to intervene himself:

> *"Quick, quick; fear nothing; I'll be at thy elbow.*
> *It makes us, or it mars us; think on that."*

His daring confidence will prove his undoing.

This time too there are loopholes in Iago's scheme. Roderigo fails to wound Cassio and Iago wounds him in the leg, but Cassio lives to expose Iago. Roderigo is wounded but Iago has to kill him, but not before he exclaims:

> *"O damn'd Iago! O inhuman dog!"*

Iago claims credit for avenging the attack on Cassio. His direct and open action in his own scheme may tell against him.

Iago tries to turn suspicion on to Bianca but Cassio may save her. In the heat of the moment, Emilia too helps to turn suspicion on Bianca but she may soon realise who was really to blame. She is slow to leave and inform Othello, as Iago has anxiously instructed her:

> *"Will you go on afore?"*

He is still anxious to evade suspicion:

> *"'... This is the night*
> *That either makes me or fordoes me quite."*

Ironically, Iago's real success this night is in confirming Othello in his decision to kill Desdemona. This Iago does by the example of his own zeal to avenge his friend, Cassio:

> *"'Tis he: O brave Iago, honest and just!*
> *That hast such noble sense of thy friend's wrong;*
> *Thou teachest me. Minion, your dear lies dead."*

Whether Iago is discovered or not he will have succeeded in destroying Desdemona and, through her, Othello. We wait anxiously to see if Iago's schemes will be exposed in time to save Desdemona.

Character Development

IAGO
FALSE SECURITY
Iago plans his master stroke – to eliminate the danger of exposure by plotting the deaths of both Cassio and Roderigo:

> *"Whether he kill Cassio,*
> *Or Cassio him, or each do kill the other,*
> *Every way makes my gain."*

He knows the risks of exposure but stakes all on the events of this night. In his desire for security of power, he underestimates the risks. For the first time he plots murder and presumes that, as usual, good luck will favour him.

As events begin to go wrong, with the untimely arrivals of Lodovico, Gratiano and Bianca, Iago realises:

> *"This is the night*
> *That either makes me or fordoes me quite."*

He has killed Roderigo in public and Cassio lives to tell the tale. He has played for high stakes and begins to lose. His downfall is imminent.

RODERIGO
CALLOUS SELF-SEEKING

Roderigo does not wish to be involved in murder and has misgivings:

> *"I have no great devotion to the deed."*

Yet he allows self-interest to dominate him:

> *"... yet he has given me satisfying reasons:*
> *'Tis but a man gone: forth, my sword; he dies."*

He has little conscience in him. Yet Roderigo acknowledges that he did wrong:

> *"O! villain that I am!"*

As he dies he attempts to expose Iago's villainy:

> *"O damn'd Iago! O inhuman dog."*

Perhaps this is not conscience but a desire to be even with Iago, who deceived and betrayed him.

OTHELLO
GRIM DETERMINATION

Othello is still confirmed in his purpose of killing Desdemona. He admires Iago for keeping his word and resolves to follow this example:

> *"'Tis he: O brave Iago, honest and just!*
> *That hast such noble sense of thy friend's wrong;*
> *Thou teachest me. Minion, your dear lies dead,*
> *And your unblest fate hies; strumpet, I come."*

He struggles to blot out his love of Desdemona and replace it with firm justice:

> *"Forth of my heart those charms, thine eyes, are blotted,*
> *Thy bed, lust-stain'd, shall with lust's blood be spotted."*

Scene II

A Bedchamber in the Castle.
Desdemona in bed asleep. A light burning.
Enter Othello.

Othello	It is the cause[1], it is the cause, my soul;
	Let me not name it to you, you chaste stars!
	It is the cause. Yet I'll not shed her blood,
	Nor scar that whiter skin of hers than snow,
	And smooth as monumental alabaster[2].
	Yet she must die, else she'll betray more men.
	Put out the light[3], and then put out the light[4]:
	If I quench thee, thou flaming minister[5],
	I can again thy former light restore
	Should I repent me; but once put out thy light, 10
	Thou cunning'st pattern[6] of excelling nature,
	I know not where is that Promethean heat[7]
	That can thy light relume[8]. When I have pluck'd the rose,
	I cannot give it vital growth again,
	It needs must wither: I'll smell it on the tree.
	[Kisses her.
	O balmy[9] breath, that dost almost persuade
	Justice to break her sword[10]! One more, one more.
	Be thus when thou art dead, and I will kill thee,
	And love thee after. One more, and this the last:
	So sweet was ne'er so fatal. I must weep, 20
	But they are cruel tears; this sorrow's heavenly,
	It strikes where it doth love. She wakes.
Desdemona	Who's there? Othello?
Othello	Ay, Desdemona.
Desdemona	Will you come to bed, my lord?
Othello	Have you pray'd to-night, Desdemona?
Desdemona	Ay, my lord.
Othello	If you bethink yourself of any crime[11]
	Unreconcil'd as yet to heaven and grace[12],
	Solicit for it[13] straight.
Desdemona	Alas! my lord, what may you mean by that?
Othello	Well, do it, and be brief; I will walk by[14]: 30
	I would not kill thy unprepared spirit;
	No; heaven forfend[15]! I would not kill thy soul.
Desdemona	Talk you of killing?
Othello	Ay, I do.
Desdemona	Then heaven
	Have mercy on me!

---

[1] a reason for action; a crime (of infidelity)

[2] plaster

[3] the torch-light
[4] Desdemona's life
[5] torch

[6] well-made example
[7] fire; Prometheus stole the fire from the gods and brought it to earth
[8] restore

[9] soothing
[10] not to do justice; Justice is seen in mythology as a woman with a sword and a scales

[11] sin
[12] unforgiven
[13] pray for forgiveness

[14] nearby

[15] heaven forbid

Othello	Amen! with all my heart.
Desdemona	If you say so, I hope you will not kill me.
Othello	Hum!
Desdemona	And yet I fear you; for you are fatal then
	When your eyes roll so. Why I should fear I know not,
	Since guiltiness I know not; but yet I feel I fear.

Othello   Think on thy sins.   *40*

Desdemona   They are loves I bear to you[16].

Othello   Ay, and for that thou diest.

Desdemona That death's unnatural that kills for loving.
Alas! why gnaw[17] you so your nether[18] lip?
Some bloody passion shakes your very frame[19];
These are portents[20], but yet, I hope, I hope
They do not point on me.

Othello   Peace, and be still!

Desdemona I will so. What's the matter?

Othello   That handkerchief which I so lov'd and gave thee
Thou gav'st to Cassio.

Desdemona   No, by my life and soul!
Send for the man and ask him.   *50*

Othello   Sweet soul, take heed,
Take heed of perjury[21] thou'rt on thy death-bed.

Desdemona Ay, but not yet to die.

Othello   Yes, presently[22];
Therefore confess thee freely of thy sin;
For to deny each article with oath
Cannot remove nor choke the strong conception[23]
That I do groan withal[24]. Thou art to die.

Desdemona Then Lord have mercy on me!

Othello   I say, amen.

Desdemona And have you mercy too! I never did
Offend you in my life; never lov'd Cassio
But with such general warranty of heaven[25]   *60*
As I might love; I never gave him token.

Othello   By heaven, I saw my handkerchief in's[26] hand.
O perjur'd woman! thou dost stone my heart[27],
And mak'st me call what I intend to do
A murder, which I thought a sacrifice:
I saw the handkerchief.

Desdemona   He found it then;
I never gave it him. Send for him hither;
Let him confess a truth.

Othello   He hath confess'd.

Desdemona What, my lord?

Othello   That he hath us'd[28] thee.   *70*

Desdemona   How? unlawfully?

Left margin notes:

[16] my only sins are for love of you (eloping with Othello)

[17] bite
[18] lower
[19] body
[20] signs of disaster

[21] lying on oath

[22] immediately

[23] belief
[24] with

[25] approval of heaven

[26] in his
[27] harden my heart

[28] enjoyed sexually

Othello	Ay.
Desdemona	He will not say so.
Othello	No; his mouth is stopped:

Honest Iago hath ta'en order[29] for't.

Desdemona   O! my fear interprets[30]. What! is he dead?

Othello   Had all his hairs been lives, my great revenge
Had stomach[31] for them all.

Desdemona   Alas! he is betray'd and I undone.

Othello   Out, strumpet! Weep'st thou for him to my face?

Desdemona   O! banish me, my lord, but kill me not!

Othello   Down, strumpet!

Desdemona   Kill me to-morrow; let me live to-night!   *80*

Othello   Nay, if you strive[32], –

Desdemona   But half an hour!

Othello   Being done[33], there is no pause.

Desdemona   But while I say one prayer!

Othello   It is too late.   *[He smothers her.*

Emilia   *[Within.]* My lord, my lord! what, ho! my lord, my lord!

Othello   What noise is this? Not dead? not yet quite dead?
I that am cruel am yet merciful;
I would not have thee linger in thy pain.
So, so.

Emilia   *[Within.]* What, ho! my lord, my lord!

Othello   Who's there?

Emilia   *[Within.]* O! good my lord! I would speak a   *90*
word with you!

Othello   Yes; 'tis Emilia: by and by. She's dead.
'Tis like she comes to speak of Cassio's death;
The noise was high[34]. Ha! no more moving?
Still as the grave. Shall she come in? Were't good?
I think she stirs again: no. What's best to do?
If she come in she'll sure speak to my wife:
My wife! my wife! what wife? I have no wife:
O, insupportable! O heavy[35] hour!
Methinks it should be now a huge eclipse
Of sun and moon, and that the affrighted globe   *100*
Should yawn at alteration[36].

Emilia   *[Within.]* I do beseech you
That I may speak with you, O! good my lord.

Othello   I had forgot thee: O! come in, Emilia:
Soft, by and by: let me the curtains draw.
Where art thou?   *[Unlocks the door.*

Enter Emilia.

---

29 taken steps
30 becomes a reality

31 appetite

32 struggle

33 since it must be done

34 loud

35 woeful

36 the earth should gape in an earthquake at such a momentous event

	What's the matter with thee now?
Emilia	O! my good lord, yonder's foul murder done.
Othello	What! now?
Emilia	But now, my lord.
Othello	It is the very error of the moon[37];
	She comes more near the earth than she was
	wont[38].
	And makes men mad. *110*
Emilia	Cassio, my lord, has kill'd a young Venetian
	Call'd Roderigo.
Othello	Roderigo kill'd!
	And Cassio kill'd?
Emilia	No, Cassio is not kill'd.
Othello	Not Cassio kill'd! then murder's out of tune[39],
	And sweet revenge grows harsh.
Desdemona	O! falsely, falsely murder'd.
Emilia	Alas! what cry is that?
Othello	That! what?
Emilia	Out[40], and alas! that was my lady's voice:
	Help! Help, ho! help! O lady, speak again!
	Sweet Desdemona! O sweet mistress, speak. *120*
Desdemona	A guiltless death I die.
Emilia	O! who hath done this deed?
Desdemona	Nobody; I myself; farewell:
	Commend me to my kind lord. O! farewell! *[Dies.*
Othello	Why, how should she be murder'd?
Emilia	Alas! who knows?
Othello	You heard her say herself it was not I.
Emilia	She said so; I must needs report the truth.
Othello	She's like a liar gone to burning hell;
	'Twas I that kill'd her.
Emilia	O! the more angel she,
	And you the blacker devil. *130*
Othello	She turn'd to folly, and she was a whore.
Emilia	Thou dost belie[41] her, and thou art a devil.
Othello	She was false as water.
Emilia	Thou art rash as fire to say
	That she was false: O! she was heavenly true.
Othello	Cassio did tup[42] her; ask thy husband else[43].
	O! I were damn'd beneath all depth in hell
	But that I did proceed upon just grounds
	To this extremity[44]. Thy husband knew it all.
Emilia	My husband!
Othello	Thy husband. *140*
Emilia	That she was false to wedlock[45]?
Othello	Ay, with Cassio. Nay, had she been true,
	If heaven would make me such another world

[37] deviation of the moon; the moon was said to cause madness
[38] accustomed

[39] out of place

[40] Alas!

[41] accuse falsely

[42] make love to
[43] if it was otherwise

[44] drastic step

[45] unfaithful

	Of one entire and perfect chrysolite[46],
	I'd not have sold her for it.
Emilia	My husband!
Othello	Ay, 'twas he that told me first:
	An honest man he is, and hates the slime
	That sticks on filthy deeds.
Emilia	My husband!
Othello	What needs this iterance[47], woman? I say thy
	husband.
Emilia	O mistress! villainy hath made mocks with
	love.
	My husband say that she was false!
Othello	He, woman;
	I say, thy husband: dost understand the word?
	My friend, thy husband, honest, honest Iago.
Emilia	If he say so, may his pernicious[48] soul
	Rot half a grain a day! he lies to the heart:
	She was too fond of her most filthy bargain.
Othello	Ha!
Emilia	Do thy worst:
	This deed of thine is no more worthy heaven
	Than thou wast worthy her.
Othello	Peace[49]! you were best.
Emilia	Thou hast not half the power to do me harm
	As I have to be hurt. O gull! O dolt[50]!
	As ignorant as dirt! thou hast done a deed, –
	I care not for thy sword; I'll make thee known,
	Though I lost twenty lives. Help! help, ho! help!
	The Moor has kill'd my mistress! Murder!
	murder!

Enter Montano, Gratiano, Iago, and Others.

Montano	What is the matter? How now, general!
Emilia	O! are you come, Iago? you have done well,
	That men must lay their murders on your neck.
Gratiano	What is the matter?
Emilia	Disprove this villain if thou be'st a man:
	He says thou told'st him that his wife was false.
	I know thou didst not, thou'rt not such a villain.
	Speak, for my heart is full[51].
Iago	I told him what I thought, and told no more
	Than what he found himself was apt[52] and true.
Emilia	But did you ever tell him she was false?
Iago	I did.
Emilia	You told a lie, an odious damned lie;
	Upon my soul, a lie, a wicked lie.
	She false with Cassio! Did you say with Cassio?

Line numbers in margin: 150, 160, 170, 180

[46] semi-precious jewel

[47] repetition

[48] villainous

[49] be quiet

[50] fool

[51] full of passion

[52] likely

[53 be silent]	

Iago   With Cassio, mistress. Go to, charm your tongue[53].

Emilia   I will not charm my tongue; I am bound to speak.
My mistress here lies murder'd in her bed.

[54 heavens forbid]

All   O heavens forfend[54]!

[55 instigated the murder]

Emilia   And your reports have set the murder on[55].

Othello Nay, stare not, masters; it is true, indeed.

Gratiano 'Tis a strange truth.

Montano O monstrous act!

Emilia   Villany! villany! villany!
I think upon't, I think, I smell't; O villany!   190
I thought so then; I'll kill myself for grief.
    O! villany, villany!

[56 order]

Iago   What! are you mad? I charge[56] you, get you home.

Emilia   Good gentlemen, let me have leave to speak:
'Tis proper I obey him, but not now.

[57 perhaps]

Perchance[57], Iago, I will ne'er go home.

Othello O! O! O!   *[Falls on the bed.*

Emilia   Nay, lay thee down and roar,
For thou hast kill'd the sweetest innocent
That e'er did lift up eye.

Othello   O! she was foul.
I scarce did know you, uncle. There lies your niece,
Whose breath, indeed, these hands have   200
    newly stopp'd;
I know this act shows terrible and grim.

Gratiano Poor Desdemona! I am glad thy father's dead.

[58 fatal]
[59 cut the thread of his life in two]

Thy match was mortal[58] to him, and pure grief
Shore his old thread in twain[59]: did he live now.

[60 something desperate]

This sight would make him do a desperate turn[60],
Yea, curse his better angel from his side,

[61 damnation]

And fall to reprobation[61].

Othello 'Tis pitiful; but yet Iago knows

[62 adultery]

That she with Cassio hath the act of shame[62]
A thousand times committed; Cassio
    confess'd it: 210

[63 seduction]

And she did gratify his amorous works[63]

[64 token]

With that recognizance[64] and pledge of love
Which I first gave her. I saw it in his hand:
It was a handkerchief, an antique token
My father have my mother.

Emilia   O heaven! O heavenly powers!

[65 be quiet]

Iago   Come, hold your peace[65].

Emilia   'Twill out, 'twill out; I hold my peace, sir? no;

[66 freely]
[67 the north wind]

No, I will speak as liberal[66] as the north[67];
Let heaven and men and devils, let them all,
All, all, cry shame against me, yet I'll speak.   220

Iago   Be wise, and get you home.

Emilia	I will not.
	[Iago offers to stab Emilia.
Gratiano	Fie!
	Your sword upon a woman?
Emilia	O thou dull Moor! that handkerchief thou speak'st of
	I found by fortune and did give my husband;
	For often, with a solemn earnestness,
	More than, indeed, belonged[68] to such a trifle,
	He begg'd of me to steal it.
Iago	Villanous whore!
Emilia	She gives it Cassio! no, alas! I found it,
	And I did give't my husband.
Iago	Filth, thou liest!
Emilia	By heaven, I do not, I do not, gentlemen. 230
	O murderous coxcomb[69]! what should such a fool
	Do with so good a wife?
Othello	Are there no stones[70] in heaven
	But what serve for the thunder? Precious villain!
	[He runs at Iago. Iago stabs Emilia, and exit.
Gratiano	The woman falls: sure, he has kill'd his wife.
Emilia	Ay, ay; O! lay me by my mistress' side.
Gratiano	He's gone; but his wife's kill'd.
Montano	'Tis a notorious villain. Take you this weapon,
	Which I have here recover'd[71] from the Moor.
	Come, guard the door without; let him not pass,
	But kill him rather. I'll after that same villain, 240
	For 'tis a damned slave.
	[Exeunt Montano and Gratiano.
Othello	I am not valiant neither,
	But every puny whipster[72] gets my sword.
	But why should honour outlive honesty[73]?
	Let it go all.
Emilia	What did thy song bode[74], lady?
	Hark, canst thou hear me? I will play the swan[75],
	And die in music: –
	Willow, willow, willow.
	Moor, she was chaste; she lov'd thee, cruel Moor;
	So come my soul to bliss as I speak true;
	So speaking as I think, I die, I die.
	[Dies.
Othello	I have another weapon in this chamber; 250
	It is a sword of Spain, the ice-brook's temper[76].
	O! here it is. Uncle, I must come forth.
Gratiano	*[Within.]* If thou attempt it, it will cost thee dear:
	Thou hast no weapon, and perforce[77] must suffer.

[68] was appropriate

[69] fool

[70] thunderbolts (to punish Iago)

[71] taken

[72] weak troublemaker
[73] why should valour outlive integrity?

[74] foretell
[75] sing before I die

[76] hardened in icy water

[77] necessarily

Othello	Look in upon me then, and speak with me,
	Or, naked[78] as I am, I will assault thee.

Re-enter Gratiano.

Gratiano	What is the matter?
Othello	Behold! I have a weapon;
	A better never did itself sustain
	Upon a soldier's thigh: I have seen the day,
	That with this little arm, and this good sword, *260*
	I have made my way through more impediments
	Than twenty times your stop[79]: but, O vain boast!
	Who can control his fate? 'tis not so now.
	Be not afraid, though you do see me weapon'd;
	Here is my journey's end, here is my butt[80],
	And very sea-mark of my utmost sail[81].
	Do you go back dismay'd? 'tis a lost fear;
	Man but a rush[82] against Othello's breast,
	And he retires. Where should Othello go?
	Now how dost thou look now? O ill-starr'd *270*
	wench[83]!
	Pale as thy smock[84]! when we shall meet at compt[85],
	This look of thine will hurl my soul from heaven,
	And fiends will snatch at it. Cold, cold, my girl!
	Even like thy chastity.
	O! cursed, cursed slave. Whip me, ye devils,
	From the possession of this heavenly sight!
	Blow me about in winds! roast me in sulphur!
	Wash me in steep-down[86] gulfs of liquid fire!
	O Desdemona! Desdemona! dead!
	Oh! Oh! Oh! *280*

Enter Lodovico, Montano, Cassio carried in a chair,
and Officers with Iago, prisoner.

Lodovico	Where is this rash and most unfortunate man?
Othello	That's he that was Othello; here I am.
Lodovico	Where is that viper[87]? bring the villain forth.
Othello	I look down towards his feet; but that's a fable.
	If that thou be'st a devil[88], I cannot kill thee.
	[Wounds Iago.
Lodovico	Wrench his sword from him.
Iago	I bleed, sir; but not kill'd.
Othello	I am not sorry neither; I'd have thee live;
	For, in my sense[89], 'tis happiness to die.
Lodovico	O thou Othello! that wert once so good,
	Fall'n in the practice[90] of a damned slave[91], *290*
	What shall be said to thee?

[78] unarmed

[79] power to stop

[80] goal
[81] destination

[82] wield only a reed

[83] unfortunate woman
[84] night-dress
[85] the Last Judgement

[86] sheer

[87] poisonous snake

[88] the devil was said to have cloven hooves

[89] in my state of mind

[90] victim of the plots
[91] villain

Othello	Why, any thing:
	An honourable murderer, if you will;
	For nought did I in hate, but all in honour.
Lodovico	This wretch hath part confess'd his villany:
	Did you and he consent in Cassio's death?
Othello	Ay.
Cassio	Dear general, I never gave you cause.
Othello	I do believe it, and I ask your pardon.
	Will you, I pray, demand that demi-devil[92]
	Why he hath thus ensnar'd my soul and body? *300*
Iago	Demand me nothing: what you know, you know:
	From this time forth I never will speak word.
Lodovico	What! not to pray?
Gratiano	Torments will ope[93] your lips.
Othello	Well, thou dost best.
Lodovico	Sir, you shall understand what hath befall'n[94],
	Which, as I think, you know not. Here is a letter
	Found in the pocket of the slain Roderigo,
	And here another; the one of them imports[95]
	The death of Cassio to be undertook
	By Roderigo. *310*
Othello	O villain!
Cassio	Most heathenish and most gross[96]!
Lodovico	Now here's another discontented[97] paper,
	Found in his pocket too; and this, it seems,
	Roderigo meant to have sent this damned villain,
	But that, belike[98], Iago in the interim[99]
	Came in and satisfied him.
Othello	O the pernicious caitiff[100]!
	How came you, Cassio, by that handkerchief
	That was my wife's?
Cassio	I found it in my chamber;
	And he himself confess'd but even now
	That there he dropp'd it for a special purpose *320*
	Which wrought to[101] his desire.
Othello	O fool! fool! fool!
Cassio	There is besides in Roderigo's letter
	How he upbraids[102] Iago that he made him
	Brave[103] me upon the watch; whereon it came
	That I was cast[104]: and even but now he spake,
	After long seeming dead, Iago hurt him,
	Iago set him on.
Lodovico	You must forsake this room and go with us;
	Your power and your command is taken off[105],
	And Cassio rules in Cyprus. For this slave, *330*
	If there be any cunning cruelty
	That can torment him much and hold him long[106],

[92] half-man, half-devil

[93] open

[94] happened

[95] suggests

[96] terrible
[97] expressing discontent

[98] it is likely
[99] meanwhile

[100] villainous wretch

[101] served

[102] criticises
[103] defy, provoke
[104] dismissed

[105] removed

[106] keep him alive long

107confined

108wait a moment!

109unfortunate
110tone down

111manipulated

112confused, frustrated

113grief-stricken

114although
115crying

116myrrh
117Alexandria
118rebellious
119betrayed
120Moslem

121ending
122ruined

123fierce dog
124cruel

125possessions

126sentence and punishment

127tragic, woeful
128sad, grief-stricken

Othello

It shall be his. You shall close107 prisoner rest.
Till that the nature of your fault be known
To the Venetian state. Come, bring him away.
Soft you108; a word or two before you go.
I have done the state some service, and they
    know't;
No more of that. I pray you, in your letters,
When you shall these unlucky109 deeds relate,
Speak of me as I am; nothing extenuate110,   *340*
Nor set down aught in malice: then, must you
    speak
Of one that lov'd not wisely but too well;
Of one not easily jealous, but, being wrought111,
Perplex'd112 in the extreme; of one whose hand,
Like the base Indian, threw a pearl away
Richer than all his tribe; of one whose subdu'd113
    eyes
Albeit114 unused to the melting mood115,
Drop tears as fast as the Arabian trees
Their med'cinable gum116. Set you down this;
And say besides, that in Aleppo117 once,   *350*
Where a malignant118 and a turban'd Turk
Beat a Venetian and traduc'd119 the state,
I took by the throat the circumcised120 dog.
And smote him thus.
                              [Stabs himself.

Lodovico   O bloody period121!
Gratiano   All that's spoke is marr'd122.
Othello   I kiss'd thee ere I kill'd thee; no way but this,
                              [Falling upon Desdemona.
Killing myself to die upon a kiss.   *[Dies.*

Cassio   This did I fear, but thought he had no weapon;
                    For he was great of heart.   *360*

Lodovico   *[To Iago]* O Spartan dog123!
                    More fell124 than anguish, hunger, or the sea.
                    Look on the tragic loading of this bed;
                    This is thy work; the object poisons sight;
                    Let it be hid. Gratiano, keep the house,
                    And seize upon the fortunes125 of the Moor,
                    For they succeed on you. To you, lord governor,
                    Remains the censure126 of this hellish villain,
                    The time, the place, the torture; O! enforce it.
                    Myself will straight aboard, and to the state *370*
                    This heavy127 act with heavy128 heart relate.
                              Exeunt.

The Plot
(Day Three – A Bedchamber in the Castle)

OTHELLO'S FATAL RESOLUTION

In her room Desdemona is sleeping as Othello enters. Othello convinces himself that it is not jealousy that drives him to kill her but a sense of justice to prevent her from further wrongdoing. He is overcome by her beauty but his tears are cruel tears and he is determined to kill her.

OTHELLO SMOTHERS DESDEMONA

When Desdemona awakens, Othello tells her to pray. She realises he intends to kill her but does not feel guilty of any crime. Othello accuses her of giving her handkerchief as a love-token to Cassio and says that Cassio has confessed to their love and is dead. She is horrified that Cassio cannot clear her name but Othello thinks she is grieving for her lover. Despite her pleas, he smothers her, as mercifully as he can.

DESDEMONA DIES FOR LOVE

Emilia comes in with news of Roderigo's murder. Othello is appalled to think that Cassio has escaped Desdemona's fate. Desdemona, dying, protests her innocence of any crime but shields Othello from blame. Othello claims she is a liar gone to hell and confesses that he killed her.

EMILIA DISCOVERS THE TRUTH

Emilia accuses Othello of rashness. He explains that he killed Desdemona for having a love-affair with Cassio, as Iago can confirm. Emilia is horrified to learn of her husband's role in Desdemona's murder. She abuses Othello and Iago for what has happened and cries out for help.

EMILIA EXPOSES IAGO

Emilia's cries are answered by Montano, Gratiano and Iago. Emilia accuses Iago of villainy and he admits he told Othello about Cassio and Desdemona. He tries to quieten Emilia, but she defies him and criticises Othello. Othello claims to Gratiano, Desdemona's uncle, that he killed her for being unfaithful to him with Cassio.

Emilia explains how she found the handkerchief and gave it to Iago. Iago denies this, but Othello attacks Iago and is disarmed. Iago stabs Emilia and runs away. Montano pursues Iago and Gratiano prevents Othello's escape. Emilia dies protesting Desdemona's innocence.

Yet I'll not shed her blood,
Nor scar that whiter skin of her than snow.

(Othello, Act 5, Scene II)

IAGO'S VILLAINY IS REVEALED

Othello finds another sword and tells Gratiano that he will not fight against anyone. He regrets killing Desdemona and wishes to be punished severely. Iago is brought in a prisoner and Cassio is carried in on a chair. Othello wounds Iago with his sword and asks Cassio's forgiveness for what he has done, saying he acted in honour not in malice. Iago refuses to explain why he plotted against Othello.

Lodovico clarifies the matter by producing two letters from Roderigo's pockets. In the first letter, Iago explained to Roderigo how he was to kill Cassio. The second letter, which was not sent, contained Roderigo's complaints against Iago. Cassio explains how he found the handkerchief and how Roderigo's letter told how Iago had persuaded him to start the brawl, which led to Cassio's dismissal.

RETRIBUTION

Lodovico tells Othello that he is to be a prisoner until Venice decides his future. Cassio is to be governor of Cyprus and Iago is to be punished as he deserves.

Before they go, Othello is allowed to speak. He recalls his service to the state and wishes to be remembered not as a murderer but as one who was manipulated and misguided. Recalling an incident where he stabbed a Turk, he kills himself with his sword and falls upon Desdemona's bed. Cassio speaks kindly of him.

Lodovico closes the play with a speech condemning Iago to extreme torture and giving Othello's possessions to Gratiano.

Dramatic Significance

THE CATASTROPHE

Desdemona is asleep as Othello enters the room as her executioner. He is clear that justice demands her death:

> *"Yet she must die, else she'll betray more men."*

Yet his love wishes to spare her life.

> *"O balmy breath, that doth almost persuade
> Justice to break her sword."*

He weeps but his tears are *"cruel tears"* and his resolution stands firm.

When Desdemona wakes, his forced composure hides his inner anxiety, as he questions her harshly and reminds her to pray for forgiveness. He charges her, like a harsh judge, with betraying him by giving the handkerchief to Cassio. When she denies betraying him, he believes she is damning her soul, by lying on her death-bed.

Alas! he is betray'd and I undone.   (Desdemona, Act 5, Scene II)

Finally he reveals to her that Cassio confessed that she was unfaithful and that Cassio is dead. She expresses great concern that Cassio cannot now clear her name. Othello sees her concern as an admission of her infidelity and smothers her in a frenzy of impatience:

> *"Out, strumpet! Weep'st thou for him to my face?"*

Now that justice is done, as Othello thinks, he tries to be merciful and ensures that she dies as painlessly as possible:

> *"I that am cruel am yet merciful;*
> *I would not have thee linger in thy pain."*

Realising that she is dead, he laments the loss of his love in a fit of grief:

> *"My wife! my wife! my wife? I have no wife:*
> *O, insupportable! O heavy hour!"*

OTHELLO'S ILLUSIONS ARE SHATTERED

Later, Desdemona revives in the presence of Emilia and excuses Othello from blame:

> *"Nobody; I myself; farewell:*
> *Commend me to my kind lord."*

Othello takes responsibility for killing Desdemona but claims to Emilia that she was *"a liar gone to burning hell"*. He killed her because she betrayed his love with Cassio:

> *"I did proceed upon just grounds*
> *To this extremity. Thy husband knew it all."*

When Emilia later reveals the truth about the handkerchief, Othello finally loses his illusions that he acted in justice, since he now knows that Desdemona was true to him:

> *"Are there no stones in heaven*
> *But what serve for the thunder? Precious villain!"*

OTHELLO TAKES RESPONSIBILITY

Othello realises that he has betrayed his own integrity:

> *"Why should honour outlive honesty?"*

He would welcome death:

> *"Here is my journey's end, here is my butt."*

He feels guilty for killing his beloved and chaste Desdemona:

> *"This look of thine will hurl my soul from heaven,*
> *And fiends will snatch at it. Cold, cold, my girl!*
> *Even like thy chastity.*
> *O! cursed, cursed slave!"*

From this time forth I never will speak word.
                                    (Iago, Act 5, Scene II)

He desires that retribution should fall on him for his betrayal of love:

> *"Blow me about in winds! roast me in sulphur!*
> *Wash me in steep-down gulfs of liquid fire!*
> *O Desdemona, Desdemona! dead!*
> *Oh! Oh! Oh!"*

OTHELLO CONFRONTS THE REALITY

Othello has already learned, before his final speech, that Desdemona has been faithful to him and that he murdered her, through his own jealous rage, imposed on him by Iago's villainy. In his final speech, Othello reaches a peak of clear judgement about himself and his situation. He tries to evaluate for us his qualities and his weaknesses of character as he begins to discover and understand his real self:

- He recognises that he loved *"too well"* but lacked wisdom and insight into love and the one he loved.

- He realises that he was not prone to jealousy but that he became extremely confused about his own real feelings, when *"wrought"* by Iago's cunning attacks on his weaknesses.

- He regrets that he rashly threw away the *"pearl"* of most value to him – Desdemona and her pure love.

- He takes responsibility for the consequences of his actions and grieves in atonement for them.

- He recognises his part in the betrayal of his love and kills himself to undo this betrayal. He sees himself as the *"turban'd Turk"* (pagan) who beat a Venetian (Christian), i.e. as one who undermined Christian values.

Othello dies just as he begins to discover what he most needed to learn in order to avert tragedy – more insight into his own character and a better understanding of others and of the ways of love. Othello's death is tragic, since he is now powerless to undo the unnecessary catastrophe he has helped to cause. Just as Othello begins to learn the true reality of his life, he dies by his own hand, in an attempt to recover what he has so cruelly and tragically lost forever.

THE UNMASKING OF IAGO

As soon as Othello asserts, *"thy husband knew it all"*, Emilia realises that her husband's villainy has caused Othello's fury and Desdemona's death. At great risk to herself she defies Iago and denounces him:

> *"Let heaven and men and devils, let them all,*
> *All, all, cry shame against me, yet I'll speak."*

Here's my journey's end, here is my butt,
And very sea-mark of my utmost sail.

(Othello, Act 5, Scene II)

She finally exposes his villainy dramatically:

> *"O thou dull Moor! that handkerchief thou speak'st of*
> *I found by fortune and did give my husband;*
> *For often, with a solemn earnestness,*
> *More than, indeed, belonged to such a trifle,*
> *He begg'd of me to steal it."*

Iago's cunning schemes are stopped by the one person who he thought posed no threat to him. His false sense of security has finally thwarted him. He then gives the game away by trying to stab Emilia and then running away. The letters in Roderigo's pockets confirm his guilt and Iago is finally reduced to a sullen silence:

> *"From this time forth I never will speak word."*

Retribution catches up with Iago in the form of slow torture:

> *"... For this slave,*
> *if there be any cunning cruelty*
> *That can torment him much and hold him long,*
> *It shall be his."*

We feel that no punishment can match the irreversible harm that Iago's villainy has wrought.

Character Development
OTHELLO
COLD JUSTICE

At first Othello is composed and in control of his emotions, as he tries to justify killing Desdemona. Despite his love, he knows that she must die for her infidelity:

> *"O balmy breath, that dost almost persuade*
> *Justice to break her sword! Once more, one more.*
> *Be thus when thou art dead, and I will kill thee,*
> *And love thee after. One more, and this the last."*

He hardens himself to Desdemona's protestations of love:

> *"O perjur'd woman! thou dost stone my heart,*
> *And mak'st me call what I intend to do*
> *A murder, which I thought a sacrifice:*
> *I saw the handkerchief."*

Even when he has killed her, he continues to maintain the justice of his action:

> *"I did proceed upon just grounds*
> *To this extremity. Thy husband knew it all."*

He sees himself as a just executioner not a murderer.

INNER TURMOIL

Within Othello's mind, love and resolution compete for supremacy and his outward calm hides his inner agitation. As he questions Desdemona, he is trying to strengthen his resolve to kill her for justice sake. Finally, it is on impulse that he kills her, believing that she has confessed to infidelity with Cassio:

> "Out, strumpet! Weep'st thou for him to my face?"

Yet the killing is, in a sense, an act of perverted love. Othello allows Desdemona time to repent of her sins and is merciful in ensuring that she dies without too much pain:

> "I that am cruel am yet merciful;
> I would not have thee linger in thy pain."

He declares his love in his first soliloquy:

> "So sweet was ne'er so fatal. I must weep,
> But they are cruel tears; this sorrow's heavenly,
> It strikes where it doth love."

RESPONSIBILITY

Later Othello accepts responsibility for killing Desdemona:

> "There lies your niece,
> Whose breath, indeed, these hands have newly stopp'd;
> I know this act shows terrible and grim."

When Iago is exposed, Othello desires to atone for the death of Desdemona:

> "Wash me in steep-down gulfs of liquid fire!
> O Desdemona! Desdemona! dead!
> Oh! oh! oh!"

He apologises to Cassio for wronging him:

> "I do believe it, and I ask your pardon."

RECOGNITION

Othello recognises his mistaken judgements:

> "Why should honour outlive honesty?"

He sees himself as honourable but still a murderer:

> "An honourable murderer, if you will;
> For nought did I in hate, but all in honour."

Othello regains some of his former nobility and greatness.

In his final soliloquy Othello shows clearer judgement and the beginning of insight into his own character:

> *"Then, must you speak*
> *Of one that lov'd not wisely but too well;*
> *Of one not easily jealous, but, being wrought,*
> *Perplex'd in the extreme; of one whose hand,*
> *Like the base Indian, threw a pearl away*
> *Richer than all his tribe."*

He has just begun to learn what he most needed to know in order to avert the tragic destruction of his love and life.

RECONCILIATION AND REDEMPTION

Othello dies loving Desdemona and attempting a spiritual reconciliation with her as he confronts his fate:

> *"I kiss'd thee ere I kill'd thee; no way but this,*
> *Killing myself to die upon a kiss."*

He redeems himself through his suffering and death but tragically he is powerless to undo the disaster which has befallen:

> *"He was great of heart."*

IAGO

AN UNREDEEMED VILLAIN

When Emilia reveals Iago's evil schemes, he continues to show utter contempt for her:

> *"Villanous whore ...*
> *... Filth, thou liest:"*

He shows no regret for his ruthless destruction of others but is reduced to a contemptuous silence:

> *"Demand me nothing: what you know, you know:*
> *From this time forth I never will speak word."*

Othello regards him as a demon:

> *"If that thou be'st a devil, I cannot kill thee."*

Iago will not speak even to pray. He is amoral and beyond redemption. No punishment can atone for his crimes:

> *"if there be any cunning cruelty*
> *That can torment him much and hold him long,*
> *It shall be his."*

Tragically he has triumphed, since the pure Desdemona and the noble Othello are now dead at his instigation. His evil deeds cannot be undone nor his evil genius outdone:

> *"O Spartan dog!*
> *More fell than anguish, hunger, or the sea.*
> *Look on the tragic loading of this bed;*
> *This is thy work; the object poisons sight;*
> *Let it be hid."*

DESDEMONA
A LOVING SACRIFICE

Desdemona retains her love for Othello, despite his actions against her:

> *"They are loves I bear to you."*

Gently she tries to convince Othello of her innocence:

> *"... guiltiness I know not; but yet I feel I fear."*

She pleads for her life, at last realising that there is a foul plot against her:

> *"Alas, he is betray'd and I undone."*

As she dies she declares her innocence:

> *"A guiltless death I die."*

Desdemona's death is a selfless sacrifice for love. She dies defending Cassio and protecting Othello from blame:

> *"Nobody; I myself; farewell:*
> *Commend me to my kind lord."*

She dies as she lived, a paragon of love and virtue:

> *"O! she was heavenly true!"*

EMILIA
THE COURAGE OF CONVICTION

Emilia fearlessly defends Desdemona's honour against both Othello and Iago:

> *"O! the more angel she,*
> *And you the blacker devil!"*

She realises that villainy has been done but is slow to realise that Iago was the instigator of it:

> *"Villany, villany, villany!"*

When Emilia realises the significance of the handkerchief, she denounces Othello and Iago courageously:

> *"O murderous coxcomb! what should such a fool*
> *Do with so good a wife?"*

Iago stabs her, and she dies with honour, having vindicated Desdemona:

I never did offend you in my life.   (Desdemona, Act 5, Scene II)

"Moor, she was chaste; she lov'd thee, cruel Moor;
So come my soul to bliss as I speak true."

CASSIO
FORGIVENESS

Cassio has been wounded and takes little part in the events of the final scene.
He gracefully forgives Othello for wronging him:

"Dear general, I never give you cause."

He shows his admiration for Othello's nobility:

"This did I fear, but thought he had no weapon;
For he was great of heart."

Cassio denounces Iago's villainy as

"Most heathenish and most gross!"

He reveals Roderigo's evidence against Iago, which finally unmasks the silent Iago. It is he
who has the unwholesome task of punishing Iago, as the new Governor of Cyprus.

LODOVICO, MONTANO AND GRATIANO
THE VOICES OF NORMALITY

These minor characters play minor roles in the scene and throw the light of common sense
on the dramatic events. They highlight the tragedy of Desdemona's murder and the villainy
of Iago, and help to restore Cyprus to normality.

Part 3

Further Study

Tragedy

Man's Tragic Sense

The genre of tragedy reflects a view of life which we all share to some degree. Tragedy portrays the precariousness of man's existence and attempts to find answers to man's quest for truth and meaning in his life. The great literary and dramatic tragedies, of which *Othello* is one, raise fundamental questions about the meaning of human existence and the mystery of suffering and death, and attempt to explore answers to such important and basic questions. In the great works of tragedy, we are exposed to the anguish of man's own quest for meaning in life and, in the process, we may learn much about ourselves and the conditions of our human existence on earth. Tragedy expresses and portrays man's deepest visions of human life and so opens up the paths to man's ultimate happiness and redemption, despite the precarious world in which he lives.

What Is Tragedy?

Tragedy, as a literary or dramatic genre, has continued to evolve and be refined, from the time of Aristotle and the Greek tragedy-writers, Sophocles and Euripides. Despite many attempts to define tragedy, since Aristotle's first attempt in the *Poetics*, tragedy continues to elude precise definition. Reflecting on the great classical tragedies and the more down-to-earth modern tragedies, we realise that the only real common factor they both possess is that they reflect or embody a tragic process or pattern which is inherent in human life. Yet there is a vast difference between the *Hecuba* of Euripides, Shakespeare's *"great"* tragedies, and Beckett's *Waiting for Godot,* which are all regarded as tragedy.

The Tragic Hero

The tragic hero or heroine should command our **earnest goodwill**. He or she need not be a king/queen or superhuman, but should command our respect, so that we can identify with them in the course of action they undertake, and sympathise with them in the tragic consequences of their action.

Usually the tragic hero will possess some flaw (**hamartia**) in character or judgement, which may initiate or partly cause the catastrophe that befalls the hero in a tragedy. This flaw emphasises the humanity of the hero and earns our sympathy for the plight of a human being, caught like us in the web of human existence.

The Tragic Process

The hero, in a tragedy, should undertake a serious course of action of some importance, which will, through a series of actions, lead to some grave suffering or misfortune, usually death in extreme circumstances **(catastrophe)**.

In the world in which the hero undertakes the tragic course of action, it should be credible that the actions undertaken should lead, with some **sense of inevitability**, to the misfortunes incurred by the hero. Accidental misfortunes do not make great tragedies.

In *"great"* tragedies also, the hero will usually realise his own part in bringing about his misfortunes **(recognition)**. He need not necessarily cause his catastrophe, but he should at least recognise that he is somehow caught on a path to inevitable disaster and that his own judgements or actions have contributed to his plight.

The Tragic Sense

A tragedy should arouse in an audience tragic emotions of *"pity and fear"* and should lead to a release or purging of these emotions **(catharsis)**. Usually an audience's emotions will be heightened, because the extent of the disaster which befalls the hero will be out of all proportion to what the hero's human failings or actions deserve. The release or refining of these heightened emotions will usually come through our relief that the hero's sufferings are over and our hope that a better future is ahead.

In summary then, in a tragedy, a hero, whom we respect, undertakes a serious course of action, which leads inevitably to catastrophe, through a credible sequence of events, involving reversals of fortune and recognition of his situation by the hero himself, and the audience experiences heightened emotions of pity and fear, which are refined with a note of hope for the future.

Shakespearean Tragedy

Shakespeare gradually shaped his own kind of tragedy, from *Romeo and Juliet* and *Richard III* to *Julius Caesar* and *Hamlet* and, in 1604, *Othello*. *Othello* is sometimes classified as a *"domestic"* tragedy, distinguished for its directness and simplicity in plot.

Shakespearean tragedy involves the ruin and death of a man of outstanding greatness and intensity of spirit, by the interaction of an outward hostile environment with some weakness in his own character. Sometimes the hero's noblest and most outstanding qualities contribute to his ruin.

Othello as a Tragedy

Othello is outstanding among Shakespeare's tragedies in that the situation which becomes tragic is invented by Iago. A tragedy based on a fatal misunderstanding by the hero is all the more heart-rending. Our deepest sympathy and understanding are evoked for Othello in his predicament. What *Othello* may lack in scope and depth of vision, it provides in psychological insight into human character and motivation. For all these reasons, *Othello* is outstanding among Shakespeare's great tragedies and cannot but appeal to any audience.

The Tragic Process in *Othello*

A Serious Course of Action

It is difficult to define what purpose or course of action Othello undertakes that leads to the catastrophe. Othello, a Moor, impetuously elopes and marries a noble Venetian lady. He undertakes to command the defence of Cyprus and Christian society against the threat of the Turks and paganism. He undertakes to listen to a friend he believes honest, in order to know the truth about his lieutenant's and his wife's conduct. All this is admirable and natural behaviour on Othello's part – designed to be loving, patriotic and fair to all around him:

> *"My parts, my title, and my perfect soul*
> *Shall manifest me rightly."*   Othello (Act 1, Scene II)

The Environment of Tragedy

Even before Othello initiates any action that might lead to disaster, the world in which he lives, particularly that of Iago and Roderigo, begins to assert its influence on his destiny:

> *"Call up her father;*
> *Rouse him, make after him, poison his delight,*
> *Proclaim him in the street, incense her kinsmen,*
> *And, though he in a fertile climate dwell,*
> *Plague him with flies; though that his joy be joy,*
> *Yet throw such changes of vexation on't,*
> *As it may lose some colour."*   Iago (Act 1, Scene I)

Thus it is Iago who initiates the series of actions which will culminate in Othello's ruin.

Tragic Inevitability

Iago's determination and outstanding skill in orchestrating events and in devising schemes to manipulate Othello's mind and emotions make disaster likely if not inevitable:

"And nothing can or shall content my soul
Till I am even'd with him, wife for wife;
Or failing so, yet that I put the Moor
At least into a jealousy so strong
That judgment cannot cure."

Iago (Act 2, Scene I)

Iago is persistent in preying on Othello's character and gives him no chance to look at events realistically. Successively he bombards Othello:

- with insinuations and half-truths about Desdemona's infidelity with Cassio

- with the circumstantial evidence of Cassio's dream and the handkerchief

- and finally with the more direct proof in Cassio's alleged confession and an orchestrated conversation with Cassio, which Othello overhears.

All these, coupled with Othello's free and open nature, make tragedy inevitable.

Reversals of Fortune

The more Othello tries to disentangle himself from Iago's web of deceit, the more he becomes entangled. Each time common sense begins to prevail, Iago asserts his power over Othello's mind.

In Act 3 Scene III, Othello asserts:

"If she be false, O! then heaven mocks itself,
I'll not believe it."

and

"Avaunt! be gone! thou hast set me on the rack."

However, Iago reaffirms Othello's conviction of Desdemona's infidelity using the invented evidence of Cassio's dream and the handkerchief, which Iago just now happens to have received from Emilia.

"Such a handkerchief –
I am sure it was your wife's – did I to-day
See Cassio wipe his beard with."

Iago (Act 3, Scene III)

Iago's evidence and his good luck that Desdemona has lost her handkerchief effectively eliminate any possibility of Othello's recovery of his senses.

Lucky coincidences, such as Bianca's timely entry with the handkerchief (Act 4, Scene I) or Desdemona's inopportune pleas for Cassio (Act 3, Scenes III and IV), contribute to the success of Iago's schemes. Throughout the play, Iago's ingenuity, Othello's personality and these coincidences combine to defeat Othello's efforts to recover his sense of reality.

Recognition and Catastrophe

Othello's catastrophe is not so much his own suicide but the mental agony he suffers. He realises that Desdemona is dead and cannot be brought to life:

> *"My wife! my wife! what wife? I have no wife:*
> *O, insupportable! O heavy hour!"*   *Othello (Act 5, Scene II)*

He sees at last that his own corrupted love has caused this disaster:

> *"This look of thine will hurl my soul from heaven,*
> *And fiends will snatch at it. Cold, cold, my girl!*
> *Even like thy chastity.*
> *O! cursed, cursed slave. Whip me, ye devils,*
> *From the possession of this heavenly sight!*
> *Blow me about in winds, roast me in sulphur!*
> *Wash me in steep-down gulfs of liquid fire!*
> *O Desdemona! Desdemona! dead!*
> *Oh! oh! oh!"*   *Othello (Act 5, Scene II)*

He dies repentant and reconciled to his love, but powerless to undo the catastrophe he has caused:

> *"I kiss'd thee ere I kill'd thee; no way but this,*
> *Killing myself to die upon a kiss."*   *Othello (Act 5, Scene II)*

The good must suffer even if the evil are justly punished.

Othello as a Tragic Hero

Othello fits the Shakespearean mould of a tragic hero. However, he is not a king or prince nor is his *"tragic flaw"*, which contributes to the tragedy, easily identifiable. Nevertheless his character has potential for tragedy.

Status and Position

Othello is of royal lineage and is commander of the Venetian armed forces. His status and position qualify him as a fit hero of a tragedy. Apart from this, he is noble and upright in character and attitude. He is an outsider to Venetian society and is at a disadvantage because of this. He easily earns our sympathy and understanding for all of these reasons.

> *"For he was great of heart."*   *Cassio (Act 5, Scene II)*

Tragic Flaws

Othello is human and it is his human traits and failings that prove to be his undoing at the skilful hands of merciless Iago. While Othello does not undertake any action, which is sufficient to cause tragedy, he shows some natural flaws of knowledge and of character, which make him an easy prey to Iago, the agent of tragedy.

Flaws of Knowledge

Othello's skill and knowledge are second to none in military affairs, but he lacks knowledge of his own character and feelings. He is therefore an easy prey to doubts and unfounded fears.

Othello's experience of life is extensive as regards adventure and military campaigns, but he has little experience of women, love or sexual relationships. This breeds insecurity and makes him an easy target for unfounded jealousy, created by Iago's cunning.

Flaws of Character and Judgement

Othello is egoistic and justly proud of his own position and military achievements and especially of his own wife's choice of him as a husband. Thus he is vulnerable to any attack on what he values highly.

Othello, as a military man, prides himself on his firmness and fairness. This leads him to act rashly and impulsively to vindicate his authority and reputation (as he does in dismissing Cassio and *"executing"* Desdemona).

Othello has a free and open nature, which makes him a little credulous of others, and is easily manipulated by the honest-seeming Iago. He is not easily jealous, so that, when he is made jealous by Iago's deception, he is all the more vehement and furious.

Othello cannot cope with uncertainty and greatly desires to be sure of others, especially those he loves. Iago's technique in Act 3, Scene III seems to be geared towards using this trait especially to manipulate Othello's mind. It is Othello's desire to be sure that clinches Iago's entrapment of him:

> *"Avaunt! be gone! thou hast set me on the rack;*
> *I swear 'tis better to be much abus'd*
> *Than but to know't a little."*

In this sense, it is Othello himself who implores Iago to convince him of the truth and thereby trap him in his web of deceit:

> *"Make me to see 't, or, at the least, so prove it,*
> *That the probation bear no hinge nor loop*
> *To hang a doubt on; or woe upon thy life!"*

It is this *"flaw"* of Othello around which the others revolve which makes Othello accessible to Iago's manipulations.

Tragic Emotions

As Othello dies, an audience must have many conflicting feelings. We pity Othello that he has been driven to such extremes of spiritual suffering. We sympathise with him that he has lost what we too prize highly – love, happiness and life. We feel horror and fear that the world is such a place that misfortune may come to those who least deserve to suffer. We are relieved that Othello is now beyond suffering and we hope that the future will hold better fortune for all of us, without requiring from us the same extremities of suffering and endurance. In general, our emotions reach a high pitch, as we witness the tragic waste of goodness, and are refined, not so much with a note of hope for the future as with a sense of the tragic nature of the world in which we live, a place where a simple misunderstanding may be fatal and bring a great catastrophe:

> "O, insupportable! O heavy hour!
> Methinks it should be now a huge eclipse
> Of sun and moon, and that the affrighted globe
> Should yawn at alteration."

The Themes of *Othello*

Shakespeare hardly wrote *Othello* according to some preconceived ideas or themes. He was primarily an actor and a dramatist, who explored life's meaning by creating plots and characters. Through the interaction of the characters with each other, as they weave the plot, we may glimpse a little of the meaning of life's ups and downs.

Theme-hunting is a poor substitute for the total experience of the drama of *Othello*. However, an understanding of the issues or themes raised in *Othello* should serve to enrich our appreciation of the dramatic experience.

Some general guidelines follow, but the student should think for himself/herself and form an individual viewpoint.

All the themes listed are closely interrelated. The opposition between evil and good is exemplified in the conflict between hate and love. Deception and dishonesty are particular aspects of hatred and are the root causes of jealousy and misunderstanding, which in turn lead to passion and revenge.

Good and Evil

This theme is a basic theme in *Othello* and is inherent in the characters on a symbolic level.

- Iago is the prime agent of evil, almost a devil.
- Desdemona is pure and good, almost an angel.

- Othello is noble, loving and good, but is corrupted and turned towards evil by Iago.
- Cassio and Emilia embody varying shades of goodness, especially loyalty and devotion to their master and mistress.
- Roderigo is Iago's ally in evil.

Each character performs his or her own particular style of good or evil actions and examples are easily identifiable from the notes after each scene and from the scenes themselves.

Love and Hate

This theme brings the previous theme down to earth in the form of characters whose basic drive is hate or love. There are many different shades of love and hate in *Othello*.

- The marriage relationship of Othello and Desdemona is built on a romantic, idealistic and spiritual affinity for each other.
- Iago and Emilia are an estranged husband and wife – Iago has contempt for Emilia and cheats on her, while Emilia feels degraded by Iago, yet she tries to please him.
- Cassio seems to have some affection for Bianca, but does not intend to marry her.
- Bianca seems infatuated by Cassio, yet she sells her love for money.
- Desdemona shows loving concern for Cassio and Cassio displays admiration and respectful friendship towards her.
- Roderigo professes love for Desdemona, which is really lust and self-love.
- Cassio admires Othello and Emilia shows devotion for Desdemona.
- Othello's love for Desdemona is corrupted by jealousy, aroused in him by Iago's hatred and spite.

Deception, Trust, Misunderstanding

These are central themes in *Othello*, as the tragedy is caused by the fatal misunderstanding on Othello's part, based on Iago's deception.

- Othello is free and open and trusts Iago's honesty: Iago is deceitful in the extreme and betrays Othello's trust.
- Cassio and Desdemona show their loyalty to Othello and Emilia is loyal to Desdemona.
- Desdemona is innocent and naive: Emilia is deceitful and worldly-wise.
- Iago disguises his hatred and spite in a false mask of honesty. Desdemona projects her true personality throughout the play.
- Othello is deceived into believing Iago's false insinuations about Desdemona's

infidelity with Cassio. He deceives himself, when he asserts that he is not jealous and when he believes that Desdemona's murder is an act of justice. This fatal misunderstanding is central to the tragedy of *Othello* and might be regarded as the principal theme.

Jealousy and Revenge

This theme is central to the tragedy since it is jealousy, a fatal tension between love and loathing for Desdemona, which leads to Othello's tragic plan of revenge on the forgiving Desdemona.

- Othello becomes jealous of Desdemona, through Iago's deceptive schemes, and performs vengeance on her by murdering her in bed. Othello also plans the murder of Cassio in revenge for his seduction of Desdemona.
- Iago envies Cassio and Othello and devises schemes of vengeance on them throughout the play.
- Roderigo is jealous of Othello's marriage to Desdemona.
- Bianca is jealous when she suspects Cassio received the handkerchief as a love-token from some other woman.

Other Themes

Many more recurring themes are raised in *Othello,* both in word and in action, and are well worth exploration:

- Power: is a thirst for power Iago's main motivation?
- Reason versus Passion: Iago is coldly rational – Othello is charming and passionate.
- The Nature of Knowledge: various kinds of knowledge.
- Violence and War: fights, brawls, war, blows, murder and suicide.
- Race and Prejudice: Othello is a Moor in sophisticated Venetian society.
- The Role and Status of Women in society.
- Love and Lust.
- The Nature of Evil and Villainy.
- Christian values versus Pagan values.
- Justice and Retribution.
- Crime and Punishment.
- Reputation and Self-Image.

Shakespeare's Craftsmanship

Over the years, since Shakespeare wrote his great tragedies, his mastery of the English language and of dramatic craft has continued to highlight his unique talents. Not only were his plays a sound basis for the subsequent development of drama, but he also helped to develop the English language by adding new words and meanings to Elizabethan English. The Elizabethan Period was a time of transition and expansion for the English language. Elizabethan English was abandoning inflections in words and adopting and coining many new words. Foreign words as well as Classical Latin and Greek words expanded and enriched the English language. Shakespeare's English, with its emphasis on energy, clarity and vigour, rather than on correct grammar and syntax, was a major stage in building up Modern English with its rich suggestiveness and creative power.

Shakespeare's craftsmanship in *Othello* is remarkable in three distinct but interrelated areas:

1. His skilful arrangement and manipulation of plot to express his themes and vision of life, to develop his lifelike characters and to create a mood and atmosphere suitable for his purposes.

2. His deep insight into human character and motivation and his skill in delineating real characters, who are credible in any age.

3. His creative use of language, imagery and rhythm to develop his themes, to create atmosphere and to portray character.

These three areas are well worth exploration by the serious student for the Leaving Certificate, who might perhaps be enticed by the following guidelines to select his/her own examples and passages from *Othello*, to examine and discuss them and to achieve an individual view. The approach in this section is necessarily selective, as reams of research and writing would be required in order to attempt to be definitive or dogmatic on these topics. What is aimed for here is not long-winded scholarship, but some "tools of the trade" to help the student to form a personal opinion.

1. Skilful Arrangement of Plot

Many aspects of Shakespeare's skill in weaving the plot of *Othello* have been referred to in earlier sections in this book – his skilful use of the five-part structure of Classical Drama; his skilful use of the traditional elements in the plot of a tragedy. These might be re-examined here by the student. However, there is much more to Shakespeare's skill with plot than these important aspects.

(a) Cinematic Movement

Shakespeare's arrangement of scenes involves constant movement and changes of scene. Contrasting scenes flash back and forth between the principal characters, weaving an intricate web of relationships and ensuring continuing tension and development.

Our avid interest is maintained throughout, as if we were present and involved in the developing drama. An air of inevitability is achieved, as action leads to action and the events of the play, whether arranged by Iago or coincidental, begin to establish a pattern. As we watch the three-dimensional picture created by Shakespeare's skill, we identify with the fortunes of Othello and Desdemona, and condemn the villain, whose sly schemes seek to destroy the love and happiness of our heroes.

(b) Foreshadowing

Events that happen earlier in the play can assume a new significance later on and so it is necessary to focus the audience's minds and emotions on where events are leading. The simple device of foreshadowing, or creating a general mood that hints at what is to happen, is a technique which helps to add an air of expectancy to the unfolding drama: examples are frequent in *Othello*:

— Act 1, Scene I foreshadows Othello's entry in the following scene. Othello is mentioned constantly by Iago, Roderigo and Brabantio. The vague information we receive about Othello whets our curiosity to meet him and to judge for ourselves whether their low opinion of him is true.

— Act 1, Scene II prepares us for the scene in the Council Chamber, where the Duke will sort out the animosity between Othello and Brabantio.

(c) Suspense

Suspense is the opposite to foreshadowing. It is a device to heighten our anxiety that events will turn out more happily than we fear for our heroes.

Iago's many conversations, towards the end of various scenes, make us curious as to what he will do against Othello and anxious that he will not succeed.

• Act 1, Scene III gives us the outline of Iago's plan to make Othello jealous:

> *"if thou canst cuckold him, thou doest thyself a pleasure, and me a sport."*

• Iago's soliloquy at the end of Act 2, Scene II prepares us for Iago's plan to destroy Cassio, Desdemona and Othello, by insinuating infidelity between Desdemona and Cassio. We hope against hope that he will fail.

We are repeatedly kept in suspense, wondering if Othello will succeed in escaping from Iago's web of insinuation and see the reality of his situation:

> "Think'st thou I'd make a life of jealousy,
> To follow still the changes of the moon
> With fresh suspicions?"   (Act 3, Scene III)

> "If she be false, O! then heaven mocks itself.
> I'll not believe it."   (Act 3, Scene III)

> "O! Iago, the pity of it, Iago!"   (Act 4, Scene I)

> "How goes it now? he looks gentler than he did."   Emilia (Act 4, Scene III)

> "... When I have pluck'd the rose,
> I cannot give it vital growth again,
> It must needs wither; I'll smell it on the tree."   (Act 5, Scene II)

Each time our hopes are dashed, as suspense gradually gives way to the certainty that Othello will be driven by Iago's poison to destroy the innocent Desdemona.

(d) Dramatic Irony

Dramatic irony is an important device in a tragedy, as it heightens tension and expectancy and increases the audience's sense of the inevitability of disaster. Basically irony involves any contradiction between appearance and reality, but there are various different kinds of irony both in the words and in the situations in *Othello*.

Dramatic irony may involve:

- the contradiction between what the hero believes is happening and what is actually happening
- the contradiction between what the hero believes is happening and what the audience knows or suspects is happening
- the tragic irony that the hero's situation or course of action is bringing him where he least expects he is going
- the tragic irony that the more the hero tries to solve his problem the worse he makes it.

> "My soul hath her content so absolute
> That not another comfort like to this
> Succeeds in unknown fate."   Othello (Act 2, Scene I)

The irony here is that Othello believes he has reached the peak of his happiness – ironically he has, since he will never again be as happy. He has no idea that the future holds the very opposite to what he expects – torment and agony. Ironically too, his "unknown fate" is already being manipulated by Iago.

> *O balmy breath, that doth almost persuade*
> *Justice to break her sword."*   *Othello (Act 5, Scene II)*

Ironically Othello believes that he is acting according to justice in killing Desdemona, when in fact he is perverting the course of justice. He believes that Desdemona's beauty is perverting the course of justice by making him unwilling to kill her. Ironically if Othello were to respond to his love of Desdemona, he would be acting justly. The more Othello tries to do justice, ironically the more he perverts it and hastens his own ruin.

There is irony too in Othello's repeated comments on Iago's "honesty" and his indebtedness to Iago for informing him of Desdemona's infidelity. One of the most tragic ironies in the play is Desdemona's complete unawareness of the hellish plot by which Iago has poisoned her husband against her and her absolute trust in Othello's freedom from jealousy:

> *"O good Iago*
> *What shall I do to win my lord again?"*

(e) Creation of Atmosphere

Shakespeare excels in creating atmosphere in *Othello*. The play has been described as "claustrophobic", since the main actions take place in the confined space of a castle in Cyprus and within a compressed sequence of time (less than three days). Much of the action takes place within doors and the main characters confront each other at close quarters in a psychological battle of wits.

Shakespeare has succeeded in weaving a pattern of finely contrasting scenes, using variations in language, stage-setting and action. Each scene has its own peculiar atmosphere to suit the developing drama:

ACT 1

Scene I takes place at night-time in a dimly-lit street and opens with the puzzling argument of Iago and Roderigo. We hear news of the sudden elopement and marriage of Desdemona and Othello and witness Iago's resentment at Cassio's promotion. It is a night of intrigue and confrontation, as Brabantio's anger is roused against Othello. Iago's crude language creates suspense, as we anxiously await the entrance of Othello and his coming confrontation with Brabantio.

Scene II begins with the false declaration of Iago's loyalty to Othello, which forebodes ill for Othello. The search parties' drawn swords, and Othello's quiet authority increase the drama. The suspense continues, as we anxiously await the outcome of the coming confrontation between Othello and Brabantio.

Scene III is a scene of high drama, as we witness a national emergency, conflicting reports of the Turks' movements and the appointment of Othello as commander in Cyprus. It is a scene of contrasts, as we witness the accusations of Brabantio in heightened language, the quiet romance of Othello's tales of adventure and love, Desdemona's spirited and open declaration of love and Iago's sinister scheming.

ACT 2

Scene I opens with the tension and suspense of the raging storm and the anxiously awaited arrival of Othello. The blissful reunion of the lovers increases our foreboding, as we see the sheer knavery of Iago's scheming in his final soliloquy.

Scene II heralds the eventful night of the celebration of victory over the Turks and of Othello's marriage.

Scene III begins with the comic relief of Cassio's drinking session, which soon gives way to the highly dramatic brawl and Cassio's sudden disgrace. Iago's feigned honesty and treacherous friendship for Cassio increase our tension and foreboding.

ACT 3

Scene I provides slight comic relief, as Cassio dismisses the musicians and uses the Clown to try to arrange a meeting with Desdemona. With Scene II it provides a brief respite before the oppressive crisis scene.

Scene III is a scene of fatal misunderstanding and swift action. The atmosphere is stifling and oppressive, as Iago poisons the noble Othello's mind and takes control of his whole personality. Tension and suspense increase, as Iago and Othello form a sinister alliance to perform vengeance on Desdemona and Cassio.

Scene IV opens with the slight comic relief of Desdemona's conversation with the Clown. Tension mounts, as Othello romantically tells Desdemona of the magic of the handkerchief and obsessively questions her about its loss. We hope against hope that Othello will recover and see the true reality of Desdemona's fidelity.

ACT 4

Scene I is a scene of high tension, as Othello loses control and falls down in an unconscious fit. We witness the intrigue and deception of Iago, as he finally convinces Othello of Desdemona's infidelity with Cassio. Drama increases as Bianca's entry with the handkerchief at an opportune moment finally devastates Othello. We are shocked and outraged at Othello's striking of Desdemona and the disintegration of his mind as he begins to use Iago's style of language – "Goats and Monkeys!"

Scene II is the oppressive "brothel scene", where Othello falsely accuses Desdemona and she is driven to beg Iago for help. We are outraged at the perversion of goodness. We begin to hope that Roderigo's threats to Iago will prove real and that Iago's plot of murder on Cassio and Roderigo will not succeed.

Scene III is a scene of pathos and pity as we see the innocent Desdemona singing the willow song and loving and forgiving her kind lord despite his cruelty and violence against her. We realise that she is doomed and feel for her.

ACT 5

Scene I is a dramatic night-time scene of noise, confusion and violence. We hope that Iago's anxiety about his failure and exposure will materialise and we are glad when his plans begin to go wrong. We anxiously hope that Emilia will expose him in time to save Desdemona. It is a scene of high drama and suspense.

Scene II is a fearful, claustrophobic scene full of tension, pathos and horror as the wavering Othello confronts Desdemona and kills her, just moments before he discovers she is innocent and true. It is a scene of great drama, as Emilia exposes Iago's villainy and he tries to escape but is caught. The heated arguments and violence contribute to the drama of the scene. At the end we feel a great sense of waste, as Othello recovers some of his honour and kills himself as an act of reconciliation and atonement. Finally, normality is restored but what is done cannot be undone.

2. Skilful Characterisation

(a) Real People

Shakespeare's skill in characterisation is best examined as the individual characters develop and grow, as the scenes progress. Each character is an individual and has his own distinct role in weaving the events of the play. Some may have an additional symbolic significance as embodiments of good or evil, love or hate or other human values. Characters come to life as the plot is woven and are rarely the result of a preconceived idea or principle. They become real and credible people, who inhabit the world we live in, whatever may be their additional symbolic significance. It is important to consider the individuality, the role and the symbolic significance of a character to assess properly the portrayal of that character, as Shakespeare perhaps intended.

(b) Methods

Characters create actions and actions mould characters and reveal them to us. In general, characters are revealed by what they say themselves, by what others say of them, by asides and soliloquy, by contrast and comparison and, above all, by their actions and roles in weaving the plot. It is through language and imagery that the finer points of character are portrayed and this is where Shakespeare excels.

(c) Distinctive Language

Each character uses his own distinctive type and pattern of language to suit his character and moods.

In Act 1 Brabantio's language, which is normally polite and respectful, is heightened and sometimes broken, reflecting his anger with Othello and his real concern for his seduced daughter (e.g. Act 1, Scene I, lines 160 and following; Act 1, Scene II, lines 62 and following; Act 1, Scene III, lines 211 and following).

Othello's language is dignified and flashy in Act 1, Scene II, lines 17 and following and lines 59–60, showing his egoism and pride in himself.

In Act 1, Scene III, Othello's language, in speaking of his adventures and of wooing Desdemona, is calm, assured, descriptive and forceful. His constant self-reference shows he is self-centred and possessive in his love.

This contrasts with Desdemona's language, which is natural but sometimes descriptive and romantic. This shows how idealistic and blindly romantic her love is (e.g. Act 1, Scene III, lines 181 and following and lines 251 and following).

Iago's language in Act 1, Scene I is forceful and rhetorical, crude and obscene (e.g. lines 86 ff., and lines 108 ff.). This is typical of Iago throughout the play and reflects his hatred of goodness (e.g. Act 2, Scene I, lines 268 ff.; Act 3, Scene III throughout; Act 4, Scene I throughout).

In Act 3, Scene III the carefully built dialogue is compressed and tense, as Iago gradually tightens his grip on Othello (Act 3, Scene III, lines 35–59; lines 93–106; lines 205–227).

As Othello is poisoned and corrupted by Iago, he begins to adopt Iago's images and speech patterns (Act 3, Scene III, lines 213–227; lines 258–279; lines 346–358; Act 4, Scene I, lines 35–44; Act 4, Scene II, lines 46–93).

Further examples abound throughout the play and are well worth examination.

(d) Contrasting Characters

Another aspect of Shakespeare's skill is his various sets of contrasting characters: Othello and Iago are the two most outstanding opposites in the play. Othello is basically good and loving: Iago is evil and full of hate. Othello is open and trusting: Iago is mysterious and deceitful. Othello is noble and great: Iago is detestable and shallow.

Perhaps these opposites are alike in some respects – Othello is obsessed with knowing the bitter truth; Iago is obsessed with corrupting it. Both are driven by extreme passions. Othello is passionate in his love: Iago is passionate in his desire for the sheer pleasure of doing evil for its own sake. Ironically, both are destroyed by the extremity of the passions which devour them. However, Othello's ruin is orchestrated by Iago, while Iago destroys himself.

There are other striking contrasts too in *Othello*. There is a contrast between Desdemona's love, selflessness and concern and Iago's hatred and self-seeking. Cassio's firm loyalty to Othello contrasts with Iago's treachery and deceit. There is a further contrast between Desdemona's pure idealistic love and Othello's rather self-centred passion. Emilia's worldliness and experience highlight Desdemona's chastity and inexperience, just as Bianca's mercenary attitude to love contrasts with Emilia's common decency. All these contrasts in character serve to highlight the various combinations of good and evil, love and hate, which make up the personalities of the play.

3. Patterns of Language and Imagery

Language is the many-faceted tool of the dramatist's trade. Shakespeare tends to create patterns of language and imagery to reflect and portray his characters, to create atmosphere and to express his themes and vision of life. A few selected examples of language and imagery in *Othello* are mentioned in the following sections to entice the more serious student to explore further.

Language Patterns

Some examples of patterns of language used to portray character have already been mentioned in the section "Distinctive Language" on p. 205.

(a) Poetry

In *Othello*, Shakespeare uses both poetry and prose to great effect. The basic line of his dramatic verse is "Blank Verse", unrhymed iambic pentameter, with five feet, each consisting of an unstressed syllable followed by a stressed syllable. This is used for most of the play by the major characters.

Sometimes the lines are rhymed, like the Duke's pronouncements in Act 1, Scene III or the final lines of some scenes. This adds solemnity or formality to what is being said. Frequently, the rhythm becomes flexible, as Shakespeare tries to reflect complex states of mind. The rhythm of Brabantio's speech becomes broken in Act 1, Scene III and Othello frequently loses his normal pattern of speech in Act 3, Scene III and Act 4, Scenes I and II. This reflects their confusion and inner turmoil.

(b) Prose

In *Othello* prose is used:

- for formal proclamations, such as the Herald's announcement in Act 2, Scene II and the Duke's explanation of the gravity of the Turkish threat in Act 1, Scene III.

- for ordinary conversation, especially intimate private conversations like Iago's frequent conversations with Roderigo.

- as the language of people of lower status in life, such as the Clown and the musicians, Bianca and sometimes Emilia.

- to represent a breakdown in personality or an extreme mental confusion, as in Act 4, Scene I before Othello falls unconscious.

(c) Descriptive Language

Descriptive language, which may be loosely termed imagery, is used to set a scene or create atmosphere.

In Act 2, Scene I, the descriptions and comments of various characters tell us of the ongoing raging storm at sea and the defeat of the Turks.

Assonance and alliteration, which are figures of speech rather than imagery, are used frequently to reveal a character's feelings or to create atmosphere. The final lines of the play are worth examination:

> *"To you, lord governor,*
> *Remains the censure of this hellish villain,*
> *The time, the place, the torture; O! enforce it.*
> *Myself will straight abroad, and to the state*
> *This heavy act with heavy heart relate."*

Many examples of alliteration, assonance and cacophony co-operate with the rhythm to suggest the horror of Iago's crimes and the tragic events that have just happened.

Many examples of descriptive language are to be found in *Othello* and are worth exploration.

Iterative Imagery

The role of imagery in *Othello* is complex. Imagery is used to reveal character and theme and to create atmosphere. Imagery establishes patterns, as the drama and the characters develop. Shakespeare's strands of imagery have been called "Iterative", since they suggest or reiterate common ideas or qualities in the play and its characters. Some important patterns of imagery are listed below.

(a) The Web Imagery

Perhaps the central strand of imagery in *Othello* is the imagery of the poisonous spider (Iago) trapping the unwary fly (Othello) in its deceptive but powerful web. It suggests the entrapment and destruction of goodness by evil:

> *"With as little a web as this will I ensnare as great a fly as Cassio."*
>
> > Iago (Act 2, Scene I)

> *"And, by how much she strives to do him good,*
> *She shall undo her credit with the Moor.*
> *So will I turn her virtue into pitch,*
> *And out of her own goodness make the net*
> *That shall enmesh them all."*
>
> > Iago (Act 2, Scene III)

> *"The Moor already changes with my poisons ...*
> *Which at the first are scarce found to distaste."*
>
> > Iago (Act 3, Scene III)

> *"'Tis true; there's magic in the web of it."*
>
> > Othello (Act 3, Scene IV)

> *"Will you, I pray, demand that demi-devil*
> *Why he hath thus ensnar'd my soul and body?"*
>
> > Othello (Act 5, Scene II)

(b) The Imagery of Animals and Insects

This imagery of repulsive preying animals and annoying corrupting insects is used by Iago, mainly in the first three acts of the play, and reflects his evil, preying mind. Significantly, Othello adopts this animal imagery in Acts 3 and 4, as Iago preys on his mind and destroys his nobility and love. The main examples of animal imagery are: goats and monkeys, monsters, rams and ewes, wolves and wild-cats, asses and jennets, toads, daws and flies and many others:

> *"Even now, now, very now, an old black ram*
> *Is tupping your white ewe."*
>
> > Iago (Act 1, Scene I)

> *"I'll make the Moor thank me, love me, and reward me,*
> *For making him egregiously an ass."*
>
> > Iago (Act 2, Scene I)

> *"O! beware, my lord, of jealousy;*
> *It is the green-ey'd monster which doth mock*
> *That meat it feeds on."*
>
> > Iago (Act 3, Scene III)

> *"I had rather be a toad,*
> *And live upon the vapour in a dungeon,*
> *Than keep a corner of the thing I love*
> *For others' uses. yet 'tis the plague of great ones."*
>
> > Othello (Act 3, Scene III)

"It is impossible you should see this,
Were they as prime as goats, as hot as monkeys,
As salt as wolves in pride."   Iago (Act 3, Scene III)

"Yield up, O love! thy crown and hearted throne
To tyrannous hate. Swell, bosom, with thy fraught,
For 'tis of aspics' tongues!"   Othello (Act 3, Scene III)

"A horned man's a monster, and a beast."
"... Goats and monkeys!"   Othello (Act 4, Scene I)

"Or keep it as a cistern for foul toads
To knot and gender in."   Othello (Act 4, Scene II)

"I took by the throat the circumcised dog,
And smote him thus."   Othello (Act 5, Scene II)

(c) The Imagery of Hell and Heaven

Many images of heaven and hell, devils and damnation are employed in Othello. The images
of hell and devils originate with Iago and identify him as an agent of evil. They are adopted
by Othello later in the play, as Iago asserts his influence for evil over Othello. The heavenly
imagery is frequently used to portray Desdemona's purity and goodness:

"Hail to thee, lady! and the grace of heaven,
Before, behind thee, and on every hand,
Enwheel thee round!"   Cassio (Act 2, Scene I)

"She is of so free, so kind, so apt, so blessed a disposition,
that she holds it a vice in her goodness not to
do more than she is requested."   Iago (Act 2, Scene III)

        "Divinity of hell!
When devils will the blackest sins put on,
They do suggest at first with heavenly shows,
As I do now."   Iago (Act 2, Scene III)

"O, 'tis the spite of hell, the fiends arch-mock,
To lip a wanton in a secure couch,
And to suppose her chaste."   Iago (Act 4, Scene I)

        "O, the more angel she,
And you the blacker devil,"
"...O! she was heavenly true!"   Emilia (Act 5, Scene II)

"This look of thine will hurl my soul from heaven,
And fiends will snatch at it. Cold, cold, my girl!
Even like thy chastity.
O! cursed, cursed slave. Whip me, you devils,
From the possession of this heavenly sight!
Blow me about in winds! roast me in sulphur!
Wash me in steep-down gulfs of liquid fire!"   Othello (Act 5, Scene II)

(d) The Storm Imagery

The raging sea storm in Act 2, Scene I becomes a symbol of the destructive forces at work in human life and within man himself. It prefigures the chaos that will come to Othello's whole personality and world, just like to a wandering ship in a storm. Iago will soon release raging destructive passions in Othello, which will ruin his whole personality and love for Desdemona:

> *"O my soul's joy!*
> *If after every tempest comes such calms,*
> *May the winds blow till they have waken'd death!*
> *And let the labouring bark climb hills of seas,*
> *Olympus-high, and duck again as low*
> *As hell's from heaven!"*   *Othello (Act 2, Scene I)*

> *"Never, Iago. Like to the Pontic sea,*
> *Whose icy current and compulsive course*
> *Ne'er feels retiring ebb, but keeps due on*
> *To the Propontic, and the Hellespont,*
> *Even so my bloody thoughts, with violent pace,*
> *Shall ne'er look back, ne'er ebb to humble love,*
> *Till a capable and wide revenge*
> *Swallow them up."*   *Othello (Act 3, Scene III)*

> *"Here is my journey's end, here is my butt,*
> *And very sea-mark of my utmost sail.*
> *... Where should Othello go?"*   *Othello (Act 5, Scene II)*

(e) Other Imagery

Many more interrelated patterns of imagery are worth exploration:

- False Appearance; Clothing
- Disease and Corruption
- Witchcraft and Magic
- Light and Darkness

- Taste and Sweetness
- Colours
- Precious Stones

Questions

Act 1

Scene I

1. Outline Iago's grievances in this scene. Which is his main grievance? Give reasons.

2. What do you think is Iago's main motive for plotting against Othello?

3. Describe Iago's philosophy of life in this scene.

4. What does Iago really think of Roderigo?

5. What methods does Iago use to persuade Roderigo to join in his plans?

6. What view of Othello does this scene present to us?

7. Discuss the contrasts of character in this scene.

8. Do you have sympathy for the main characters in this scene: Iago, Roderigo and Brabantio? Give reasons.

9. What themes and images predominate in this scene? Give examples.

Scene II

1. What do we learn of Othello's character (a) from others; (b) from what he says; and (c) from his behaviour?

2. Who is the most outstanding character in this scene – Othello or Desdemona?

3. Describe the relationship between Othello and Desdemona in this scene.

4. Does Othello's character in this scene seem different from the previous scene?

5. Is Iago different in this scene? Give reasons.

6. Are there any potentially tragic elements in this scene? Give reasons.

7. Contrast the good characters with the bad characters in this scene.

8. What is your attitude to Iago and Roderigo in this scene?

Act 2
Scene I

1. What is the role of the storm in this scene?

2. How does this scene advance Iago's plans?

3. Compare and contrast Cassio and Othello in this scene.

4. What do we learn of Othello's relationship with Desdemona in this scene?

5. With what is Iago really concerned in this scene? How does this compare to previous scenes?

6. How is this scene a turning point in the play?

7. Looking back to Act 1 Scene I, how credible does Iago's hatred of Othello now seem?

8. What themes are evident in this scene?

9. What potentially tragic elements are present in this scene?

Scene II

1. What role does this short scene play in *Othello*?

Scene III

1. What is amusing and comic in this scene?

2. Why does Iago's manipulation of Cassio succeed so well?

3. How does Iago manage to maintain his reputation for honesty in this scene?

4. What character traits of Othello does this scene emphasise most?

5. How much sympathy do you have for Cassio, Iago and Othello from the events of this scene?

6. Account for the relatively easy success of Iago's schemes in this scene.

7. What insight does this scene give us into Iago's inner personality?

8. Describe the contrasts and inconsistencies in Iago's behaviour.

Act 3

Scene I

1. What is humorous about this scene?

2. How does this scene help Iago's plans?

3. Describe Cassio's attitude to himself and to others in this scene.

Scene II

1. What is the role of this scene in the play?

Scene III

1. Compare Othello's character at the beginning of this scene with his character at the end.

2. What elements contribute to Iago's success in this scene?

3. How do the other characters in this scene help to advance Iago's plans?

4. What is Iago's most successful piece of evidence in persuading Othello of Desdemona's infidelity?

5. List Iago's arguments to convince Othello, in the order he uses them.

6. Describe the main effects on Othello of Iago's arguments and insinuations.

7. How does good luck help Iago's schemes in this scene?

8. How does Iago's attitude to and relationship with Othello change, as the scene progresses?

9. How much are (a) Iago, (b) Othello and (c) other characters to blame for what happens to Othello in this scene?

10. How is this scene a major turning point in the play?

11. Iago succeeds in trapping Othello more by what he doesn't say than by what he actually says. Discuss.

12. Shakespeare could have achieved the same results with a much shorter scene. Discuss.

13. Describe the main conflicts which become clear in Othello's character in this scene.

14. Does Othello ever have a chance, in this scene, of recovering his senses?

15. What causes Othello most pain and torment in this scene?

Scene IV

1. How does Othello's character seem different in this scene?

2. Describe Othello and Desdemona's marriage relationship from the evidence of this scene.

3. Is Desdemona a credible character in this scene?

4. Does your sympathy for Othello lessen in this scene?

5. What in this scene makes tragedy likely?

6. Compare and contrast the women in this scene.

Act 4
Scene I

1. What is most despicable about Iago's character in this scene?

2. Describe Othello's changes of mood in this scene.

3. What is demonic about Iago in this scene?

4. What really motivates Iago to humiliate Othello?

5. How is this scene a major turning point in the play?

6. What chances does Othello have of escaping from Iago's power, at this stage in the play?

7. Discuss the role of contrasts in this scene.

8. Is Desdemona's behaviour faultless in this scene?

9. Does Othello become repulsive in this scene? Give reasons.

Scene II

1. Is Othello trying to be fair or cruel to Desdemona in this scene?

2. What is Emilia's role in this scene?

3. Compare Desdemona's character in this scene to her character earlier in the play.

4. Iago shows remarkable skill and cruelty in this scene. Discuss.

5. Describe Iago's attitude to Emilia in this scene.

6. How does Emilia's character in this scene differ from previous scenes?

7. How much success have Iago's plans had so far in the play?

8. How has Roderigo's character changed in this scene?

Scene III

1. Describe Desdemona's attitude to Othello and to life in this scene.
2. Compare and contrast Emilia and Desdemona in this scene.
3. How does this scene contribute to our sense of tragedy?
4. Is it credible that Desdemona should so passively submit to her fate?
5. What is the role of the "willow song" in this scene?

Act 5
Scene I

1. Iago becomes an opportunist in this scene and takes too many risks – Discuss.
2. This scene marks the turning point in Iago's schemes – Discuss.
3. How is Iago's attitude different in this scene?
4. Has Othello's attitude changed in this scene?
5. What does this scene contribute to our understanding of Iago's motives?
6. Does Roderigo deserve sympathy in this scene?
7. Iago makes the best of bad luck in this scene – Discuss.
8. Why does Iago plot murder in this scene?
9. Is Iago worthy of any sympathy in this scene?

Scene II

1. To what extent do you accept Othello's reasons for killing Desdemona, in his first speech in this scene?
2. To what extent is Othello's killing of Desdemona cruel, just, or merciful?
3. Is Desdemona a little too passive to be credible?
4. Our sympathy for Othello increases as the scene progresses – Discuss.
5. To what extent does Othello show himself to be a fool in this scene?
6. Describe Emilia's role in this scene.
7. Iago's villainy is emphasised in this scene – Discuss.
8. Othello's nobility of character is restored in this scene – Discuss.
9. To what extent does Othello redeem himself in this scene?
10. Is Desdemona's death the real tragedy?
11. How is Othello's death a relief rather than a disaster?
12. How do Othello's character and moods change as this scene progresses?
13. Who wins and who loses in this scene?
14. What elements in this scene make *Othello* a tragedy?
15. What really causes the downfall of Iago?

Leaving Certificate Questions and Sample Answers

Sample Exam Question for Ordinary Level

1. (a) How does Brabantio react to the news that his daughter, Desdemona, married Othello? (10)

   (b) Briefly explain how Iago manages to create distrust between Othello and Michael Cassio. (10)

2. What is your opinion of Desdemona? (10)

3. Answer one of the following [Each part carries 30 marks]:

   (i) Iago is the most interesting character in the play Othello. Do you agree with this statement?

   OR

   (ii) Relationships often make drama interesting. Select one of the following relationships from the play and explain why you think it is interesting:

   (a) The relationship between Iago and Emilia

   OR

   (b) The relationship between Othello and Desdemona.

   OR

   (iii) "The final scene of *Othello* is both dramatic and memorable." Do you agree with this statement? Give reasons for your answer.

Sample Exam Question for Ordinary Level

1. (a) What reasons does Iago give Roderigo for his hatred of Othello in Act 1, Scene I? (10)

   (b) Do you feel sympathy for Michael Cassio in the play? (10)

   (c) From the following statements, choose one which, in your opinion, best describes what the play is about. Give reasons for your choice :

   • It is a play about jealousy.

   • It is a play about love.

   • It is a play about evil.   (10)

2. Answer **ONE** of the following [Each part carries 30 marks]:

   (i) What is your opinion of the behaviour and actions of Emilia in the play *Othello*? Support the points you make with reference to the text.

   OR

   (ii) *Othello* is filled with moments of great tension and drama. What, in your opinion, is the most dramatic scene in the play? Support the points you make with reference to the play.

OR

(iii) It has been suggested that *Othello* is a very funny play. Do you agree with this opinion? Support your answer with reference to the play.

Past Ordinary Level Exam Questions

2008 EXAM

1. (a) Do you feel sorry for Brabantio, Desdemona's father, when he learns that she has married Othello? Explain your answer. (10)

   (b) From your reading of the play, why do you think Desdemona falls in love with Othello? Explain your answer. (10)

2. *"Yet she must die, else she'll betray more men."* Describe the murder of Desdemona by Othello in Act 5, Scene II. (10)

3. Answer **ONE** of the following [each part carries 30 marks]:

   (i) At the very end of the play, Lodovico describes Iago as a *"hellish villain"*. Do you think this is a fair description of Iago? Support your answer by reference to the play.

   OR

   (ii) You have been invited to play the part of a character in a production of the play *Othello*. Describe the qualities of your chosen character which you would wish to make clear to the audience. Support your answer with reference to the text.

   OR

   (iii) Write a report putting forward the view that *Othello* is, or is not, a suitable text for Leaving Certificate candidates.

1998 EXAM

Note: for extract referred to in question below, see Act 3, Scene IV, pp.111–113. The first and last quotes from the extract are below:

Desdemona   Where should I lose that handkerchief, Emilia?   [p.111]
…
Emilia   Is not this man jealous?   [p.113]

Having read the extract above, answer **ONE** of the following questions, 1 or 2 or 3.

1. (a) What does Othello reveal about himself in this extract? Support your answer by reference.

   (b) Outline what has occurred prior to this scene which has caused Othello to behave as he does in the extract.

2. (a) What evidence is there in this extract to support the view that Desdemona is not aware that Othello has changed in his attitude towards her? In your answer you should refer closely to the extract.

   (b) In this extract, Desdemona reveals herself as a complete innocent. Does what you know about her elsewhere in the play support this impression? Support your answer by reference.

3. In the above extract, Desdemona is attempting to have Cassio restored to the position of Lieutenant. From your knowledge of the character of Cassio, do you think him worthy or unworthy of Desdemona's efforts on his behalf? You should support the points you make with reference to the play as a whole.

Sample Answer to 2008 Ordinary Level Exam Question

1. **(a) Do you feel sorry for Brabantio, Desdemona's father, when he learns that she has married Othello? Explain your answer.**

No, I do not feel sorry for Brabantio. He is a racist, a bully and a hypocrite. He is very angry when he hears of the marriage. This happens in Act 1, Scene I, when he is woken by Iago and Roderigo shouting that he has been robbed. They know that, as a senator, Brabantio is a proud man. At this time, a daughter was regarded as her father's property. He is shocked when Iago tells him, *"An old black ram is tupping your white ewe."* Iago then tells Brabantio, *"Your daughter and the moor are now making the beast with two backs."* Of course, Brabantio is hurt that his daughter has married without his permission. However, his reaction shows him to be a racist and a hypocrite.

Brabantio complains to the Duke about Othello's behaviour. He tells Othello, *"Damned as thou art, thou hast enchanted her."* He believes Othello must have tricked Desdemona, for that is the only way she would marry a black man. He says his daughter would not have *"to incur a general mock, run from her guardage to the sooty bosom of one such as thou."* This reveals Brabantio as a bigot. He is also hypocritical, as Desdemona met Othello when Brabantio invited him to his home. He did this because he was a hero of Venice, yet he is not good enough to marry his daughter. **Therefore, I do not feel sorry for Brabantio when he learns of Desdemona's marriage to Othello.**

   (b) From your reading of the play, why do you think Desdemona falls in love with Othello? Explain your answer.

Desdemona falls in love with Othello because he is a hero. Othello first saw Desdemona when he was invited into her home by Brabantio. Having just returned from the wars, Othello was something of a hero. Brabantio invited him to his home to tell the stories of his adventures. Othello told him his life story. He told him of his victories and of his defeats; of the time he was captured and sold into slavery; of his escape from slavery and his encounters with cannibals and of other fascinating people he had met on his travels.

As he sat with Brabantio recounting these stories, night after night, Desdemona sat quietly in the back of the room, and Othello noticed that she listened closely to his tales. He says, *"This to hear would Desdemona seriously incline."* Desdemona approached him, without her father's knowledge, and asked him to tell his stories again, but this time to her alone, and

Othello remembers how *"she'd come again, and with a greedy ear, devour up my discourse."* Desdemona wept to hear of his suffering and gasped to hear of his adventures.

Eventually, Desdemona told Othello that she could love a man like him, telling him, *"if I had a friend that lov'd her, I should but teach him how to tell my story, and that would woo her."* He took the hint and declared his love for her. **It is for these reasons that Desdemona fell in love with Othello.**

2.   *"Yet she must die, else she'll betray more men."*
     Describe the murder of Desdemona by Othello in Act 5, Scene II.
The final scene of the play opens with Othello's last soliloquy. He says he does not want to shed his wife's blood, yet must kill her, if only to prevent her harming other men. He says, *"Yet she must die, else she'll betray more men."* He compares his wife to candlelight. Like the candle, Desdemona's life can easily be put out. However, unlike the candle, life cannot easily be re-ignited once it is taken.

He leans over and kisses the sleeping Desdemona, tears staining his cheeks. She wakes, and is frightened to find her trembling husband standing over her. He tells her, *"If you bethink yourself of any crime unreconcil'd as yet to heaven and grace, ask for it straight."* She understands immediately what is to become of her, and begs for her life. She once again repeats her innocence regarding Cassio, and knows there is no hope when she learns from Othello that Cassio has been murdered. It is impossible to reason with Othello, and he smothers her until he believes she is dead.

Emilia comes and knocks on the bedroom door. She has come to tell Othello of the terrible attack on Roderigo, and when she enters the room it is in darkness. She tells Othello that Roderigo is dead, and shocks him when she says Cassio was merely wounded and did not die in the attack. At that point, the dying Desdemona speaks, saying she dies without guilt, and Emilia is startled. She pushes past Othello and hugs the body of her mistress just at the point when Desdemona dies. **Desdemona's last words claim that Othello is not guilty for her death.**

3.   (i) **At the very end of the play, Ludovico describes Iago as *"a hellish villain"*. Do you think this is a fair description of Iago? Support your answer with reference to the play.**
Yes, I do think this is a fair description of Iago. He is a villain because he is wicked and cruel. He **manipulates** Othello, Brabantio, Roderigo, Cassio and Desdemona. While he is corrupt, he also has a **brilliant** mind. Other than his intelligence, Iago possesses no **redeeming qualities**. Throughout the play, he takes particular pleasure in boasting about just how **cruel** he is. He enjoys the suffering of others and, despite his early attempts to justify his hatred of Othello for a variety of reasons, his actions appear to be motivated purely by moral **corruption**. His takes advantage of the idiotic Roderigo in a **ruthless** way, and he has no hesitation in murdering his "friend" in Act 4 when his continued existence presents a threat

to the success of Iago's schemes. Iago is a **sinister** character, and the events of Act 5, Scene II confirm that he is a man without any redeeming qualities.

Nowhere is Iago's corruption more clearly stated than in Act 2, Scene III, when he says of Desdemona, *"So I will turn her virtue into pitch, / And out of her own goodness make the net / That shall enmesh them."* It is this kind of **shameless** declaration of **wicked** intent that makes Iago the villain he is, and confirms his status as the most interesting and fascinating character in the play. Iago wants to destroy Desdemona simply because she is good. He sees her goodness as a weakness. This shows that he is a cruel villain.

For Iago, the end justifies the means. He wants to destroy Othello, so he lies. His first words to Othello in Act 1, Scene II are, *"I lack iniquity."* Othello trusts him completely, continuously referring to him as *"honest Iago"*. Iago is extremely **intelligent** and is an **excellent judge of character**. He recognises that Othello's *"constant, loving, noble nature"* is in fact a weakness to be exploited. He sees Cassio is *"rash and very sudden in choler"*, and sets in place a plan to make Othello distrust the loyal Cassio. The fact that he deliberately destroys the innocent Cassio's life is another sign that he is a *"hellish villain"*.

Iago's scheme to cause distrust between Cassio and Othello succeeds when, following his drunken assault on Montano, Cassio is told *"never more be officer of mine"*. Iago makes Othello distrust Cassio; makes him jealous. He encourages Desdemona to ask Othello to forgive Cassio while at the same time planning to *"pour this pestilence into his ear, / That she repeals him for her body's lust."* He **successfully exploits** the weakness he has identified in Othello's character, until Othello declares, *"Perdition catch my soul / But I do love thee! And when I love thee not, chaos is come again."* Iago is not only fascinating and interesting and intelligent, he is also highly successful. His aim was to make Othello jealous of Cassio's friendship with Desdemona. This aim has largely been reached by the end of Act 3.

The destruction of Othello's character is surprisingly easy. Iago takes pleasure in the effects of his schemes. In Act 4, Scene II he celebrates Othello's emotional breakdown with the words, *"Work on, my medicine, work! Thus credulous fools are caught."* He creates the circumstances for Othello to overhear Cassio say, *"She haunts me in every place"*, and allows him to believe his former lieutenant is boasting about Desdemona. When Othello decides to kill Desdemona, Iago advises him, *"Do it not with poison, strangle her in her bed."* Iago then murders Roderigo in Act 4 to ensure his own safety, and succeeds in leading Othello to his destruction in Act 5. There can be no doubt that Iago really is a vicious and cruel villain.

When Iago's villainy is revealed at the end of the play, he shows no sorrow for any of his actions. His final words are, *"Demand me nothing, what you know you know / From this time forth I will never speak a word."* He is taken away to be tortured and leaves behind him the the bodies of Othello, Desdemona and Emilia in a heap on Desdemona's bed. **There can** be no doubt that Iago is by far the most interesting character in the play. He is a cruel and hellish villain who causes great suffering and pain in the play.

Sample Exam Questions for Higher Level

1. Is Othello's downfall due to his own weakness or circumstances beyond his control? Support your answer with reference to and quotation from the play.

2. "It is difficult to see Othello as a hero. Rather, he is a weak, gullible, proud man, whose tragic fate leaves the audience feeling little sympathy." Do you agree with this statement? Support your answer with reference to and quotation from the play.

3. "It is easy to feel sympathy for Othello. He is a decent man who is undone by Iago, a consummate villain." Discuss this statement, supporting your answer with reference to and quotation from the play.

4. "Iago is a master manipulator who exploits weakness in order to make people destroy themselves by making them instruments of his will." Discuss this statement, supporting your answer with reference to and quotation from the play.

5. "Iago is a disgusting villain who is unusual because he possesses no redeeming qualities." Discuss this statement, supporting your answer with reference to and quotation from the play.

6. The critic Thomas Rymer described Iago as "a close, dissembling, false, insinuating rascal." Do you agree with this statement? Support your answer with reference to and quotation from the play.

7. "*Othello* is a play about contrast – between black and white, good and evil, love and hate." Discuss the theme of contrast in the play, supporting your answer with relevant reference and quotation.

8. "*Othello* is a play about the powerful force of envy." Do you agree with this statement? Support your answer with reference to and quotation from the play.

Past Higher Level Exam Questions

(*Note: Othello* has only been examined twice in the last fifteen years. The 2008 exam was the only time it has been examined since the introduction of the new Leaving Certificate syllabus in 2000.)

2008 EXAM

(i) "Othello's foolishness rather than Iago's cleverness leads to the tragedy of Shakespeare's *Othello*." Discuss this statement supporting your answer with the aid of suitable reference to the text.

OR

(ii) "Shakespeare's play *Othello* demonstrates the weakness of human judgement." Discuss this statement, supporting your answer with the aid of suitable reference to the text.

(i) "Irony is a powerful dramatic device used by Shakespeare to heighten the dramatic tension of his play *Othello*." Discuss this view, supporting your answer by reference to or quotation from the play.

OR

(ii) "Despite the striking portrayals of goodness and nobility, the play *Othello* leaves the audience with a sense of dismal despair." Discuss this view, supporting your answer by reference to or quotation from the play.

Sample Higher Level Answers

"The play may be called *Othello*, but there is no doubt that Iago is the most interesting character in Shakespeare's drama." Discuss this statement with reference to and quotation from the play.

Iago is the most **interesting** character in Shakespeare's *Othello*. He is the force which drives the drama of the play. His **manipulation** of Othello and, indeed, the rest of the characters in the play, is evidence of a quite **brilliant** mind. Unlike other Shakespearean villains, such as Edmund and Lady Macbeth, Iago possesses no **redeeming qualities**. He is **amoral** rather than immoral and, throughout the play, takes particular pleasure in boasting about just how **cruel** and **malevolent** he is. He revels in the suffering of others and, despite his early attempts to justify his hatred of Othello for a variety of slights, real or imagined, his actions appear to be motivated purely by **malicious** intent and moral **corruption**. His exploitation of the hapless Roderigo is **Machiavellian** and **ruthless**. He has no hesitation in murdering his dupe in Act 4 when Roderigo's continued existence presents a threat to the success of Iago's schemes. Iago is a **sinister** character, and the events of Act 5, Scene II confirm that he is a man without any redeeming qualities. He murders Emilia, and is dragged away to be tortured without asking for forgiveness or expressing any remorse for his **wicked** actions. **It is for these reasons that Iago, Othello's trusted Ancient, is without question the most interesting character in Shakespeare's *Othello*.**

Samuel Taylor Coleridge described Iago's justifications for his actions in the play as "**the motive-hunting of a motiveless malignity**". The fact is that, throughout the play, Iago presents a long line of grievances to explain his resentment of Othello. Act 1, Scene I clearly establishes his **vicious** intent. Roderigo comments, "*Thou told'st me thou did hold him in thy hate.*" Iago confirms this, saying he hates Othello because he appointed Cassio, "*A Florentine / A fellow almost damned in fair wife*", as lieutenant, overlooking "*I – of whom his eyes had seen the proof at Rhodes*". However, this reason for despising Othello is quickly forgotten, and he then says he hates Othello because he hates being a servant. He says, "*I follow him to serve my turn on him*", and adds, "*In following him I but follow myself.*" This indicates that he needs no motivation for his actions. Later, in Act 2, Scene I, his soliloquy reveals, "*I do suspect the lusty Moor / hath leaped into my seat*", *and "nothing can or shall content* *my soul / Till I am evened with him."* Again, the idea that he is motivated by jealousy of a possible relationship between Othello and Emilia seems spurious given the fact that he does not mention it again in the rest of the play. The source of Iago's motivation is simple. **He is a malignant villain who takes pleasure in creating mayhem and misery in the lives of others.**

Nowhere is Iago's malignancy more clearly stated than in Act 2, Scene III, when he says of Desdemona, *"So I will turn her virtue into pitch, / And out of her own goodness make the net / That shall enmesh them."* He is **excited** by the prospect of using Desdemona's virtue against her. Earlier, in Act 1, Scene II, he uses vile racist and sexist language: *"An old black ram is tupping your white ewe"*, and *"Your daughter and the Moor are now making the beast with two backs."* He is coldly **cynical**, and the language he uses to describe his schemes is graphic and visceral. In Act 1, Scene III, he says Cassio has *"a person and a smooth dispose to be suspected"* and calculates that *"The Moor is of a free and open nature / That thinks men honest that but seem to be so, / And will as tenderly be led by the nose as asses are."* It is this kind of **shameless** declaration of **wicked** intent that makes Iago the unremitting villain he is, **and confirms his status as the most interesting and fascinating character in the play**.

Iago is **Machiavellian**. For him, the end unquestionably justifies the means. In his case, the means are manipulation and deception. His first words to Othello in Act 1, Scene II are, *"I lack iniquity."* These words confirm Iago as a master **dissembler**, for his last words in the previous scene were, *"I do hate him as I do hell-pains, / Yet, for necessity of present life, / I must show out a flag and sign of love."* Othello trusts him completely, continuously referring to him as *"honest Iago"*. Iago is extremely **intelligent** and is an **excellent judge of character** (the sole exception being his underestimation of his wife, Emilia). He recognises that Othello's *"constant, loving, noble nature"* is in fact a weakness to be exploited. He sees Cassio is *"rash and very sudden in choler"*, and sets in place a plan to make Othello distrust the loyal Cassio. The anticipatory pleasure can hardly be concealed from his voice as he says, in Act 2, Scene I, *"I'll have our Michael Cassio on the hip / Abuse him to the Moor in the rank garb."* He ends that speech by declaring, *"Knavery's plain face is never seen till used"*, a most **sinister** and **malevolent** observation from the character whose presence and actions drives the drama of the play.

The ultimate blame for Othello's tragedy must lie within the hero himself. However, there is no doubt that Othello is unfortunate to have such a **wicked** character as his trusted aide. Iago's scheme to cause distrust between Cassio and Othello succeeds when, following his drunken assault on Montano in Act 2, Scene III, Cassio is told, *"never more be officer of mine."* Once that bond of trust is broken, Iago determines to exploit the breach. He encourages Desdemona to plead with Othello on Cassio's behalf, while at the same time planning to *"pour this pestilence into his ear, / That she repeals him for her body's lust."* Iago organises a meeting between Cassio and Desdemona, and then brings Othello along to witness the "assignation". When Othello asks, *"Was not that Michael Cassio parted from my wife?"*, Iago brilliantly replies, *"Cassio, my lord? No, sure, I cannot think it / That he would steal away so guilty-like."* He **successfully exploits** the weakness he has identified in Othello's character and, by the end of the scene, Othello is declaring, *"Perdition catch my soul / But I do love thee! And when I love thee not, chaos is come again."* **Iago is not only fascinating and interesting and intelligent, he is also highly successful**. His aim was to break Othello through his relationship with Desdemona. This aim has largely been reached by the end of Act 3.

It is in Act 3, Scene III that Iago's **duplicity** is perhaps best illustrated. He has pitched Othello into a fit of jealousy, and then, with immense cynicism, tells his master, *"O! beware, my lord, of jealousy; / It is the green-eyed monster which doth mock / The meat it feeds on."* He then, shockingly, tells Othello, *"I would not have your free and open nature / Out of self-bounty be abused"*, before twisting the knife further by reminding Othello, *"She did deceive her father, marrying you."* He is utterly **vindictive** and **his character lacks empathy and compassion**.

The demolition of Othello's character is surprisingly easy, and is proof that the ultimate blame for the Moor's destruction lies within his own character. However, that does not prevent Iago from revelling in **sadistic** pleasure at the effects of his schemes. In Act 4, Scene I he celebrates Othello's emotional breakdown with the truly sinister words, *"Work on, my medicine, work! Thus credulous fools are caught."* He creates the circumstances for Othello to overhear Cassio say, *"She haunts me in every place"*, and allows Othello to believe his former lieutenant is boasting about Desdemona. When Othello, his rational mind now destroyed, decides to kill Desdemona, Iago advises him, *"Do it not with poison, strangle her in her bed."* He then uses the incredible stories of Cassio's dream and Desdemona's handkerchief to push the hero over the line into pathetic anti-hero. He murders Roderigo in Act 4 to ensure his own safety, and succeeds in leading Othello to his destruction in Act 5.

Iago is a **villain**, and, as such, must be exposed and meet his fate before the end of the play. He is exposed by Emilia, who exclaims to Othello, *"O, thou dull Moor, that handkerchief thou speak'st on / I found by fortune, and did give my husband…he begged of me to steal it."* Iago's reaction is unsurprising. He stabs his wife, fatally, and then flees for his life. He is captured, but, remarkably, **shows no remorse for any of his actions**. His final words are, *"Demand me nothing, what you know you know / From this time forth I will never speak a word."* He is taken away to be tortured and leaves behind him the wreckage of his Machiavellian schemes and his cynical cruelty, as the bodies of Othello, Desdemona and Emilia lie in a heap on Desdemona'a bed. **There can be no doubt that Iago is by far the most interesting character in the play. His malevolence, his duplicity and his corruption make for an appalling, and an utterly hypnotic, character.**

"Iago may be a ruthless villain, but there can be no doubt that Othello is at fault for his own downfall." **Discuss this statement, supporting your answer with reference to and quotation from the play.**

Othello is a tragic hero. His journey in the play takes him along a **tragic arc**. He begins the play as **a representative of all that is admirable in the human character**. He is an **experienced and talented soldier and general**. He has the trust of the Doge, the Venetian head of state, who, when faced with a crisis in the empire, turns to Othello to ensure the safety and security of the key island of Cyprus. He is **deeply loved by the beautiful Desdemona**, a senator's daughter who loves Othello so much that she is prepared to defy her father to elope with him. He has **an easy authority**, and is **respected, calm and rational under pressure**. However, the Othello of Act 1 is almost the complete opposite of the Othello of Act 5. By the end of the play, he is a rather **pathetic, paranoid and obsessive killer**, and his earlier status as admirable hero is scarcely credible. Any analysis of how this remarkable transformation has come about must take two factors into account: firstly, Othello is an **unwitting victim** of the calculating, Machiavellian Iago; secondly, and most importantly, Othello's transformation comes about because of a **fatal flaw,** or weakness, that lies at the heart of his character. Othello is a great man, but his greatness is undermined by **jealousy**. As he acknowledges in his moving final speech, he is *"one not easily jealous, but being wrought / Perplexed in the extreme."*

Shakespeare takes care to establish Othello's heroic status from the outset. In Act 1, Scene I, Iago expresses his contempt for his general by saying, *"I follow him to serve my turn upon him."* However, he also acknowledges that, *"the state, / However this may gall him with some check / Cannot with safety cast him."* That confidence in the strength of his position is echoed by Othello in the following scene when he tells Iago, *"My services which I have done the signiory / Shall out-tongue his* [Brabantio's] *complaints."* He is a noble and sincere man, who traces his ancestry from *"men of royal siege",* and his love for Desdemona is real and heartfelt. He tells his ancient, *"For know, Iago / But that I love the gentle Desdemona."* He is clearly a **heroic** man, whose character is marked by **nobility** and **dignity**.

This exposition of Othello as admirable **hero** is furthered by his reaction to Brabantio's racist vitriol. Brabantio believes Othello must have used witchcraft to bewitch his daughter, for that is the only reason he can conceive of as to why *"a maid so tender fair and happy…/ Would ever have, to incur a general mock, / Run from her guardage to the sooty bosom / Of one such as thou."* Othello is **calm** in the face of such insults, and, when asked by the Duke to explain his behaviour, he delivers a beautiful speech that confirms his **heroic** status. He begins **modestly**, saying, *"Rude am I in my speech / And little blessed with the soft phrase of speech."* He recounts how he was invited into Brabantio's home by the senator himself, and was asked to tell his life story. As he told of his adventures and his escapades, we, the audience, are left in no doubt of his **heroism**. He goes on to tell how Desdemona listened to his tales, and, when the opportunity came, declared, *"if I had a friend that lov'd her / I should but teach him how to tell* *my story, and that would woo her."* This incredibly romantic story is extremely well told, and the audience is left in no doubt about how a woman like Desdemona could fall in love with the **dashing, sensitive warrior**.

It does not take long for this heroic façade to crumble. Iago is aware that *"The Moor is of a free and open nature / That thinks men honest that but seem to be so."* The fact that Othello trusts Iago so much is worrying, and indicates his **poor character judgement**. Othello's arrival on Cyprus following a storm reunites him with Desdemona, and his love for her is reiterated when he tells her, *"It gives me wonder great as my content / To see you here before me. O my soul's joy!"* Iago recognises Othello's essential dignity in his soliloquy at the end of Act 2, Scene I when he says Othello is *"of a constant, loving, noble nature / And I dare think he'll prove to Desdemona / A most dear husband."* Iago is an astute and clever man, and is determined to *"put the Moor into a jealousy so strong / That judgement cannot cure."* It is Iago's adroit exploitation of this weakness that leads Othello to his destruction.

Iago's schemes isolate Othello from his friend, Cassio. Iago then goes on to nurture a **paranoia** and **envy** that overwhelms Othello's noble qualities. Iago is sinister and states his intentions clearly when he says, *"When devils will the blackest sins put on / They do suggest at first with heavenly shows / As I do now."* he decides to *"pour this pestilence into his ear / That she repeals him for his body's lust."* It is vital to recognise that **Iago**, wicked and malicious as he is, **is merely exploiting a weakness that already exists in Othello's character. Iago leads Othello to his destruction, but that would not be possible if the hero's character was not already corrupted by his fatal flaw.**

Iago's brilliance at exploiting Othello's fatal flaw is clear from Act 3, Scene III. He organises a meeting between Cassio and Desdemona, and then arranges for Othello to walk in on the meeting. As Othello approaches, Cassio leaves, too shamed to face his general, and Othello asks Iago, *"Was not that Cassio parted from my wife?"* Iago's response, *"Cassio my lord? No, sure, I cannot think it that / He would steal away so guilty-like"*, is maliciously suggestive. Othello's jealously is irrational, but is immediately aroused. Desdemona has given him no reason to doubt her fidelity. **The ease with which he becomes suspicious clearly shows that the source of his final despair lies within his own character.** He says, *"Perdition catch my soul / But I do love thee! And when I love thee not, chaos is come again."* Iago, with immense cynicism, warns him, *"beware my lord, of jealousy / It is the green-eyed monster which doth mock the meat it feeds on."* He then furthers Othello's insecurity by reminding him, *"She did deceive her father, marrying you."* Othello's envy has been awakened, and it does not take long for Iago to demolish the character of the hero who, one day previously, had seemed so **imperious**.

Act 3 Scene III ends with Othello ordering Cassio's murder. This is a **wicked** act, and **Othello's moral fibre has been proved to be paper-thin.** The ease with which the **malleable** Othello is manipulated by Iago in Act 4 sees him transformed into a **pathetic shadow of his former self**. He overhears Cassio talk about Bianca and accepts immediately he is boasting of an affair with Desdemona. He hears Iago's ridiculous and illogical story of Cassio's sleep talk and accepts its truth without question. He strikes Desdemona in a fit of jealous rage, prompting Lodovico to ask, *"Is this the noble Moor whom our full senate / Call in all sufficient?"* The answer to that question is, of course, no. The Othello of Act 1 is gone, replaced by the **violent paranoid** of Act 4. **There is no doubt that the hero is the author of his own destruction**. He questions Emilia about Desdemona's relationship with Cassio and is given a definitive answer: *"I durst, my lord, to wager she is honest / lay down my soul at stake."* This is real evidence of Desdemona's fidelity, but Othello chooses to reject it, dismissing Emilia as a *"simple bawd"*.

The tragic arc that takes Othello from hero to tragic hero ends in Act 5. By that stage, he is almost **anti-heroic**. He reacts with glee when he hears what he believes is Cassio's murder. This is an **abhorrent** reaction, born of envy. His pathetic comment, *"O brave Iago, honest and just"*, serves to accentuate how **pathetic** he has become. He is fully aware of the consequences of his actions when he kills Desdemona, comparing her to a candle, knowing *"not where is that Promethean heat / That can thy light relume."* He kills the innocent Desdemona to satisfy his irrational desire for vengeance, and tells Emilia, *"She was a whore."* When Cassio's duplicity is revealed, he despairs at his folly, and attempts to kill Iago. However, it is clear that no matter how cruel Iago has been, **the fault for Desdemona's death and the implosion of Othello's world lies squarely with the Moor himself**.

Othello is the quintessential Shakespearean tragic hero. He has many heroic qualities but those qualities are undone by his fatal flaw: jealousy. His speech at the end of the play, in which he accepts both his guilt and his punishment, remind the audience of the great, heroic man of Act 1. **He was the victim of Iago's sadistic character, but there can be no doubt that he is responsible for his own tragedy.**

What, in your opinion, are the most striking images and symbols in Shakespeare's *Othello*? Support your answer by reference to the text.

> *"Whip me, you devils,*
>
> *From the possession of this heavenly sight,*
>
> *Blow me about in winds, roast me in sulphur,*
>
> *Wash me in steep-down gulfs of liquid fire!"*

Othello is one of Shakespeare's greatest plays. Like the other celebrated Shakespearean tragedies, *Hamlet*, *King Lear* and *Macbeth*, *Othello* delves into the passions and motivations that dictate our lives, and deals with profound thematic concerns such as the nature of loyalty and betrayal, power and its abuse, and the devastation wrought by passionate love infected by paranoid jealousy. Shakespeare's use of soliloquy lends power, poignancy and tension to the play, and there can be no doubt that his innovative use of this device makes this play great. However, it is **his ability to manipulate language and to conjure up startlingly accurate imagery and symbols which really makes this play memorable**. Sex, racism, evil, love and jealousy are all brought vividly to life. Shakespeare was a playwright who understood the power of the imagination. His determination to stimulate his audience's imagination through the use of **powerful**, **cinematic** and at times **visceral** imagery is one of the defining characteristics of *Othello*.

Act 1, Scene I sets the rhythm for the rest of the play. The cruelty, malevolence and malicious intent of Iago's character is immediately established. The dramatic tension of the play is conveyed to the audience as Iago outlines his plan to destroy his master, and this is achieved though the **vivid use of symbols and imagery**. Iago is intensely self-aware, and describes himself as one who is *"trimm'd in forms and visages of duty"*. A crucial and recurring **motif** is established for the play. Iago is deliberately and cynically duplicitous. He then goes on to say, *"In following him I but follow myself / I am not what I am."* This very striking use of **juxtaposition** leaves an unmistakeable impression on the audience. Iago is a wicked and sinister man. The audience have yet to meet the hero, Othello, but are in no doubt that his story must be a tragic one. Iago viciously informs Roderigo, *"I do hate him as I do hell pains / Yet, for necessity of present life / I must show out a flag and sign of love."* This **photographic metaphor** for determined deceit is one of the great **symbols** of the play, and is one of the reasons why Act 1, Scene I is such an effective and engaging opening to the tragedy.

Nowhere is Shakespeare's **language** more **powerful** and **evocative** than in the **sexual imagery** that permeates the play. Othello and Desdemona are lovers and Iago debases their love by describing it in vile terms. He employs **animal imagery** when referring the sexual act as making *"the beast with two backs"*. He uses a deliberately **provocative image** to shock Brabantio by telling him, *"An old black ram / Is tupping your white ewe"*, and, later in Act 1, he suggests Othello has seduced Desdemona for her fortune by again employing a coarse **image**, *"Faith, he tonight hath boarded a land carrack."*

Iago's base morality is further developed in sexual terms when in Act 2 he says, *"I do suspect the lusty Moor / hath leap'd into my seat; the thought whereof / Doth, like a poisonous mineral, gnaw my inwards."* This is a very powerful piece of **imagery**. Shakespeare combines **metaphor and simile** and the **precision of the verb** "gnaw" to communicate the intense hatred Iago feels when he thinks Othello may have slept with his wife. The sexual **imagery** in the play is potent and shocking, and sex itself is debased by Iago's corruption. He stokes the fires of Othello's jealousy by suggesting Desdemona slept with Cassio, that there is nothing wrong with being *"naked with her friend a-bed / An hour or more, not meaning any harm."* His tactic is successful and, by the end of the play, Othello's rage with his wife is explained when he describes her as a *"subtle whore"*. **Again, the precision of the language serves to create a powerful image.**

One of the major thematic concerns of the play, certainly in its initial phases, is racism. Endemic racism pervades Venice. Shakespeare uses the racist attitudes of the Venetians to build the image of Othello as a hero. He is a noble and dignified black man who remains stoic in the face of racial abuse and has risen to a position of eminence and respect despite the racism that surrounds him. The realities of this bigotry are brought to life by Shakespeare through his **adroit use of symbolism and imagery**. When attacking Othello in Act 1, Scene III, Brabantio accuses the Moor of using magic to bewitch his daughter: *"Damned as thou art, thou hast enchanted her…If she in chains of magic were not bound / whether a maid so tender, fair and happy… Would ever have, to incur a general mock, / Run from her guardage to the sooty bosom / Of one such as thou."* Brabantio then goes on to say *that "…my particular grief is of so flood gate and overbearing nature / That it engluts and swallows other sorrows."* Again the **power of the images** here is unmistakable, and the audience is left in no doubt that Brabantio's despair lies not in the fact that his daughter has eloped, but that she has eloped with a black man.

If *Othello* has one primary thematic concern, it is with the destructive power of jealousy. Iago draws out the latent fatal flaw in the hero, and its force destroys him completely. The power of Othello's jealousy is communicated through a series of **effective symbols and images**. Iago is malicious and despises Othello for his trusting character. In Act 1, Scene III, his soliloquy chillingly describes his intentions. He says, *"The Moor is of a free and open nature / That thinks men honest that but seem to be so / And will as tenderly be led by the nose as asses are."* The **simile** is brilliant and successfully captures the idea of a powerful animal being led towards his destruction. Iago is fully aware of the power of envy, as he feels it himself. Having stated his belief that Othello slept with Emilia, he says, *"nothing can or shall content my soul / Till I am evened with him, wife for wife."* His revenge, he says, will be to *"put the Moor / At least into a jealousy so strong / That judgement cannot cure."* These are clear **images** of Iago's wicked intent, and he succeeds in his aims. Later, in Act 4, he cynically warns Othello, *"Beware, my lord, of jealousy; / It is the green-eyed monster which doth mock the meat it feeds on."* The **metaphor** sums up jealousy's effect on Othello, and he is left paranoid and obsessive, saying, *"I had rather be a toad / And live upon the vapour of a dungeon / Than keep a corner in the thing I love for other's uses."* The **images** here are dark and rancid, and reflect the corruption eating away at the hero from within.

Of course, *Othello* is a play that is famous for the depiction of the evil of which human beings are capable. That malevolence is embodied by Iago, and is expressed through **imagery and symbolism**. He is a wicked and utterly ruthless man. Nowhere is this more powerfully evoked than in Act 2, Scene I when, in soliloquy, he outlines his plans to ensnare and destroy the innocent Michael Cassio. He says, *"I'll have our Michael Cassio on the hip / Abuse him to the Moor in the rank garb."* This is a **visceral image** of violence, and is expressed with salacious intensity. Later in the same speech, the deception **motif** is repeated when he boastfully states, *"Knavery's plain face is never seen till used."* He puts in train a plan to destroy Cassio's reputation by exploiting Roderigo, and again, **simile and metaphor** are utilised in order to communicate the evil that lies within him. He says once Cassio gets drunk he'll be *"as full of quarrel and offence as my mistress' dog…If consequences do but approve my dream /*

My boat sails freely, both with wind and stream." Probably the most memorable **symbol** of Iago's cruelty comes in Act 2, Scene III when he describes his plan to *"pour this pestilence in his ear / That she repeals him for her body's lust…So will I turn her virtue into pitch / And out of her own goodness make the net that shall enmesh them."* This **metaphor** symbolises Iago's twisted and distorted view of the world. He has contempt for decency and will exploit it to destroy his enemies.

The play ends in tragedy with the death of the hero, of Desdemona and of Emilia. It is an absorbing piece of drama that is brought to life by **Shakespeare's determination to excite and stimulate our imaginations through the use of symbolism and imagery.** Act 5 is filled with moving images of Othello's diseased mind. He is devastated because the *"fountain, from which my current runs"* has, he believes, betrayed him. He kills her, but not before he notes the finality of the act in another apposite **metaphor**. He holds the candle in his hands, aware that it is easy to relight it, but also knowing that once he puts the life out of Desdemona, *"I know not where is that Promethean heat /That can thy light relume."* This extraordinary **image symbolises** the fact that Desdemona's love brings light to Othello's life, and his feeling that once that love is gone, only darkness remains, typifies the greatness of the play. *Othello* is a remarkable account of one man's tragic fall, and another man's malicious malevolence. **The play is gripping from start to finish, not merely because of the narrative, but also because Shakespeare so brilliantly harnessed imagery and symbolism to tell his story.**

General Questions

1. *Othello* is concerned not so much with jealousy as with misunderstanding – Discuss.
2. *Othello* is concerned with no major issues: it simply portrays the ups and downs of ordinary life – Discuss.
3. *Othello* is a pessimistic play; in it anything that can go wrong does go wrong – Discuss.
4. *Othello* portrays human relationships at their very worst – Discuss.
5. Othello is not a tragic hero: he really has no idea what is happening to him – Discuss.
6. *Othello* dramatises the hidden conflicts in human life – Discuss.
7. Despite his sufferings, Othello learns little of himself or of human relationships – Discuss.
8. Iago is the real hero of *Othello*: he attempts remarkable feats of skill and he triumphs in the end, despite his exposure and punishment – Discuss.
9. Iago is a likeable villain: he cannot be blamed for making the most of his opportunities – Discuss.
10. Iago's schemes succeed, not only because of his skill in manipulation but because there is nobody else with the talent to defeat him – Discuss.
11. Desdemona's character is just not credible: her innocence and passiveness border on stupidity – Discuss.

12. Desdemona is just too good to be true – Discuss.

13. Desdemona is a woman not an angel: she lives and loves with her whole person, both body and soul – Discuss.

14. Iago and Desdemona are at opposite extremes of virtue and vice, but Othello is somewhere in between them – Discuss.

15. Iago's evil schemes succeed since Othello is so noble and not because he is weak – Discuss.

16. Iago is no villain: he merely defends himself against the hard knocks he has received in life – Discuss.

17. Iago is motivated not so much by revenge or natural evil as by a thirst for power – Discuss.

18. A combination of Iago's skill, Othello's weakness and a measure of good luck bring about the tragedy in *Othello* – Discuss.

19. Othello is not a tragic hero – he is really only a victim of circumstances and Iago's cunning – Discuss.

20. Love and the corruption of love is a major theme in *Othello* – Discuss.

21. Jealousy, imposed on a man of openness and trust, is the central theme in *Othello* – Discuss.

22. Othello cannot be blamed for trusting Iago's false show of honesty: others too are totally deceived – Discuss.

23. It is really Othello's egoism and lack of self-knowledge, and not Iago's evil schemes, which cause the tragedy – Discuss.

24. Discuss the roles of Desdemona, Cassio, Brabantio, Emilia, Roderigo and Bianca in contributing to the tragedy.

25. *Othello* is somewhat far-fetched as a tragedy: the unlikely and the coincidental play a major role in bringing disaster – Discuss.

26. Discuss the roles of language and imagery in the creation of the atmosphere of tragedy in *Othello*.

27. *Othello* is an unexciting play: the main action is confined to two characters, Othello and Iago – Discuss.

28. The basic plot or action of *Othello* is simple and undramatic, but Shakespeare's skill in characterisation and language makes it a memorable drama – Discuss.

29. The ending of *Othello* is an anti-climax: everything that happens is predictable and this spoils the drama – Discuss.

30. Iago cannot be blamed for the tragedy of *Othello*: he never intended the deaths of Desdemona and Othello – Discuss.

31. *Othello* abounds in extremes and contrasts, both in character and in events – Discuss.

32. Discuss the roles of the minor characters in *Othello*.